Discourse Analysis in the Language Classroom

Discourse Analysis in the Language Classroom

Volume 1. The Spoken Language

Heidi Riggenbach, University of Washington

Ann Arbor

THE UNIVERSITY OF MICHIGAN PRESS

Copyright © by the University of Michigan 1999
All rights reserved
Published in the United States of America by
The University of Michigan Press
Manufactured in the United States of America
⊗ Printed on acid-free paper

2002   2001   2000   1999   4   3   2   1

A CIP catalog record for this book is available from the British Library.

Library of Congress Cataloging-in-Publication Data

Riggenbach, Heidi.
    Discourse analysis in the language classroom / Heidi
Riggenbach.
        v.<1> ; cm.
    ISBN 0-472-08541-7 (pbk. : acid-free paper)
    1. Language and languages—Study and teaching. 2. Discourse
analysis. I. Title.
P53.2965 .R54   1998
418'.007—dc21   98-40287
                                                        CIP

Acknowledgments

To friends and colleagues Brian Lynch and Peter Master, and friends/colleagues/mentors Russ Campbell and Mary McGroarty: Thank you, simply and sincerely. You're the best. Also, in this same category but closer to home, Sandy Silberstein and Jim Tollefson. Without you, where would I be? Kansas City?

For early (and sustained?) encouragement (and interest?) in this project, thank you to Donna Brinton, Marianne Celce-Murcia, Evelyn Hatch, Diane Larsen-Freeman, and Gin Samuda.

At this point it would be appropriate to say that I accept responsibility for my viewpoint, which those mentioned here may disagree with, and I accept responsibility for any remaining problems, real or imagined, with the content of this book. That should cover it.

To Ann Wennerstrom, Maria Mohr Amonette, and Laurie Stephan: Thank you, friends and colleagues, for your careful reading(s) of the manuscript. I foresee collaboration in our future.

Wendy Asplin, Betsy Branch, and Terry Perez; Keven Gozho, Rebecca Gonyouro, Olleyn Kashiri, and Hilary Kowino: You all deserve mention for your creative input. Thank you, too, to the many teachers, students, and student-teachers around the globe who have tried out activities from the book and have given me useful feedback. This book would not have been possible without your help. This also includes instructors and writers/materials developers from the University of Washington ESL Center and the greater Seattle area. Some of you have been more helpful than I'm sure you realize and have influenced my thinking. I'm talking about *you* in particular, Ann Wennerstrom, Anita Sokmen, Stacy Hagen, Pat Grogan, Wendy Asplin, Patricia Brenner, and Mary Kay Seales, among others. In this "others" category are Bill Harshbarger and Patty Heiser, who have been (and are) consistently supportive and positive.

Gin Samuda, although you were mentioned earlier, you're also in a category of your own. I love the way you can turn misery into fun.

Thank you, thank you, friends and colleagues.

And Dan, Lily, and Robin—You're at the top of any and all of my lists, you know.

Contents

Part 1
Introduction

· ·

Chapter 1
Overview: Discourse Analysis in the Language Classroom

· ·

1. Discourse and Context Described
2. Communicative Competence and Discourse Analysis Activities
3. Other Recent Trends in Theory and Pedagogy
4. Materials Design and Teacher Preference Considerations
For Teachers: Discussion Questions
Suggested Readings and References

The purpose of this chapter is to provide you with some background about discourse analysis and its potential for use with language students. As is the tradition in texts for language teachers and for students of applied linguistics, the first section is provided to familiarize you with the terms associated with the study of discourse. Next, there is a discussion of the ways in which different types of discourse analysis activities can address the development of communicative competence in language learners. Third, the way that recent trends in second language acquisition theory and pedagogy support the use of discourse analytic techniques in the language classroom are examined. Together, these three sections of the book provide an overview and general orientation to *discourse analysis*, since some readers of this book may be new to this discipline.

Also in this chapter are suggestions about ways that discourse analysis activities can be adapted for different levels and different course situations: settings where skills are taught as independent courses, settings where skills are integrated, settings with institutional constraints (e.g., where teachers have little or no say in textbook and materials choice or in course design), and settings with different kinds of student populations. Teacher preferences and teacher style are also discussed.

1. Discourse and Context Described

The notion of discourse analysis may vary from discipline to discipline. But are there areas of agreement among discourse analysts? What do discourse analytic approaches have in common? In addition to the result of discourse analysis research—evidence of systematicity as an explanation for the occurrence of particular language features—discourse analysts consider context to be of primary importance (Schiffrin 1994; Duranti and Goodwin 1992).

Examining language features in isolation is not considered particularly fruitful by those trained in discourse analysis. Rather, the surrounding text and the sociocultural environment offer important clues to the systematicity. Discourse analysts look at extended text, beyond a sentence (in writing) or an utterance (in speaking). A unit shorter than a single sentence or single utterance may provide information, but what is interesting to discourse analysts is how that unit is situated in and affected by its broader context.

Language learners can study discourse by analyzing not only the linguistic regularities found in ways of speaking and ways of writing (as in Lee 1992; Saville-Troike 1989) but also the social and cultural meanings that frame the production and interpretation of messages. This wider definition of discourse implies that constituents of text are not the only worthy areas of study and that equally important are such matters as the inferencing of meaning by readers and listeners and the social dynamics that shape speech events and influence the learning environment of the language student. Such topics are perhaps the broadest areas to be included within a discourse framework.

This broad definition of discourse is sometimes associated with post-structuralist practices. For example, Foucault (1980) calls a cultural domain of knowledge a discourse. Discourse here, then, is not simply text longer than a sentence, or the flow of conversation, as it might be according to those in some academic disciplines. Rather, discourse in this sense is a "cultural complex of signs and practices" that contribute to regulating how we live socially (Goodwin and Duranti 1992). Though not all discourse analysts would endorse a perspective of discourse that is so broad and encompassing, they would agree that even from this more macro perspective, patterns can be observed, and they would also agree that context is of utmost importance.

In contrast to macro structures such as power, value systems, and prestige or status, micro-level features of discourse are much more concrete and much less wide-ranging and abstract. Micro-level features are individual, identifiable constituents. In an example of a discourse analysis activity that targets the micro level, language learners audiotape conversations, television sitcoms, academic lectures, or taped telephone announcements and then listen for contrasts between rising intonation and falling intonation or for contrasts between stressed and unstressed syllables. By doing this, learners have the opportunity to see for themselves how these prosodic features function meaningfully in authentic live communication; they are not simply features deemed important by a teacher or a language professional. This act can provide learners with a sense of ownership of the learning process since they themselves are the researchers: they are the discoverers of facts rather than the recipients of the "expert" knowledge of others.

Another example of a discourse analysis activity that targets the micro level examines particular grammatical structures in real language as it is spoken or written—the use of the present perfect, the passive, or the definite article *the*. One objective of this kind of activity is that grammatical structures "gain life" from a language student's perspective. Students observe grammar as it is used in real language targeted at real people rather than as it is presented in grammar textbooks targeted at ESL learners. These are examples of discourse analysis activities that target micro-level structures, since the structures are limited both in scope and length, usually to a single identifiable constituent.

Macro-level structures look instead at "the big picture" and are thus much larger in scale and also often less localized and less tangible. A macro-oriented discourse analysis activity, for example, might ask learners to explore the social factors that influence their learning environment: How are learners viewed (or how do they feel they are viewed) by their teachers, by other students, and by members of the community in which they live and interact? What effect does this perception have on students? Another example of a macro-level discourse analysis activity directs learners to view a film in order to "unpack" the dominant themes and the dominant social and cultural structures. What general background concepts must students be familiar with? What "gaps" in contextual or cultural knowledge must be addressed in order for students to fully understand the film?

Most analysts of oral discourse believe it is important to recognize that spoken discourse is structured by speaker-hearer conceptions of the social activity or social event taking place (Hymes 1974; Ochs 1986). Parallel to this in the analysis of written text are the beliefs that readers collaborate with text to disclose meaning (Eskey and Grabe 1988) and that an essential task is to recognize genre (Swales 1990). In interacting with discourse and making sense of context, communication is achieved, in part, when there is an exploration of the assumptions that operate beyond text as well as those that are evident and observable in text. For example, in a language classroom, what types of student behavior does a teacher appear to value, and what are the social, academic, and institutional influences that drive or contribute to this teacher's preferences? Exploring these assumptions would indeed be considered a macro-level activity, since it is aimed not necessarily at specific features but at broader, more abstract social and cultural structures.

An example of a discourse analysis activity that targets a slightly less macro level is one in which learners use an audiotaped classroom discussion as their data. In contrast to a micro-level-oriented activity, where analysts examine patterns of occurrence of individual features, a discussion is a larger, identifiable speech event, with a recognizable beginning and ending. Thus, it is, in a sense, a closed "structure" that is neither as broad nor as abstract as more macro-level social issues are. What happens from one discussion to the next may be quite different, but on closer examination, discussions resemble each other and are thus recognizable as speech events that adhere to certain "rules": participants express their opinions in a relatively orderly fashion (they cannot all talk at once); claims are made that other participants agree with, disagree with, ignore, or use as the basis for further claims; and often one or two people tend to lead or direct the discussion (this may or may not be determined beforehand). Thus, such a speech event may be perceived as a structure that is neither as micro as individual, isolated constituents located within text nor as macro as the social and cultural influences that operate from without to shape text.

The study of discourse, then, can take many forms. Learners can explore a range of language phenomena, from more micro-oriented linguistic constituents to more macro-oriented social structures. Like the term *discourse,* these terms, *micro* and *macro,* are defined somewhat differently from discipline to discipline (e.g., see van Lier 1988). In this book, however, you are encouraged to think of specific language phenomena as relative to particular points on a continuum, which ranges from broader macro-level structures on one end to more narrow micro-level structures on the other:

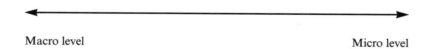

Macro level   Micro level

Another term that may be interpreted differently by discourse analysts is the word *text.* Some people may associate the word *text* only with writing. In fact, discourse analysts from some disciplines do not consider that the examination of written text is discourse analysis. But opening up an interpretation of discourse analysis to include not only the study of the structure of spoken language but also the study of how people understand language in context (as in Short 1990; Schiffrin 1994) does in fact imply that discourse analyses can be conducted on both written and spoken texts. (This volume concentrates on the spoken language. A second volume, written with Laurie Stephan, concentrates on the written language. This section of this chapter discusses discourse analysis in general terms, and thus both the written mode and the spoken mode are treated.)

Kramsch (1993) points out that face-to-face interaction involves a "sphere of intersubjectivity" between two or several people, which is the source of problems and successes in expression, interpretation, and negotiation of meaning. Similarly, written communication involves a "sphere of intertextuality" that encompasses texts and their readers; writing and reading also require skill in expression, interpretation, and negotiation of meaning. Therefore, although the definition of text may differ slightly from discipline to discipline (e.g., see Widdowson 1983), for the purposes of this book, text is synonymous with discourse: it is any extended piece of writing or talk in its natural context.

A text's "natural context" is its setting and sociocultural environment. To determine and to understand context in spoken discourse, information is needed about the speakers, their relationship to one another, the *genre* (Is it a political speech, a church sermon, a conversation?), and the setting. To determine and to understand context in written discourse, information is needed about the writer and/or the writer's intention, the audience, the genre (Is it a print advertisement, an academic journal article, a poem?), and the setting. These contextual factors help to situate text for the discourse analyst.

Context can also refer to the utterances (in speaking) or the sentences (in writing) that situate a particular structure—that precede and follow it. A specific illustration of context in this sense involves the article system. Most practitioners think the article system is not effectively taught at the sentence level, because accurate article choice is dependent on surrounding text—the information shared by the speaker and listener or the reader and writer (i.e., whether or not a noun can be identified by both producer and receiver of the message, which is possible only if the context provides adequate clues). This sense of context is relevant for micro-level discourse analysis activities, since an appropriate objective is to explore how particular features function in the discourse.

Context, then, is both the surrounding text (the utterances or sentences that precede and follow) and the surrounding sociocultural setting. These two interpretations of context, though quite distinct, actually illustrate an area of agreement among discourse analysts from different disciplines: they agree that language features/structures must be considered as part of, rather than separate from, their larger context. Examining a word or structure in isolation, void of its surrounding text, is of little use to researchers analyzing discourse. Particular language features are affected by their textual and sociocultural environment.

In addition to the importance of context, most discourse analysts agree that authenticity of text is essential for insight into actual language use. Rather than create examples of sentences and structures by introspective or intuitive methods, most language researchers interested in discourse use "real" data—talk, audiotaped or videotaped, or writing. This writing or talk may be naturally occurring, or it may be elicited. For example, it may be a response to instructions, to prearranged interview questions, or to tasks intended to elicit written or spoken exchanges. Either way, actual language use is considered a primary data source, if not the only valid data source.

This idea of a text's natural context, then, is of vital interest to discourse analysts from various disciplines. Generally, researchers who are interested in how language is actually used agree that language is complex, affected by and dependent on an array of factors. The job of the discourse analyst is not simply to speculate on "what might be," given our intuitions about language, but to study "what is," given samples of language produced by actual users of a language.

Initial impressions about a text may be intuitively motivated, but researchers agree that, in order for these impressions to be of any use, evidence from authentic discourse is crucial. Thus, evidence must be data based. In other words, for most discourse analysts the only evidence that "counts" as valid are observations about actual discourse or actual interactions, with the goal being to detect patterns that can offer a systematic explanation about phenomena that appear in the discourse. Since this book concentrates on the study of the spoken language, the discourse analysis activities described here primarily consider oral text.

2. Communicative Competence and Discourse Analysis Activities

The notion of communicative competence can serve as the basis for developing different kinds of discourse analysis activities. Communicative competence, as described by Savignon (1983) and earlier by Hymes (1972), recognizes the complexity of communicating, especially in a foreign or second language. Besides acquiring linguistic and sociolinguistic competence—accuracy and social appropriateness, respectively—a learner also needs other skills to effectively communicate. Canale and Swain 1980 and Canale 1983 identify these other skills as related to discourse competence (the ability to connect utterances or sentences so that there is cohesion and coherence) and strategic competence (the ability to avoid breakdown of communication).

The concept of communicative competence, then, is compatible with a discourse orientation to language: language is intricate and multidimensional, yet it is systematic. Truly proficient or communicatively competent learners must be cognizant of the complex of factors that affect perceptions about their language abilities. In other words, how learners exhibit these different types of competence can link with judgments that others have of their proficiency level. Discourse analysis activities can target these different competencies. An emphasis on negotiating meaning both in reader-text and speaker-listener contexts can stimulate development in learners' strategic competence. Activities intended to reveal how social and cultural dynamics interact with text and shape speech events can foster sociolinguistic competence. Textual coherence and cohesion and the ways these affect the inferencing of meaning by readers and listeners can serve as the foundation for activities that target discourse competence. And finally, activities that stimulate the recognition of form-genre relationships address linguistic competence, beyond simply the goal of accuracy of form.

Thus, the model of communicative competence proposed in Canale and Swain 1980 and Canale 1983 is applicable to this discussion, since each of these different types of competence can serve as the basis for discourse analysis activities. It is important to note, however, that the notion of communicative competence has come to be associated primarily with oral language skills, although many teachers and researchers have worked to expand the concept to include written language skills as well. In order to illustrate to teachers ways in which they might develop activities that incorporate discourse analysis techniques for both written and spoken language, I will now elaborate on each of these four different kinds of competencies: sociolinguistic competence, linguistic competence, discourse competence, and strategic competence.

Sociolinguistic Competence

The development of learners' sociolinguistic competence is essential. Kramsch (1993) points out that culture in language learning is not an "expendable fifth skill," tacked on to the four traditionally taught skills: speaking, listening, reading, and writing. If language learning is perceived as the acquisition of new forms of discourse, a task that learners must acquire is the ability to first recognize to what extent their discourse is that of their surrounding environment. For example, what role does culture have in organizing the kinds of interactional sequences that might affect classroom teaching and thus be relevant to classroom learning (Poole 1990)?

When considering how best to stimulate the development of learners' sociolinguistic competence, interesting questions arise. Is it important to determine which usages are representative of a particular speech community? Should there be a distinction between competence and performance—knowledge about the culture and experience of and in the culture? Does sociocultural competence include the obligation to behave in accordance with the social conventions of a particular speech community (Kramsch 1993)? With respect to these issues, discourse analysis activities can be designed to be in accordance with and sensitive to learner settings and learner preferences.

Accordingly, language teachers and researchers have in recent years proposed that classroom-based, student-led action research should aim toward understanding the social structures that shape and influence a learner's world within and beyond the classroom. Much of the interesting work with adult immigrant learners shares these goals (e.g., Weinstein-Shr 1992; Peirce 1995). Such "participatory learning" activities (Auerbach 1994) that target these more macro-level social structures can be considered discourse analysis activities, given the broader definition of discourse as a complex of signs and practices that contribute to regulating our lives in society. A focus on the context of learning encourages questions about what else besides particular language skills are learned and taught (Pennycook 1989). From this perspective, of fundamental importance, then, is understanding how social and cultural factors frame the production and interpretation of messages.

Along these lines, Scollon (1995) also takes a broader, contextualizing view of discourse. Understanding discourse patterns is a means of enhancing the ability to use language to communicate. As Gee (1986) suggests, learners of a language are learning the discourse practices of the language, specifically the discourse practices associated with the standard dialect of that language. In other words, language is seen as a means of socialization. If language learning is perceived as the acquisition of new forms of discourse, a skill that learners must acquire is the ability to recognize the ways that social and cultural forces affect how interactions are organized and interpreted.

Teachers and researchers who have concentrated on the development of language learners' listening and reading skills recognize that background sociocultural knowledge can be of utmost importance in text interpretation. It is helpful to realize that readers and listeners are "active model builders" who must engage with a text in order to "unlock" its meaning (Anderson and Lynch 1988). In other words, in order to accurately and comprehensively interpret spoken messages or written text, listeners and readers usually require schemata, or background information about content and about the rhetorical structures and conventions that shape text (Silberstein 1994).

Developing skills that bring to consciousness the constructs and assumptions underlying a text is therefore a worthwhile, if not essential, endeavor. Clearly these considerations are not strictly related to sociolinguistic competence—and, in fact, the different types of competence in the model proposed in Canale and Swain 1980 and Canale 1983 are not mutually exclusive. However, most practitioners believe that the social and cultural factors that interact with text and that, in spoken communications, shape speech events must be targeted. Macro-level-oriented discourse analysis activities are an appropriate means of examining these social and cultural factors.

In fact, teachers of literature claim that it would be difficult, if not impossible, to introduce literature in the second and foreign language classroom without some attention to social and cultural schemata (Brumfit and Carter 1986). In other words, sociolinguistic aspects of the text must be given consideration. As Thiong'o (1994) points out, literature cannot escape its cultural implications. Any literature teaching is a response to a relationship between the culture of the students (and teacher) and that represented by the original readers of the literature being presented. Discourse analysis activities that are geared toward exploring these macro-level structures related to culture and society can "get at" the sociolinguistic aspects of text.

Similarly, culture affects how writing is created, as well as how it is read. One approach to teaching writing considers genre of primary importance and investigates the texts generated by specific discourse communities (Swales 1990). Genre theory grounds writing in particular social contexts and emphasizes the convention-bound nature of much discourse. According to this paradigm, then, writing involves conformity to certain established patterns, and thus it is important that learners develop ability in identifying sociocultural factors that influence and shape writing

The notional functional approach to teaching, popular in previous decades, also emphasized form-genre relationships (van Ek and Alexander 1975; Munby 1978). Two primary objectives of this approach were, first, to expose learners to speech events that they would be likely to encounter and, second, to replicate contexts that would elicit these speech events and that would thus provide learners with opportunities to practice them. This approach to teaching can most certainly be seen as discourse oriented, since learners were encouraged to associate function and form, structure and genre, and thus to sensitize themselves to social factors and to consider how language is perceived in terms of social appropriateness.

The process approach to teaching writing contrasts with an emphasis on genre identification. But this approach also recognizes the influence of social context, since consideration must be given to the context in which the message will be read and to the environment with which the written product will be received (Bamforth 1993). In the process approach, the starting point for creation of meaning is the student's own experience of the world. However, even with this emphasis on individual creativity, attention to audience is vital, since meaning is investigated and pursued by means of conferencing, team writing, drafting, and redrafting. Though "ownership" of one's own writing is stressed, meaning must be negotiated in order for a learner's writing to be accessible to others.

Sociolinguistic competence, then, can be investigated in many ways in the language classroom. In teaching reading skills, discourse analysis activities can target the social and cultural factors that frame the written text and that affect how a text is read. In producing their own writing, learners can focus on the context in which their writing will be perceived as well as on the conventions associated with particular genres. Attention to genre can also be the objective of speaking and listening activities: learners examine the ways in which vocabulary and grammar correspond with speech events and with *register*—how formal or informal they are considered. And finally, listening and speaking discourse analysis activities can explore the broader social and cultural factors that frame the production and interpretation of messages.

Linguistic Competence

In the consideration of linguistic competence, accumulating evidence suggests that focus on accuracy of form may be necessary in order to prevent fossilization (Ellis 1995; Celce-Murcia 1991). Many instructors now advocate the explicit teaching of grammar but suggest that a discourse-based, inductively oriented approach may be potentially more effective than traditional methods (Fotos 1994, 1993; Ellis 1995, 1993; Bley-Vrorman 1988).

As Rutherford (1987) points out, for more than 2,500 years the teaching of grammar was synonymous with language teaching. Grammatical structures were often presented in isolation or at the phrase or sentence level, with little regard for the ways in which form, meaning, and function interacted. Now, however, there seems to be an emerging interest in teaching grammar by using techniques that encourage students to operate in the role of language researcher: they examine grammatical structures as they naturally appear in both written and spoken discourse, and they inductively develop hypotheses about the rules regarding these structures. For example, students observe grammatical structures (e.g., verb tenses, the passive voice, article usage) as they appear in authentic written or spoken discourse, and they then make hypotheses about why particular grammatical choices were made instead of others, which ultimately leads to outlining the "rules" that determine these choices. Clearly, teaching grammar inductively can be viewed as a discourse analysis activity with a micro-level focus.

Concentrating on form is not necessarily equivalent to an explicit teaching of grammatical structures. Linguistic accuracy can be realized at different levels and with features other than morphosyntax, by means of discourse analysis activities that focus on micro-level structures. For example, Wennerstrom (1991) and Celce-Murcia, Brinton, and Goodwin (1996) have developed activities that increase learners' awareness about word stress, intonation, and other prosodic features. In writing, Kroll's 1990 study of ESL college-level compositions showed that it was possible for students to be lacking in grammar but accurate in terms of discourse features, such as logical connectors, that contribute to coherence. Similarly, Riggenbach 1991 demonstrated that learners could be perceived as being "native-like" in their use of certain conversation micro structures, such as repairs and turn-claiming devices, yet lacking in grammatical and phonological proficiency.

Beyond simply the goal of accuracy of form, activities that stimulate the recognition of form-genre relationships address linguistic competence as well as sociolinguistic competence. A challenge for learners is to develop the skills to observe that some activities and events (in spoken exchanges) and some genres (in written exchanges) may have highly predictable discourse structures, whereas others may have more variable discourse organization. Developing discourse analysis activities that stimulate an awareness of these associations can certainly benefit learners.

Discourse Competence

Given that it may not always be possible or desirable to isolate linguistic features from their larger discourse context, it is logical and worthwhile to explicitly target discourse competence. This area of communicative competence is addressed by first language researchers interested in the notions of coherence (Gernsbacher and Givon 1995) and cohesion (Halliday 1987; Halliday and Hasan 1976) as well as by second language researchers interested in the various ways in which learners can display discourse competence (Sato 1990; Neu 1990; Frodesen 1991; Fiksdal 1990).

Though the work in these areas is not necessarily pedagogically oriented and may not claim familiarity with the notion of communicative competence proposed in Canale and Swain 1980, the findings nevertheless suggest that aspects of discourse competence can be explicitly taught. For example, activities can target cohesive devices in reading and writing (Silberstein 1994), turn-taking devices in informal conversation (Dornyei and Thurrell 1992; Riggenbach 1998), and discourse markers and transition devices in the teaching of listening strategies (Dunkel and Davis 1994; Dudley-Evans 1994) and in the planning of oral presentations (Wennerstrom 1991).

It may be helpful to note that the notion of discourse competence explicit in the model of communicative competence proposed in Canale 1983 can be said to assume a somewhat narrow view of discourse, since discourse competence is described as the ability to connect utterances or sentences so that there is cohesion and coherence. One possible implication of this notion of discourse competence is that the features targeted—specific cohesive devices and transition signals—are located more toward the micro-level pole of the continuum. However, an awareness of the greater context is a necessary condition for creating and maintaining cohesion and coherence across text. Discourse analysis activities can indeed be an appropriate means of raising this contextual awareness while at the same time encouraging a micro-level focus on the specific constituents that contribute to text-level coherence and cohesion.

Strategic Competence

The notion of strategic competence acknowledges learner autonomy and creativity in that learners find means to compensate and thus communicate when linguistic resources are not automatic or not adequate for ease of expression. Yule and Tarone (1990), Faerch and Kasper (1983), Bialystok (1983), and Meyer (1990) offer frameworks for understanding and identifying learners' communicative strategies as well as rich descriptions of learners in the act of exercising strategic competence and negotiating meaning. Others advocate the explicit teaching of such strategies (Oxford 1990; O'Malley and Chamot 1990).

Some of these "strategies" are not communicative strategies per se but discourse analytic approaches to deconstructing, comprehending, and constructing language (Dornyei 1995). For example, Oxford (1990) considers reasoning deductively one of five strategies that helps a learner use logical thinking: this involves "deriving hypotheses about the meaning of what is heard or read by means of general rules the learner already knows" (83). Though this "strategy" is not strictly aligned with the notion of strategic competence presented in Canale and Swain 1980—a notion that was biased toward spoken exchanges—researchers currently have a more expansive notion of what constitutes negotiation of meaning (e.g., see Gass and Selinker 1995; Sorace, Gass, and Selinker 1995). Accordingly, any conscious methods that, employed by the learner, result in communication—effective transmission of a spoken or written message—can be conceived of as "strategies," since learners are negotiating meaning: they are structuring new input so that it is comprehensible, they are deciphering text that was previously opaque, or they are shaping and reshaping their own communications so that they are understood by the receiver of the message.

An example of an activity that certainly requires the negotiation of meaning is the act of summarizing, considered a "cognitive strategy" by Oxford (1990) and by O'Malley and Chamot (1990) since learners must structure input and distill facts to their bare bones. Inferencing and contextualization are also considered strategies that can be consciously learned and that are useful for improving reading skills. However, they can also be perceived as means of analyzing discourse, since they encourage the development of learners' awareness of the patterns and regularities of language. Allowing students to act as discourse analysts/language researchers can stimulate an awareness of systematicity in the language. In addition, an emphasis on negotiating meaning both in reader-text and speaker-listener contexts can motivate development in learners' strategic competence.

The notion of communicative competence has been used as a means of structuring the discussion up to this point, since features of discourse can be aligned with different "types" of language competencies. To summarize, activities that target macro-level social and cultural factors can foster socio-linguistic competence. Stimulating learners' awareness of ways to negotiate meaning can help to develop learners' strategic competence. Examining coherence and cohesion in both written texts and spoken interactions can target discourse competence. And finally, beyond simply the goal of accuracy of form, linguistic competence can be addressed by implementing micro-level activities that encourage the recognition of form-genre relationships. Thus, the model of communicative competence proposed in Canale and Swain 1980 and Canale 1983 can be used as an underlying principle on which to develop discourse analysis activities.

3. Other Recent Trends in Theory and Pedagogy

The Communicative Movement

Shifts in teaching paradigms accompanied the interest in the development of learners' communicative competence. The communicative movement advocates teaching approaches that are compatible with the view that language is more than grammar and, accordingly, that language learners are more than "grammar machines"—empty vessels that a teacher can fill with knowledge or behavior (Savignon 1991). In addition, the communicative movement supports a learner-centered approach to language teaching, which shifts some responsibility from the teacher to the student and moves away from the traditional authoritarian, teacher-centered curriculum. Besides championing the concept of the learner-centered classroom, communicative teaching approaches support the use of authentic, rather than contrived, language in the classroom, and they stress the importance of there being an actual reason to communicate.

Logically, the use of discourse analytic tools by language students is one way to employ communicative teaching methods and at the same time stimulate in learners an interest in language. Yet few published texts or articles on language teaching explicitly address this use of discourse analysis—as a means of encouraging students to act as language researchers who *themselves* learn to use the tools of discourse analysis. By using these tools, students can discover the patterns in the language they are learning and the sociocultural influences that affect message production and interpretation.

A more encompassing understanding of communicative teaching supports the use of activities that incorporate exploratory, interpretive procedures for student researchers (Grotjahn 1987). The communicative movement, as interpreted by many practitioners, is in favor of group and pair work and is against the traditional teacher-centered classroom (i.e., large group or lecture format), although as Howat (1984) and Holliday (1994) point out, the practice of group and pair work is not necessarily suitable for many foreign language contexts. However, what Howat and Holliday call the "strong view" of the communicative movement is in line with a discourse approach to teaching language, since from this perspective, the basis for a communicative lesson is the text as discourse. What is valued is not only the communication between learners and text but also the solutions of language problems through text-"unlocking" activities. The outcome of such communicative activities is not only text produced by the learners but student-generated hypotheses about patterns and systematicity, the result of the text-unlocking activity. This view of a communicative activity supports student use of collaboration not just for the purposes of communication but as a means by which students can help each other solve language problems.

The rule of speaking only the target language is relevant to this discussion. Since a primary goal of a discourse-based communicative activity is to generate hypotheses about the language feature under discussion and to observe what is systematic about it, there is not necessarily strong justification for learners to be monolingual at all times, especially in foreign language settings. When target language discourse features are the subject matter, it may be a fallacy to claim that native language use will inhibit learning of the target language. When using discourse analysis activities, then, it may be appropriate to question the rule of speaking only the target language, as Auerbach (1993) and Phillipson (1992) do.

Besides arguments for adapting the "traditional" communicative approach so that it is more aligned with learner settings and learning styles, there is currently in the English language teaching field a great deal of additional support for providing language learners with the opportunity to develop skills as language researchers and discourse analysts. Three themes that Brown (1991) identifies as recent trends in approaches to teaching English are relevant: (1) focusing on the intrinsic motivation of the language learner; (2) favoring teaching methods that address learners' needs and are oriented toward communicative goals; and (3) designing curricula that cover content-centered, task-based subject matter.

Learner Motivation

The first theme Brown (1991) identifies—focusing on the learners' intrinsic motivation—is particularly relevant to the issue of the language learner as language researcher/discourse analyst. It is believed that providing learners with the tools to develop language research skills can appeal to their autonomy, build confidence, and tap into their natural inquisitiveness. If learners invest in their own learning process by observing "real" language interactions (spoken and written), by reflecting critically on these and their own language exchanges, and by collaborating on and reviewing what they have observed, the result can be an energizing and validating experience.

For many learners, involvement in their own language-learning processes helps to empower them in the sense that they are able to gain a measure of control over their own position in the target culture (Pennycook 1989). With discourse analysis activities that they themselves conduct, students develop the ability to come up with their own discoveries and need not always rely on pat answers prescribed from textbooks or on "expert" opinions provided by instructors.

Cultivating an interest in the target language is undoubtedly advantageous. There is mounting evidence that learners who have the skills and the motivation to learn about the language and the culture they are studying carry on their self-education processes beyond the institutional setting (Ellis and Sinclair 1989; Rubin and Thompson 1994). In addition, learners who have studied second language acquisition research report that their consciousness about the learning process facilitates their learning (Larsen-Freeman and Long 1991). In other words, the language development of learners interested in learning does not stop after their formal education ceases.

Focus on the Learner

Discourse analysis activities are problem-solving, language-based tasks. The talk that students generate as they do their language research may not always produce the language feature under study, but the end goal—generating hypotheses about the discourse structure being focused on—explicitly addresses language or culture. At the least, this generation of hypotheses can activate an interest in real communication, and ideally it can stimulate and develop the ability to apply learning outside the classroom.

Learner-as-researcher discourse analysis activities keep with the recent trends toward centering on learners' needs. The task-based nature of language-oriented "discovery" activities provides opportunities for students to integrate their linguistic and cognitive competence. There is evidence that a student-negotiated syllabus increases learners' receptivity and promotes a willingness for self-investment and communication (Strevens 1987). Involvement in their own language-learning processes can encourage learner "response-ability and responsibility," as Legutke and Thomas (1991) put it.

As Brown (1991) pointed out, much second language research in the last decade has focused not only on the learning process but also on the learner

(Lightbown and Spada 1993; Larsen-Freeman and Long 1991). There is evidence that learners learn more productively if they are aware of what specifically they are learning (Spada 1990; Nunan 1995). Further, if learners themselves are involved in contributing to the content of classroom lessons, they are more likely to claim that they have learned (Slimani 1992; Block 1994). Thus, discourse analysis activities may be most effectively employed when there is learner input—when tasks are selected, planned, revised, and conducted according to learners' needs and goals.

Further, work on learning styles suggests that inductive approaches suit many adult learners well, especially when the goals of a lesson are well defined and limited. Rather than a formulaic, prescriptive approach to learning about transition devices in writing, for example, students can be encouraged to form their own hypotheses about what works as a successful transition. Instead of being handed a set of "rules" about how transition devices are used, learners examine data that exhibit the structure—written texts that learners themselves choose. Another way of putting this is that learners themselves analyze discourse. It appears that this kind of autonomy is effective for many field-independent learning types who may be resistant to deductive approaches in which they are handed ready-made, prescriptive rules.

Content-Centered and Task-Based Approaches

The recent focus on content-based learning also lends support to the kind of learner-as-researcher approach that discourse analysis activities employ. A content-centered approach to materials and curriculum design contrasts with previous approaches in which language skills were taught with little substantive content (e.g., the audio-lingual method and other structural approaches). It appears to be the case that when the content is relevant and interesting to the learner, learner investment increases accordingly (Brinton, Snow, and Wesche 1989; Krueger and Ryan 1993).

A fundamental premise of content-based approaches is that students can successfully learn the content of an academic discipline and improve their proficiency at the same time. A disadvantage is that some academic disciplines tend to organize expression in limited types of texts and rhetorical conventions. However, for students pursuing degrees in these specific academic disciplines, they are provided natural opportunities for exploring genre-form relationships. In addition, when the discipline is "language arts"—English language studies—it is logical to incorporate discourse analysis activities that draw attention to genre and to the linked linguistic patterns associated with them (Widdowson 1993).

Along these lines, some teachers/researchers have begun to experiment with courses based on nonacademic content, organized around topics as diverse as jazz and baseball (Seales 1995). Such courses are prime candidates for integrating macro-level discourse analysis activities, since social and cultural background material is so crucial for a grasp of their topics. In addition, expression is not as constrained here in terms of text type and rhetorical conventions as it is in some courses based on academic content; the decrease in constraints can "open up" the possibilities for a variety of activity types.

Task-based approaches to the work of language teaching also have the potential to go beyond simply practicing language for its own sake (Breen 1987a, 1987b). Tasks optimally are designed so that the language learning that takes place *inside* the classroom is activated for application to situations *outside* the classroom and so that learners have opportunities to focus not only on language but also on content and on the learning process itself. Activities in which the learner acts in the role of language researcher can satisfy the principles of both content-centered and task-based education.

For example, discourse analysis activities incorporate what Nunan (1991) calls sound "rehearsal rationale," essential for a well-designed task. This terminology refers to the kinds of language functions learners will actually or potentially need to perform in the target language. Since discourse-oriented tasks engage learners in exploring a research agenda that they determine based on interest and need, the syllabus can address this aspect of validity. Another concern in task design is that psycholinguistic principles be considered, namely, that learning is activated so that classroom experiences are transferable to communicative exchanges that occur outside the classroom (Nunan 1989).

Experiential Learning/Learner-as-Researcher

Although the idea of experiential learning was originally intended as applicable to native language instruction, practices associated with this approach—sometimes referred to as "project work"—have been used successfully in second and foreign language classrooms (Eyring 1991; Fried-Booth 1986). In the mid-1980s, Hatch, Flashner [Wenzell], and Hunt (1986) spoke of the experience model of language learning. In brief, this model can be viewed as a framework for structuring, organizing, and clarifying experience through language and, conversely, as a way for language to grow out of experience. The claim of Hatch and her colleagues was that activities that activate the "system for the discovery of the new" have great potential for the language classroom, since learners who engage in language learning with their own language-learning processes are often the successful language learners. This is consistent with research findings that suggest that making goals conscious enables more effective learning.

Hatch and her colleagues were inspired, in part, by the Vygotskian school of psychology, which emphasizes the role that social activities can take in cognitive development and in language development specifically (Vygotsky 1962). It is believed that growth in cognitive skills is the outcome when language is used for particular, identifiable purposes and is associated with different activities. Thus, language is viewed as a tool that can be used to serve a number of ends: learners will differ in the ends for which they use language, and these differences will lead to a variability of cognitive skills.

More recently, teacher educators have shown an interest in the teacher-as-researcher concept (Freeman and Richards 1996; Graves 1996; Nunan and Lamb 1996; Auerbach et al. 1996). One of the assumptions that these researchers/teacher educators share is that instructors will benefit by an understanding of the systems operating in the language they are teaching and in the sociocultural forces inside and outside the classroom; this understanding will lead to better language instruction.

For learning about processes operating in the classroom, for example, van Lier (1988) recommends student-as-ethnographer activities. Others have suggested that teachers use similar investigation techniques when designing course syllabi (Graves 1996; Chaudron 1988), when "managing" the learning process that occurs in their classrooms (Nunan and Lamb 1996), when considering appropriate methodologies (Ulichny 1996), and when conducting needs analyses (Long and Crookes 1992). With a slightly different slant, Nunan (1992) advocates teacher action research in which teachers develop skills that can, among other things, shed light on the macro-social influences on classroom behavior.

It is interesting that the focus has been primarily on the *teacher's* development of research skills. However, Peirce (1994) and Auerbach et al. (1996) are among those who most recently appear to be challenging that focus. They describe specific techniques for learning in which the language *learner* serves in the role of language researcher: Auerbach et al. (1996; also Auerbach 1994, 1992) aptly term this learning "participatory."

Earlier, Heath (1983) trained her language students to become ethnographers who would investigate, through participant-observation techniques, the language behavior of groups of people in the community outside the classroom. Inspired by Heath's work, Hatch and Hawkins (1991) instructed their students to collect data spoken by native speakers—audiotaped narratives. Working with these data, students explored the structures essential to well-told stories, transformed the spoken narratives into written stories, and critiqued their own and each other's final products. Others (e.g., Yule and Gregory 1989; Morrison 1989) have used similar activities with their language students, although they have been less explicit about calling them research or ethnography activities. And finally, the recent interest in activities that encourage and train language learners to examine the social structures that affect their learning and their lives also puts the language learner into a researcher role; Peirce (1995) calls this classroom-based action research.

Auerbach et al. (1996) make a case for participatory learning activities in which both teachers and learners take part. Their grounds for incorporating these types of activities parallel the arguments for using discourse analysis activities in the classroom: (1) activities are based on participants' needs, interests, and day-to-day reality, rather than on the prescriptions of outside "experts"; (2) by situating their investigations in the broader social context, learners' own knowledge is validated and they gain a more critical understanding of their own experiences; and (3) a collective sharing of strategies and resources allows group problem solving and encourages learner autonomy rather than reliance on language professionals. The discourse analysis activities presented in this book employ similar principles.

Along similar lines, some teachers and teacher educators advocate project learning (Eyring 1991), an approach to materials design that promotes both student-as-researcher practices and the use of tasks (as defined in Nunan 1989). Projects can be set up so that learners participate in their own learning: they design activities to be compatible with their needs and interests, and they collaborate to meet these goals and to pool their data. Final projects may consist of reports on their findings or role plays that represent these findings. Learner-determined discourse analysis activities can be designed to be highly suitable projects.

Although some activities used by teachers in the language classroom may actually look like the discourse analysis activities described in this book, few people have explicitly linked the notion of discourse to these practices. In other words, it is novel to consider many of the language trends of the current decade from a discourse analytic perspective. The following list summarizes the topics of discussion up to this point from this perspective.

1. With discourse analysis activities, learning can take place in a communicative format. Activities can be designed to address the different dimensions of language that a truly communicatively competent learner must have skill in interpreting and in producing—from the more macro-oriented social structures to more micro-oriented linguistic features.
2. Learner motivation and investment can be heightened when content is learner determined and when student researchers are responsible for deciding what database will serve as course material.
3. Classroom tasks can be designed to incorporate a focus on the discourse

of a communicative exchange; learners reflect on the data they have collected (written or spoken text or observed interactions), with one goal being to make sense of the text's discourse features.
4. Discourse analysis techniques, which allow learners opportunities to explore the systems operating in language by inductive means, may better address adult learning styles.
5. Students learn experientially; they act both as ethnographers who research and observe interactions and as participants themselves in authentic communicative exchanges.

4. Materials Design and Teacher Preference Considerations

Discourse analysis activities are intended to help learners become aware of the patterns that operate in natural discourse. Activities are initially directed "outward": when examining spoken language, learners listen and analyze data produced by others (usually native or expert speakers), making hypotheses about possible patterns. They also explore topics of interest to them, conducting "interpretive research" (Holliday 1994) that can provide insight into the wider social environment and into the culture of the classroom. In engaging in language research, students can also gain practice in oral skills. They discuss their research findings, make cross-cultural comparisons, analyze their own self-produced language data, and brainstorm about strategies for self-monitoring and for further practice.

Despite the advantages of student-conducted language research, language teachers may initially be hesitant to use discourse analysis activities in their own classrooms for a variety of reasons. For example, experienced teachers may have strong convictions about what works and what does not, and language research activities may be unfamiliar to them. Institutional constraints may make it difficult for some teachers to introduce any new materials or activities besides those specified in a fixed syllabus. Student populations accustomed to traditional, teacher-centered approaches and large, monolingual classroom settings may not appear to be receptive to group research projects. These are just some of the reasons for an initial resistance to using discourse analysis activities. In this section of this chapter, I will counter these objections and justify the use of discourse analysis activities in any language classroom.

Student Populations

When designing a curriculum, ideally students' language needs come first. But this statement may seem overly simplistic. Language students may have widely different needs because of differences in previous education, cultural background, and age. Even students in a class that is relatively homogeneous may have varied learning styles and diverse attitudes and assumptions about what learning entails. For this reason, seasoned language instructors often advocate an ongoing, dynamic needs assessment (e.g., Peck 1991) that takes into account students' preferences. For example, in considering group size, do students like to learn alone, in small groups, or in large groups? Do students tend to be active participants, or do they prefer observing?

Discourse analysis activities are rich in potential and can be tailored to different learning styles. Language research topics can be pursued individually or in groups. How students conduct and present research findings can also vary widely. In part 2 of this book, tried-and-true sample activities are presented, with suggestions for ways to vary format and approach. It is not necessary to follow these suggestions to the letter. Instead, they are intended to provide examples of, not prescriptions for, language research activities that have been successful. My other objective in presenting these activities is to stimulate teachers to design activities that target their own students' needs and goals and that are thus situation sensitive.

Not all methodologies that are successful in one context will be successful in another. Just as individual learners differ from each other, so do the traditions, assumptions, and preferences of student populations. For example, students in many EFL classroom settings around the world are accustomed to large, teacher-centered classes that stress accuracy in grammar and translation. It requires quite a shift for students to make the transition to settings that, in contrast, decentralize the teacher and emphasize the oral communication of meaning. In his book *Appropriate Methodology and Social Context* (1994), Holliday stresses the need for English language education that considers the social context of the different teaching environments throughout the world.

Focusing on the spoken language, the discourse analysis activities presented in this book have the flexibility to be useful in different educational environments. For example, the activities can be highly structured and conducted with a great deal of teacher guidance and assistance, thus not undermining a teacher's role in a population of students unaccustomed to a more learner-centered environment. Listening comprehension can be targeted, if it is determined to be of greater usefulness for students than are oral skills. Or if spoken language accuracy is important, learners can benefit from analyzing their own spoken language data and designing further practice activities that target the areas they need to work on.

For example, I have recently used the discourse analysis activities presented in part 2 with students in a Zimbabwean university. The students were English majors in the second year of a four-year B.A. program in education and were taking my discourse analysis class as one of their required courses. Although many of the students in the class considered themselves bilingual, at least half the class considered English their second language. These latter students were much more comfortable speaking their native languages— Shona, Ndebele, and other indigenous languages spoken in countries in southern Africa. Thus, many of these students were especially appreciative of opportunities to do activities that targeted their listening comprehension, since all classes were conducted in English. But those students who considered themselves bilingual were more interested in exploring aspects of English in some depth. Some, for example, wanted to investigate macro features that they had not before explored—issues of sociolinguistic appropriateness, cultural practices, or storytelling. Others were interested in the use of particular grammatical structures in "African English" as compared to British or American English, or they wanted to familiarize themselves with the microfeatures systems in conversation—repair, turn changes, or backchannels.

Besides providing examples of how discourse analysis activities can be tailored to diverse student populations, this class in Zimbabwe can also be described in terms of how the issue of limited technological resources can be managed. The class consisted of sixty-eight students, with three audio recorders available. My students and I developed a rotating sign-up system, so that groups of three could have access to a tape recorder two or three times during the term, with individual "homework" time as well. This situation was not unlike the arrangement in my advanced speaking course in China, where only one audio recorder with taping capability was shared among forty students.

In short, students are excellent resources in finding solutions to problems that occur when using discourse analysis activities in less-than-ideal circumstances. This collaborative group problem solving can itself be a way to use English meaningfully. Once or twice, after an especially interesting discussion on how to manage a problem, I had wished in retrospect that the discussion itself had been taped and used as data. Several options for what to focus on occurred to me—the participants' turn-taking styles, the evolution of who "led" the discussion, the mechanics of reaching a consensus, or an analysis of volume and pitch increase as a floor-gaining strategy.

With discourse analysis activities, students work to understand patterns of language and to identify "structures" and influences of society. The outcome of these activities is not only spoken text produced by learners but also student-generated hypotheses about what these patterns and structures are and how they operate. This view of a communicative language research activity supports the use of collaboration not just for the purposes of communication but as a means by which learners help each other solve language problems (and problems involved with the mechanics of setting up the activity).

In designing discourse analysis activities, another "limited technology" issue of concern to teachers in foreign language contexts is limited access to spoken language data produced by native speakers. For better or for worse, technology has had an impact on all but the most inaccessible places in the world. English language newspapers, magazines, and books are widely available, and it is no longer unusual, in far corners of the world, for U.S. television programs or BBC radio news programs to be broadcast or for computer networks to be accessed. These can serve as data sources. In addition, for most of the activities described in this book, it is perfectly appropriate to ask expert speakers of English, rather than native speakers, to provide spontaneous spoken language data. (Expert speakers, as defined in this book, are people who have attained high proficiency in English and/or have lived or worked in an English-speaking country.)

In an English class in China, where I taught, we encountered the problem of limited access to native speakers. Some creative brainstorming helped to provide solutions. At that time—the early 1980s—in the capitol, Beijing, the foreign teacher and journalist population was housed primarily in a few prominent locations (e.g., a large long-term "hotel") rather than in campus housing. Thus, many of these people willingly served as members of a "subject pool" of native English speakers who could provide my students with data.

Besides the context in which language is taught, other important considerations are learner age and level of proficiency. Most of the activities described in this book have been used with adult learners at the low-intermediate level or higher, mainly in university ESL classes in the United States and elsewhere. However, some of them, such as the storytelling activity (Activity 9), have been used with children considered LEP (limited English proficiency) students (see, for example, Hatch and Hawkins 1991). Others, such as the child language acquisition activity (Activity 21) and the new words activity (Activity 23), have been used with beginning-level recent immigrants, the latter activity with a group of Hmong women whose average age was fifty-five (also see Yang 1995). The activities described in this book allow great room for adaptation for specific populations and class settings.

To illustrate, one instructor reported on how she went about creating a discourse analysis activity for her beginning-level grammar class for young adults (Perez 1996). Students in her interactive, community-based program were asked to listen for unfamiliar words and phrases in conversations that they participated in or that they overheard in public places. They then brought these words and phrases back to the class, saying them aloud and writing them on the board. The job of the other students in the class was to contextualize these words and phrases, guessing who the speakers were, what the setting was, and what the general topic of conversation was. In the process of doing this, students used the present and past progressive ("The speakers are talking about . . .") and the simple present and past ("They were probably in a restaurant"), which were the grammar forms being focused on in class. An added benefit of this activity is that students also unexpectedly got practice in using modals of prediction ("The speakers must be waiters"; "They could be talking about . . .").

Course/Syllabus Situations

Some language teachers do not have the opportunity to design their own courses. One true-life scenario is a teacher who is handed a syllabus and a textbook only hours (and that early only if the teacher is lucky) before his or her class of more than one hundred students is about to meet. The teacher has a moment to talk with the previous teacher of the course, who advises, "Just go through the textbook." Even settings as rigidly structured as this can benefit from the use of discourse analysis activities. In a grammar class, for example, students can be assigned, as homework, to record "live," in teams or individually, spoken language data. They then listen to their tapes for the use of specific grammatical structures related to what they are working on in their class textbook. They write down these examples, and they consider whether there are clear patterns or rules and whether what they are finding in their tape-recorded data is consistent with what their textbooks say. This kind of activity can be done in a relatively short amount of time, yet it can add a great deal of life and concreteness to materials that have little or none.

The degree to which specific language skills are taught as independent courses varies a great deal (Johnstone 1995). Some courses are taught as multiskills courses; some courses address discrete skill areas, such as reading, listening, speaking, writing, grammar, pronunciation, and vocabulary. There is room for discourse analysis activities in any of these course situations. This book provides examples of language research activities that target all of the skill areas related to the spoken language.

Discourse analysis activities are appropriate as supplements to a core syllabus or textbooks. They can also serve as the framework for an entire course. Teachers may want to establish the "areas," topics, or structures that their students need or want to work on. What students feel they need to work on may differ from the teacher-set objectives of a syllabus, but, as discussed earlier in this chapter, there is growing evidence that students' opinions and ideas about how to proceed with their learning matter a great deal (Block 1996). In addition, when students are conscious of the objectives of a specific lesson, it appears that they are more confident about their progress (O'Malley and Chamot 1990). Since discourse analysis activities are reliant on student input, they are appropriate activities in classes where students have a say in what is taught and how it is taught.

Also as discussed earlier in this chapter, it can be validating and energizing for learners to invest in their own learning processes by taking on the role of language researcher. Further, it is believed that learners are empowered by involvement in their own language-learning processes. Learners who are interested in the language and the culture they are studying are likely to carry on their self-education processes beyond the institutional setting (Ellis and Sinclair 1989; Legutke and Thomas 1991). In addition, discourse analysis activities that target macro-level social structures can help students feel they are able to gain a measure of control over their own position in the target culture (Pennycook 1989).

Teacher Style

The discourse analysis activities described in this book encourage the instructor to act as coresearcher and facilitator rather than expert. Many of the activities are open-ended in that there is no one right or wrong conclusion. Rather, the goal is to stimulate student interest in language, to develop learners' confidence in their own abilities to "discover" truths about the structure of language under study, and to help raise learners' consciousness not only about what is systematic about the language they are learning but also about learners' own linguistic strengths and weaknesses. In addition, learners can examine distinct, micro-level features as well as more macro-level structures that are revealed in the ways people talk—such concepts and topics as power, belief systems, and emotions.

For the benefit of the instructor, each sample activity described in this book provides general introductory background material about the feature(s) under focus in each activity. References and suggested readings are provided for instructors who want to further pursue a particular topic. However, the activities have been used by teachers with no previous knowledge about the structures or topics; also, instructors who have successfully used the activities include nonnative speakers as well as native speakers. Entering into these activities as a novice along with the language learners may, in fact, be the best way for instructors to put themselves on an equal footing with their students, since with this approach, everyone can discover something about language.

Some instructors, however, do not want to be on an equal footing with students. Some teaching environments, especially in non-Western settings, are not conducive to such equality. Some instructors, whatever the teaching context, are simply not comfortable with approaches that are anything other than "traditional" in the sense that the teacher is expert and authority. It is important that instructors be aware of their own teaching preferences and teaching "style." It has been my experience that teachers who have never been exposed to the use of discourse analysis activities with their students may initially be resistant to doing activities about which they are not fully knowledgeable. They may characterize discourse analysis techniques as activities where "the blind lead the blind," and they may think it is appropriate to first learn everything there is to know about language and about discourse analysis.

For these types of teachers, it may be helpful for them to observe colleagues using discourse analysis activities before they try it themselves in their own classrooms. Additionally, in order to feel confident of their background and expertise, these teachers may prefer doing an activity themselves before introducing it to their students. However, consistent with recent learner-centered approaches, many teachers—both new and experienced—do feel at ease entering into an activity along with their students. I have never yet encountered a teacher who has rejected outright the use of discourse analysis activities, though the degree to which this approach is embraced obviously varies.

Whatever the teacher style, there is clearly value in the use of discourse analytic approaches in the language classroom. Since students themselves take on the role of discourse analysts/language researchers, they are no longer passive recipients of previously developed materials or of the instructor's "expert" knowledge. Instead, they are responsible for providing important information about the structures. Learners themselves contribute pieces of the puzzle.

For Teachers: Discussion Questions

1. Language researchers from different disciplines use the tools of discourse analysis in their research. What do these different disciplines have in common in their approaches to and understanding of discourse analysis? Where might they disagree or differ from each other?
2. Recall the continuum of language features and structures introduced in this chapter.

Macro level   Micro level

Think of an example feature or structure for each of three different points on the continuum: (a) one that you would consider being at the micro level (a single, identifiable constituent), (b) one that you would consider being at the macro level (a broader, more abstract social and cultural feature or phenomenon), and (c) one that you would consider somewhere in between. Be prepared to justify your decisions for placing features and structures at these particular points on the continuum.

3. Explain one interpretation of context. How many different interpretations can you and your classmates come up with? Do you feel that these interpretations are all related to each other?

4. Canale and Swain 1980 and Canale 1983 describe communicative competence as a holistic kind of language proficiency with four distinctive aspects, or types: linguistic competence, sociolinguistic competence, strategic competence, and discourse competence. Do you find this concept useful? Why or why not?

5. How might discourse analysis activities be adapted to address different language-teaching contexts? Think of the range of situations that you and your colleagues have taught in—for example, a large monolingual setting in a non-English-speaking country as compared to a small multilingual class. Choose a discourse analysis activity mentioned in this chapter—or create one of your own—and imagine how the different language-teaching contexts would affect how this activity was implemented.

6. After reading this chapter, what would you tell someone who is considering using discourse analysis activities in her or his language classroom? First, describe what discourse analysis activities are. Then give reasons for using discourse analysis activities and/or discuss any reservations that you still have about using them.

Suggested Readings and References

Andrews, L. 1993. *Language exploration and awareness: A resource book for teachers.* New York: Longman.

> This book on "language arts" is intended for teachers of children and adolescents in a K–12 school context. Although the term *discourse analysis* is rarely used in it, this book offers a range of language-oriented discourse analysis activities that can be used in the classroom, all of which go beyond "traditional" grammar-based approaches. Clear and reader-friendly, this book also provides background material on various features of language, thereby "grounding" the activities that are described.

Duranti, A., and C. Goodwin. 1992. *Rethinking context: Language as an interactive phenomenon.* New York: Cambridge University Press.

> This book is recommended for readers interested in the theoretical and methodological perspectives of leading figures in the social sciences, not for readers who want an easily accessible overview of the field of discourse analysis. The essays in this collection examine the concept of context from a variety of angles, thus appealing to scholars from various disciplines who are interested in the current debates about issues of language and society.

Hatch, E. 1992. *Discourse and language education.* New York: Cambridge University Press.

> This book is a comprehensive and interesting introduction to discourse analysis for readers who want a more thorough understanding of the discipline. The many practice activities that are provided help to make this book accessible to people who are new to the study of discourse analysis. The data used in the discussions and in the practice activities are drawn from spoken and written language and from language learners of varying levels, ages, and backgrounds. Thus, this book is highly recommended for teachers who want to learn more about the study of discourse before they try out activities with their students.

McCarthy, M. 1992. *Discourse analysis for language teachers.* New York: Cambridge University Press.

> Similar to Hatch's treatment (see preceding listing), McCarthy's book offers a range of approaches for analyzing discourse. It is organized by

traditional skill areas (e.g., vocabulary, grammar), with analysis activities for each. Rather than providing an overview of the many ways discourse analysis has been used by a variety of academic disciplines, McCarthy narrows his treatment to what he considers will be of relevance to language teachers.

Anderson, A., and T. Lynch. 1988. *Listening.* New York: Oxford University Press.

Auerbach, E. R. 1994. Participatory action research. In A. Cumming, ed., Alternatives in TESOL research: Descriptive, interpretive, and ideological orientations. *TESOL Quarterly* 28 (4): 693–97.

Auerbach, E. R. 1993. Reexamining English only in the ESL classroom. *TESOL Quarterly* 27 (1): 9–32.

Auerbach, E. 1992. *Making meaning, making change: Participatory curriculum development for adult ESL literacy.* Washington, DC, and McHenry, IL: Center for Applied Linguistics and Delta Systems.

Auerbach, E., with B. Barahona, J. Midy, F. Vaquerano, A. Zambrano, and J. Arnaud. 1996. *Adult ESL/literacy from the community: A guidebook for participatory literacy training.* Mahwah, NJ: Lawrence Erlbaum.

Bamforth, R. 1993. Process versus genre: Anatomy of a false dichotomy. *Prospect* 8 (1–2): 89–99.

Bialystok, E. 1983. Some factors in the selection and implementation of communication strategies. In C. Faerch and G. Kasper, eds., *Strategies in interlanguage communication,* 100–118. New York: Longman.

Bley-Vrorman, R. 1988. The fundamental character of foreign language learning. In W. Rutherford and M. Sharwood Smith, eds., *Grammar and second language teaching,* 19–30. New York: Newbury House.

Block, D. 1996. A window on the classroom: Classroom events viewed from different angles. In K. Bailey and D. Nunan, eds., *Voices and viewpoints: Qualitative research in second language education.* New York: Cambridge University Press.

Block, D. 1994. A day in the life of a class: Teacher/learner perceptions of task purpose in conflict. *System* 22 (4).

Breen, M. 1987a. Contemporary paradigms in syllabus design. Part 2. *Language teaching* 20 (3): 157–74.

Breen, M. 1987b. Learner contributions to task design. In C. Candlin and D. Murphy, eds., *Language learning tasks.* New York: Prentice Hall.

Brinton, D., M. A. Snow, and M. B. Wesche. 1989. *Content-based second language instruction.* New York: Newbury House.

Brown, H. D. 1991. TESOL at twenty-five: What are the issues? *TESOL Quarterly* 25 (2): 245–60.

Brumfit, C. J., and R. A. Carter, eds., 1986. *Literature and language teaching.* New York: Oxford University Press.

Canale, M. 1983. From communicative competence to communicative language pedagogy. In J. C. Richards and R. W. Schmidt, eds., *Language and communication.* New York: Longman.

Canale, M., and M. Swain. 1980. Theoretical bases of communicative approaches to second language teaching and testing. *Applied Linguistics* 1:1–47.

Celce-Murcia, M. 1991. Grammar pedagogy in second and foreign language teaching. *TESOL Quarterly* 25 (3): 459–80.

Celce-Murcia, M., D. Brinton, and J. Goodwin. 1996. *Teaching pronunciation: A reference for teachers of English for speakers of other languages.* New York: Cambridge University Press.

Chaudron, C. 1988. *Second language classrooms: Research on teaching and learning.* New York: Cambridge University Press.

Dornyei, Z. 1995. On the teachability of communication strategies. *TESOL Quarterly* 29 (1): 55–86.

Dornyei, Z., and S. Thurrell. 1992. *Conversations and dialogues in action.* Hemel Hempstead, England: Prentice-Hall.

Dudley-Evans, T. 1994. Variations in the discourse patterns favoured by different disciplines and their pedagogical implications. In J. Flowerdew, ed., *Academic listening: Research perspectives,* 146–58. New York: Cambridge University Press.

Dunkel, P. A., and J. N. Davis. 1994. The effects of rhetorical signaling cues on the recall of English lecture information by speakers of English as a native or second language. In J. Flowerdew, ed., *Academic listening: Research perspectives,* 55–74. New York: Cambridge University Press.

Duranti, A., and C. Goodwin, eds. 1992. *Rethinking context: Language as an interactive phenomena.* New York: Cambridge University Press.

Ellis, E., and B. Sinclair. 1989. *Learning to learn English: A course in learner training.* New York: Cambridge University Press.

Ellis, R. 1995. Interpretation tasks for grammar teaching. *TESOL Quarterly* 29 (1): 87–105.

Ellis, R. 1993. Interpretation-based grammar teaching. *System* 21:69–78.

Eskey, D., and W. Grabe. 1988. Interactive models for second language reading: Perspectives on instruction. In P. Carrell, J. Devine, and D. Eskey, eds., *Interactive approaches to second language reading,* 223–38. New York: Cambridge University Press.

Eyring, J. 1991. Experiential language learning. In M. Celce-Murcia, ed., *Teaching English as a second or foreign language,* 2d ed., 346–59. New York: Newbury House.

Faerch, C., and G. Kasper. 1983. On identifying communication strategies in interlanguage production. In C. Faerch and G. Kasper, eds., *Strategies in interlanguage communication,* 210–38. New York: Longman.

Fiksdal, S. 1990. *The right time and pace: A microanalysis of cross-cultural gatekeeping interviews.* Norwood, NJ: Ablex.

Fotos, S. 1994. Integrating grammar instruction and communicative language use through grammar consciousness-raising tasks. *TESOL Quarterly* 28 (3): 323–51.

Fotos, S. 1993. Consciousness raising and noticing through focus on form: Grammar task performance versus formal instruction. *Applied Linguistics* 14:385–407.

Foucault, M. 1980. *Power/knowledge: Selected interviews and other writings, 1972–1977.* New York: Pantheon Books.

Freeman, D., and J. C. Richards, eds. 1996. *Teacher learning in language teaching.* New York: Cambridge University Press.

Fried-Booth, D. L. 1986. *Project work.* New York: Oxford University Press.

Frodesen, J. 1991. Aspects of coherence in a writing assessment context: Linguistic and rhetorical features of native and non-native English essays. Ph.D. diss., University of California, Los Angeles.

Gass, S., and L. Selinker. 1995. *Second language acquisition: An introductory course.* Mahwah, NJ: Lawrence Erlbaum.

Gee, J. P. 1986. Orality and literacy: From *The savage mind* to *Ways with words. TESOL Quarterly* 20 (4): 719–46.

Gernsbacher, A., and T. Givon. 1995. *Coherence in spontaneous text.* Amsterdam/Philadelphia: John Benjamins.

Goodwin, C., and A. Duranti. 1992. Rethinking context: An introduction. In A. Duranti and C. Goodwin, eds., *Rethinking context,* 1–42. New York: Cambridge University Press.

Graves, K., ed. 1996. *Teachers as course developers.* New York: Cambridge University Press.

Grotjahn, A. 1987. On the methodological basis of introspective methods. In C. Faerch and G. Kaspar, eds., *Introspection in second language studies.* Clevedon, UK: Multilingual Matters.

Halliday, M. A. K. 1987. Spoken and written modes of meaning. In R. Horowitz and S. J. Samuels, eds., *Comprehending oral and written language.* San Diego: Academic Press.

Halliday, M. A. K., and R. Hasan. 1976. *Cohesion in English.* New York: Longman.

Hatch, E., V. Flashner [Wenzell], and L. Hunt. 1986. The experience model and language teaching. In R. Day, ed., *Talking to learn: Conversation in second language acquisition,* 5–22. New York: Newbury House.

Hatch, E., and B. Hawkins. 1991. Narratives from the classroom: Linguistic features of power in the narratives of LEP children. Paper presented at the

1991 meeting of the Second Language Research Forum, Los Angeles, CA, and at the 1992 meeting of the American Association of Applied Linguistics, Seattle, WA.

Heath, S. B. 1983. *Ways with words: Language, life, and work in communities and classrooms.* New York: Cambridge University Press.

Holliday, A. 1994. *Appropriate methodology and social context.* New York: Cambridge University Press.

Howatt, A. 1984. *A History of English language teaching.* New York: Oxford University Press.

Hymes, D. 1974. *Foundations in sociolinguistics: An ethnographic approach.* Philadelphia: University of Pennsylvania Press.

Hymes, D. 1972. On communicative competence. In J. B. Pride and J. Holmes, eds., *Sociolinguistics: Selected readings,* 269–93. Harmondsworth, England: Penguin.

Johnstone, R. 1995. Research on language learning and teaching. 1994. *Language Teaching* 28 (3): 131–47.

Kramsch, C. 1993. *Context and culture in language teaching.* New York: Oxford University Press.

Kroll, B., ed. 1990. *Second language writing: Issues and options.* New York: Cambridge University Press.

Krueger, M., and F. Ryan, eds. 1993. *Language and content: Discipline- and content-based approaches to language study.* Lexington, MA: Heath.

Larsen-Freeman, D., and M. Long. 1991. *An introduction to second language acquisition research.* New York: Longman.

Lee, D. 1992. *Competing discourses: Perspective and ideology in language.* New York: Longman.

Legutke, M., and H. Thomas. 1991. *Process and experience in the language classroom.* New York: Longman.

Lightbown, P. M., and N. Spada. 1993. *How languages are learned.* New York: Oxford University Press.

Long, M. H., and G. Crookes. 1992. Three approaches to task-based syllabus design. *TESOL Quarterly* 26 (1): 27–56.

Meyer, L. 1990. It was no trouble: Achieving communicative competence in a second language. In R. Scarcella, E. Andersen, and S. Krashen, eds., *Developing communicative competence in a second language,* 195–215. New York: Newbury House.

Morrison, B. 1989. Using news broadcasts for authentic listening comprehension. *English Language Teaching Journal* 43 (1): 14–18.

Munby, J. L. 1978. *Communicative syllabus design.* New York: Cambridge University Press.

Neu, J. 1990. Assessing the role of nonverbal communication in the acquisition of communicative competence in L2. In R. Scarcella, E. Andersen, and S. Krashen, eds., *Developing communicative competence in a second language,* 121–38. New York: Newbury House.

Nunan, D. 1995. Closing the gap between learning and instruction. *TESOL Quarterly* 29 (1): 133–58.

Nunan, D. 1992. *Research methods in language learning.* New York: Cambridge University Press.

Nunan, D. 1991. Communicative tasks and the language curriculum. *TESOL Quarterly* 25 (2): 279–96.

Nunan, D. 1989. *Designing tasks for the communicative classroom.* New York: Cambridge University Press.

Nunan, D. 1988. *Syllabus design.* New York: Cambridge University Press.

Nunan, D., and C. Lamb. 1996. *The self-directed teacher: Managing the learning process.* New York: Cambridge University Press.

Ochs, E. 1986. Introduction to B. B. Schieffelin and E. Ochs, eds., *Language socialization across cultures.* New York: Cambridge University Press.

O'Malley, J. M., and A. U. Chamot, eds. 1990. *Learning strategies in second language acquisition.* New York: Cambridge University Press.

Oxford, R. L. 1990. *Language learning strategies: What every teacher should know.* Boston, MA: Heinle and Heinle.

Peck, S. 1991. Recognizing and meeting the needs of ESL students. In M. Celce-Murcia, ed., *Teaching English as a second or foreign language,* 363–71. Boston, MA: Heinle and Heinle.

Peirce, B. N. 1995. Social identity, investment, and language learning. *TESOL Quarterly* 29 (1): 9–32.

Peirce, B. N. 1994. Using diaries in second language acquisition. *English Quarterly* 26 (3): 22–29.

Pennycook, A. 1989. The concept of method, interested knowledge, and the politics of language teaching. *TESOL Quarterly* 23 (4): 589–618.

Perez, T. 1996. Course materials. University of Washington ESL Center/downtown program, Seattle.

Phillipson, R. 1992. *Linguistic imperialism.* New York: Oxford University Press.

Poole, D. 1990. Discourse analysis in ethnographic research. *Annual Review of Applied Linguistics* 11:42–56.

Riggenbach, H. 1998. Evaluating learner interactional skills: Conversation at the micro level. In R. Young and A. He, eds., *Language proficiency interviews: A discourse approach,* 53–67. Amsterdam/Philadelphia: John Benjamins.

Riggenbach, H. 1991. Towards an understanding of fluency: A microanalysis of nonnative speaker conversations. *Discourse Processes* 14 (4): 423–42.

Rubin, J., and I. Thompson. 1994. *How to be a more successful language learner.* Boston, MA: Heinle and Heinle.

Rutherford, W. E. 1987. *Second language grammar: Learning and teaching.* New York: Longman.

Sato, C. 1990. Ethnic styles in classroom discourse. In R. Scarcella, E. Andersen, and S. Krashen, eds., *Developing communicative competence in a second language,* 107–20. New York: Newbury House.

Savignon, S. 1991. Communicative language teaching: State of the art. *TESOL Quarterly* 25 (2): 261–78.

Savignon, S. 1983. *Communicative competence: Theory and classroom practice.* Reading, MA: Addison-Wesley.

Saville-Troike, M. 1989. *The ethnography of communication.* 2d ed. Oxford: Blackwell.

Schiffrin, D. 1994. *Approaches to discourse.* Oxford: Blackwell.

Scollon, R. 1995. From sentences to discourses, ethnography to ethnographic: Conflicting trends in TESOL research. *TESOL Quarterly* 29 (2): 381–84.

Seales, M. K. 1995. From blues to bebop: Teaching American culture through jazz. Paper presented at the annual meeting of TESOL, Long Beach, CA.

Short, M. 1990. Discourse analysis in stylistics and literature instruction. *Annual Review of Applied Linguistics* 11:181–95.

Silberstein, S. 1994. *Techniques and resources in teaching reading.* New York: Oxford University Press.

Slimani, A. 1992. Evaluation of classroom interaction. In J. D. Alderson and A. Beretta, eds., *Evaluating second language education,* 197–211. New York: Cambridge University Press.

Sorace, A., S. Gass, and L. Selinker. 1995. *Second language learning data analysis.* Mahwah, NJ: Lawrence Erlbaum.

Spada, N. 1990. Observing classroom behaviors and learning outcomes in different second language programs. In J. C. Richards and D. Nunan, eds., *Second language teacher education,* 293–310. New York: Cambridge University Press.

Strevens, P. 1987. Interaction outside the classroom: Using the community. In W. M. Rivers, ed., *Interactive language teaching,* 170–76. New York: Cambridge University Press.

Swales, J. M. 1990. *Genre analysis: English in academic and research settings.* New York: Cambridge University Press.

Thiong'o, N. 1994. Decolonising the mind: The politics of language in African literature. London: Currey.

Ulichny, P. 1996. What's in a methodology? In D. Freeman and J. C. Richards, eds., *Teacher learning in language teaching,* 178–96. New York: Cambridge University Press.

van Ek, J. A., and L. G. Alexander. 1975. *Threshold level English.* Oxford: Pergamon Press and Council of Europe.

van Lier, L. 1988. *The classroom and the language learner.* New York: Longman.

Vygotsky, L. 1962. *Thoughts and language.* Cambridge: MIT Press.

Weinstein-Shr, G. 1992. Family and intergenerational literacy in multilingual families. *ERIC Q&A.* Washington, DC: Center for Applied Linguistics.

Wennerstrom, A. 1991. *Techniques for teachers: A guide for nonnative speakers of English.* Ann Arbor: University of Michigan Press.

Widdowson, H. G. 1993. English language teaching and ELT teachers: Matters arising. *English Language Teaching Journal* 46 (4): 333–39.

Widdowson, H. G. 1983. New starts and different kinds of failure. In A. Freedman, I. Pringle, and J. Yalden, eds., *Learning to write: First language/second language.* New York: Longman.

Yang, K. Y. 1995. Hmong women in the U.S.: Challenges and opportunities. Paper presented at the annual meeting of TESOL, Long Beach, CA.

Yule, G., and W. Gregory. 1989. Survey interviews for interactive language learning. *English Language Teaching Journal* 13 (2): 142–49.

Yule, G., and E. Tarone. 1990. Eliciting the performance of strategic competence. In R. Scarcella, E. Andersen, and S. Krashen, eds., *Developing communicative competence in a second language,* 179–94. New York: Newbury House.

Chapter 2
Students as Discourse Analysts/Language Researchers: The Spoken Language

Chapter 1 discussed the ways in which current pedagogical practices in the language-teaching field support the use of discourse analysis in the language classroom. Since discourse analysis is often considered a kind of qualitative research, this chapter provides an introduction to qualitative research, identifying the major research concerns and procedures. It concludes with a description of the research skills necessary for students new to discourse analysis and presents a paradigm for designing language research activities for use in the ESOL classroom.

1. Qualitative Research in Perspective

Although this is a book on discourse analysis activities, there is good reason for including a discussion about qualitative research, since discourse analysis comes out of a qualitative research paradigm. Discourse analysis is sometimes viewed as a type of qualitative research. Others believe that discourse analysis is evolving as a discipline in its own right (Schiffrin 1994). I agree with this and cite as evidence a recent North American applied linguistics conference with "discourse communities" as its theme, the 1996 conference of the American Association for Applied Linguistics, in Chicago. This conference drew scholars from many disciplines, with over one hundred papers, colloquiums, and plenaries with the terms *discourse* or *discourse analysis* in their titles or abstracts (AAAL 1996 Program Guide).

The examination of discourse can be quite complex. People unfamiliar with the term *discourse analysis* or the practices of that analysis might feel intimidated by something that sounds so technical (to the layperson). Researchers, especially those not involved in language teaching, may feel it is not possible to conduct discourse analyses without extensive training in qualitative research methods and in discourse analysis techniques. Some qualitative researchers advocate an apprentice relationship as one way, if not the best way, to learn qualitative research methods. However, I believe that if a research question is focused and the task is structured, even a novice language researcher can undertake a discourse analysis project.

Doing a discourse analysis activity outlined in this book is a markedly different task than full-scale ethnographic research, or what Holliday (1994) calls pure ethnography. In contrast to pure ethnography, the individual activities presented in part 2 are designed so that data are limited and therefore manageable. These discourse analysis activities, intended for novice language researchers, resemble tasks (as described in Nunan 1989) rather than ethnographies (such as Heath's 1983 study). Thus, discourse analysts from some disciplines might not consider the activities in these books "real" qualitative research. One of the sources of bias against qualitative research is in fact disagreement about what constitutes qualitative research. Because so many disciplines employ qualitative research methods, the different histories, philosophies, and research objectives of these disciplines have shaped the ways in which research is conducted and reported.

However, this has led to another source of bias against qualitative research: that there is in fact disagreement about what constitutes "standards." Yet across different disciplines, there are certain practices and beliefs that are considered of primary importance. These will be discussed in the next section, "Overview: Qualitative Research Principles and Methodology."

Despite the consensus among qualitative researchers about principles and methodology, in some disciplines of study there are still persistent undertones of quantitative research elitism. This is evident in the proportion of published articles (in major journals across many fields) that primarily employ quantitative approaches to collecting and analyzing data. For example, in graduate programs for ESOL teachers/researchers and for students of applied linguistics, there is an imbalance of courses and textbooks in quantitatively oriented research and design (Henze 1995; Lazaraton 1995). In addition, qualitative research is still often misunderstood, as is evident in the characterization of qualitative research as "anecdotal" (e.g., Henning 1986).

Which approach—qualitative or quantitative—has the most scientific rigor is the subject of long-standing debate not just in the field of applied linguistics but in education more generally (e.g., see Eisner and Peshkin 1990; Bogden and Biklen 1992). Most open-minded researchers would agree that each approach has its place. Different research questions require different research methodologies. Some language researchers, even those who are clearly drawn to one paradigm or another (e.g., Watson-Gegeo 1988; Henning 1986; Chaudron 1986), advocate combining methods when appropriate.

Similarly, Cumming (1994) claims that in language research a choice of orientations exists, depending on the objectives and the kind of research questions asked. Descriptive research is helpful in analyzing and understanding learner language (Tarone 1994; Connor 1994). Interpretive research can provide a holistic perspective and a deep understanding of communication (Cazden 1995; Spada 1994; Hornberger 1994). Research with an ideological orientation can move toward changing situations of inequality (Pennycook 1994; Auerbach 1994).

Few would argue against the claim that different types of qualitative research have their place. One common critical comment, however, is that qualitatively oriented research is not generalizable beyond the group or case explored in a particular study. This criticism has also been applied to studies that employ discourse analytic methods. Quantitative research methods, it is argued, are superior in this way, with the appropriate attention to population and method. However, one of the strengths of qualitative research in general and discourse analysis in particular is that studies are designed to be situation sensitive. Hypotheses come out of the process of collecting and analyzing the data; they are not fixed beforehand. Thus, some say, the results are more likely to reveal "truths," or as Wolfson (1986, 697, after Erickson 1977) puts it, "potentially valid insight into functionally relevant definitions of social facts."

Until the mid-1980s, there was little available textual support to guide novice qualitative researchers. University courses in qualitative research, which were rare, primarily targeted students of anthropology and focused on ethnography, one methodological approach (Henze 1995). However, a growing interest in and need for qualitative research in language studies and other areas is increasing the availability of information in terms of qualitatively oriented collections of research (e.g., see Bailey and Nunan 1996), university courses, and introductory textbooks. In a "progress report" that describes the status of qualitative research in ESOL and applied linguistics, Lazaraton (1995) optimistically anticipates that qualitative research will at some point soon enjoy the credibility and visibility that quantitative approaches to research do.

2. Overview: Qualitative Research Principles and Methodology

It is not my intent in this section to "teach" qualitative research methodology or to present a comprehensive overview of the qualitative research that has been done in the field of language teaching. Rather, my purpose is to provide a brief overview of the concerns and practices that are central to qualitative research and to clarify the relevance of qualitative research to discourse analysis. Readers who want a more comprehensive treatment of qualitative research may be interested in pursuing some of the readings recommended at the end of this chapter (in the Suggested Readings and References section).

Certain practices and beliefs are considered of primary importance to all who do qualitative research. Researchers agree that the following areas are fundamental: the emphasis on reflexivity and the exploration of the researcher's role, the importance of considering the theory-method relationship, triangulation (multiple data collection techniques, data sources, and/or investigators) as a means of increasing validity of findings, and the central role of observation and interviewing as data collection techniques.

Guiding Practices and Beliefs in Qualitative Research

One of the important concerns for qualitative researchers is the role of theory. All methodologies are linked with theories, or as Davis (1995, 436) puts it, "inextricably bound together." An early stage in a qualitative research study is to explore what effects theories may have on the study. Researchers are taught to use a log, or reflexive journal, to examine their philosophical positions, their thought processes, and the bases for decisions they make. This is one method qualitative researchers can use to guard against bias and to explore their own frames of interpretation. Another way is to collaborate. Collaboration can provide an opportunity to debrief, to hear others' perspectives, and to "learn not only that qualitative research is an interpretive process, but also that interpretation is negotiable" (Glesne and Peshkin 1992). These two strategies for guarding against bias are also useful in discourse analysis research.

Besides examining their own "guiding theories" and characterizing biases, researchers also need to identify what other theories may be operating and thus shaping the research. Although qualitative research advocates theory generation through discovery, it is naive to think that there are no preconceived guiding theories going into a project. On the contrary, conceptual frameworks can be useful in informing and guiding a study. Geertz, a respected anthropologist, offers an understanding of theory as being neither explanatory nor predictive (Geertz 1973). Instead, according to him, theory building is interpretation—the act of making sense of a social interaction.

Being conscious of how theory operates at different levels of abstraction is a worthwhile objective as well as a principle of quality qualitative research. Attaining this consciousness is also helpful in studies that employ discourse analysis, where, similarly, researchers' interpretations are shaped by their notions and previous experiences.

How-to books in qualitative research sometimes imply that researchers who are able to place themselves more toward the "observer" pole on the participant-observer continuum will be able to remain more objective than full participants. However, Peirce (1995, 570), drawing from feminist research and critical ethnography, reminds researchers that since they play a "constitutive role in determining the progress of a research project," objectivity is neither a desirable nor a realistic goal. Rather, researchers—including discourse analysts—need to be conscious of the ways that their own histories and experiences intersect with the research at all stages.

Data Collection Issues

Qualitative researchers use a variety of methods of collecting data, called "triangulation" since it may involve multiple data collection methods as well as multiple data sources, investigators, and theoretical perspectives. The reasoning for this is that relying on a single technique or perspective can cause threats to the validity of the results.

According to Grimshaw (1974), the most common data-gathering procedures are the observation of "natural" speech in "natural" settings; the observation of "natural" speech in contrived settings (i.e., experimental situations or those organized by the researcher); and the elicitation of speech through direct inquiries. These data collection methods are used in the spoken language discourse analysis activities presented in this book. Another data collection method used by qualitative researchers, perhaps more relevant to research on the written language, involves an examination of photographs, written documents, and artifacts that can shed light on a phenomenon by providing historical context.

Interviewing is a primary method of obtaining data in qualitative research, a method that is employed in some of the discourse analysis activities presented in part 2. Since "90 percent of all social investigations use interview data," Briggs (1986, 1) argues for a deeper examination of the nature of the interview. Rather than simply accepting the interview as a valid data collection method, Briggs contends, it should be demystified and examined as a communicative event in its own right. More specifically, it should be viewed as a culture-specific speech event, unfamiliar to and uncomfortable for members of many non-Western and nonacademic cultures and subcultures.

Qualitative researchers in some disciplines aim for objectivity in their interviews, yet with such an approach, little consideration may be given to the ways in which interview data are shaped by the interview participant's role relations, by researchers' own beliefs about appropriate interviewing techniques, and by participants' perceptions of the interview (some may view the interview setting as formal and contrived and as very different from the more casual settings in which they normally interact). A clearer understanding of the interview can enhance its usefulness as a research tool. Further, as with all methodological decisions and interpretive choices in qualitative research, the goal is a heightened awareness of the intersection of theory and method and an articulation of the complex of factors involved in interpretation and the presentation of results.

Another critical issue in interviewing is the need for structuring and standardization. Structuring questions beforehand offers some assurance to the researcher that the predetermined questions will be answered; not structuring an interview allows room for tangents and for a more egalitarian contribution to the research agenda and to the form of the discourse. Following up on parts of the discussion that may seem off the interview topic might offer richer data, which may later be relevant in the context of the study, and which may take the analysis in a different direction than expected. Again, the research question will help to determine what discussions are most appropriate and if time should be allowed for both on-topic and tangential discussions. The discourse analysis activities in part 2 provide examples of structured and unstructured interview approaches.

Besides the issue of structuring, another concern in conducting an interview is the amount of rapport that the interviewer and interviewee have. Interviewing a friend encourages intimacy and perhaps more "depth" to the data; interviewing an acquaintance, someone in a culture unfamiliar to the researcher, or someone the researcher has met solely for the purposes of the interview may provide a more objective account. However, like Peirce (1995), Briggs (1986) points out that true objectivity is neither possible nor desirable, given the nature of the interview and the goals of qualitative research (also see Auerbach 1994). Beliefs about interviewing strategies, role relations between interviewer and participant, and the fact that the interviewer is primarily responsible for determining the direction of the interview all affect interpretations and thus must figure into the claims that can be made about reliability and validity. As always, the research objectives are crucial in making these decisions about methodology.

Since the research objectives for different activities in this book vary, the qualitative data collection and analysis methods employed for each activity may have a slightly different slant. The methodology is drawn and adapted from different research traditions because of their potential for addressing the specific research questions posed. However, all the traditions can be considered under the auspices of discourse analysis, if one subscribes to the broader definition of discourse, as described in chapter 1.

Working with Spoken Language Data

Preceding sections of this chapter have presented some of the principles and concerns common to qualitative researchers from a number of disciplines. Because of the close association of qualitative research and discourse analysis, this discussion can be informative when using discourse analytic approaches. The following discussion addresses concerns specific to those researchers working with oral language data. As in the previous sections, since these concerns are introduced only briefly, readers new to discourse analysis and to the study of the spoken language may want to follow up on the suggested readings.

When considering the intersection of theory and method, language researchers who work with spoken language data must contend with issues involving the contrast between native speaker speech and nonnative speaker speech. This contrast is a relevant topic, since one's own "guiding theories" and perspectives about nonnative and native speaker skills and knowledge may impact interpretations and thus figure largely into the outcome of a research project. For the nonnative speaker of English using discourse analysis as a means of studying language, the exploration of this topic can be rewarding and enlightening. Learners can discover for themselves that there is no such thing as "perfect" speech—that is, native speakers make errors, too.

The issue called "the deficiency/proficiency dichotomy" is also worth thinking about. Most language teachers and researchers do not find such a concept particularly useful (e.g., Firth 1995). Rather than perceiving language learners as moving toward target or native-like proficiency from a point of zero proficiency, it is perhaps more productive and logical to think in terms of learner interlanguage (see Larsen-Freeman and Long 1991 for a discussion of the history of this term). Perceiving learners' language as rule governed and systematic, at all stages of learning, is a more neutral perspective less oriented toward the target language. Regarding learners' language as a system in its own right may open up research on learners' language and may motivate questions and observations that might not have otherwise come up.

Most discourse analysts who work with authentic spoken language data recognize that "perfect" native speaker speech is a fallacy and that it may be more helpful to think instead in terms of a descriptive/prescriptive dichotomy. In other words, researchers who take on the task of describing language that is used in real, unrehearsed talk observe that the speech of native speakers often does not conform to a prescriptive "standard." Spoken language is notably different than written language; formal rehearsed language is notably different than language used in unrehearsed, informal contexts.

These perspectives and issues are also important since they imply that (1) native speaker speech is neither perfect nor error free; (2) spoken language differs from written language in many important ways (in fact, some think of oral language as not just a different mode but a different system altogether); and (3) since learners' language is systematic and rule governed, it is a system in its own right, not something "less" than native speaker speech. A number of language researchers either are language teachers or language learners or are interested in applications of their findings to language teaching. Thus, these three issues, among the many that may arise when analyzing spoken language data from nonnative and native speakers, have important pedagogical implications. Ideological views, conscious and unconscious, are likely to affect teacher and student attitudes and conduct, as well as students' progress in the language they are learning. These topics are rich in potential as focused discourse analysis activities that target the macro level.

Additional considerations arise when working with oral language data. With the technology available today, language researchers need not rely only on observation techniques; they can use videotaping and audiotaping to "freeze" face-to-face interactions. This is especially appropriate for discourse analysis activities that target spoken language micro features that may be largely unconscious. For example, researchers interested in what makes for a "fluent"-sounding conversation can review (repeatedly) audiotapes or videotapes of conversations in order to isolate how speakers claim, yield, and maintain their turns of talk. Simply observing conversational interactions (in real time) would not be likely to provide the kind of detail necessary to establish whether patterns exist or not.

However, the process of videotaping or audiotaping interactions can initially raise objections, since some believe that speakers unaccustomed to this procedure may not be behaving "naturally." Transcription is another challenge for researchers working with spoken language data. For ease of analysis, audiotaped or videotaped spoken exchanges are often transformed into written text. But this process can pose problems of reliability (the researcher is once removed from the original source of the data) and validity (the researcher must make decisions about what information should be recorded in writing and, from the opposite perspective, what information will be "lost").

For example, how important are the lengths of a speaker's pauses, the subtle changes in pitch and volume, the intonation contours, and the point at which one speaker's words "overlap" with another's? And, when examining videotaped material, how essential to the research questions being pursued are the nonverbal features: gestures, facial expressions, and bodily orientation/posture changes? Seasoned qualitative researchers point out that every stage of a qualitative research project must be considered interpretive (Glesne and Peshkin 1992). Thus, the act of the transcription of spoken language into written words and symbols is actually an early stage of analysis, since transcription involves determining which features are important enough to note, certainly an act of interpretation.

As with any research, it is important that researchers be aware of their limitations in observation skills. With written language, information is taken in visually, through words or graphics on a surface—in these days, a computer monitor as well as paper. But with spoken language, researchers are reliant on other observation skills—on their ability to perceive a broader range of visual phenomena, such as facial expressions and physical orientation of speakers to each other, and also on their ability to note complex aural information, conveyed by a speaker's pitch, volume, and voice quality, by hesitation phenomena, by the coordination of turns between speakers, and so on. If a transcription is to serve as an accurate and comprehensive written record for an exchange that is actually contextualized in and by such visual and aural cues, then these limitations need to be taken into consideration as possible threats to validity.

In some cases, where a micro-oriented analysis is important, additional technological support may be appropriate. For example, there is technology available that can physically chart certain aural phenomena, such as pitch changes and intonation contours (see, e.g., the research on intonation in Wennerstrom 1994). For some researchers, however, such technology may be inaccessible or prohibitively expensive, and for some research questions, an approach as micro-oriented as to require this kind of technology is inappropriate.

Many discourse analysts who work with spoken language insist that the spoken record—the videotape or audiotape—must always serve as the original data source. In other words, the written record is only used as a backup source, for ease of discussion and explanation, not as a substitute for the recorded oral/aural exchange. In working with oral data, the written transcript accompanies the original data (e.g., observation notes and/or the videotape or audiotape) rather than replaces the original data source. Transcriptions are, then, less than adequate as representations of authentic, real-time speech. However, in many of the discourse analysis activities in part 2, detailed and accurate transcriptions are not necessarily appropriate, depending on the research objective.

3. An Approach for Conducting Discourse Analysis Activities

For many of the activities presented in this book, student researchers are encouraged to use a journal as a forum for examining their philosophical positions and the bases for decisions they make as they proceed in their research. They are also encouraged to collaborate, which can provide an opportunity to hear others' perspectives and to explore the frames of inter-pretation that may be operating, and which can thus serve as a check on validity.

Since conceptual frameworks can also be useful as a way of informing and guiding a study, one way language researchers can prepare for their observations is to anticipate the features or structures that address the research question posed. They can do this by collaboratively designing their own data collection sheets or by adapting the "roughed out" data collection sheets provided in some of the activities in this book. Observing with a preset list of categories may be viewed as something other than "true" qualitative research, since a priori categorization and labeling can limit the kinds of fea-tures that the researcher notices and can thus bias the analysis. But the prac-tice of preparing a data collection sheet can be seen as appropriate for some narrowly defined research questions. The focused research objectives in this book make the data manageable and the discourse analysis studies doable in a short period of time. Preparing for the kind of data that is likely to be rele-vant is helpful to students studying discourse in a limited time frame, since it can alert them to what they might (and should) observe. In addition, the act of collaborating with others to prepare a data collection sheet can activate schema.

The following paradigm is useful for designing discourse analysis activi-ties for use in the ESOL classroom. Each stage relies on research skills consis-tent with the principles of qualitative research. The six steps also structure the discourse analysis activity so that it is a manageable research project that can be done in a limited amount of time—usually in one to five one-hour class periods.

Step 1: Predict Learners make predictions about the target structure.

Step 2: Plan Learners set up a research plan that will produce samples of the target structure.

Step 3: Collect data Learners observe and/or record the target structure in its discourse environment.

Step 4: Analyze Learners analyze the data and explain results/make conclusions.

Step 5: Generate Learners discuss the target structure or produce the target structure in its appropriate context.

Step 6: Review Learners summarize their findings or reanalyze the data that they produced, asking whether the data conform to their conclusions in Step 4.

In *Step 1* of the discourse analysis activities in this book, learners first predict what they may find. This step is designed to be schema activating in that learners draw insights from what they know about their native language or about the act of communicating in general. This step also is intended to make conscious any guiding theories that may be operating in the minds of the researchers, since their analysis and collection of data are likely to be shaped by their beliefs and attitudes.

In *Step 2,* learners plan: they discuss where and with what speakers they are likely to find samples of the target structure, and they consider questions regarding their data collection and interpretation. For example, can the learners collect the data unobtrusively, in natural settings, by audiotape or videotape? Will they need to describe their research objectives to the speaker, the "informant," or the person they are interviewing? If the structure they are interested in is not likely to occur frequently in natural circumstances, will they need to set up a situation that elicits the data? If so, how can they best do this? What are the best ways to get information about more macro-oriented topics or constructs, such as power relations and societal values? How might the researchers' own notions about the research process affect the outcome of the research?

In *Step 3,* learners collect data: they gather information about the target structure, and they observe and/or record the target structure in its discourse environment. Each activity in this book offers explicit suggestions for doing this in ways appropriate to the research question. Teachers and students, in doing these activities, may find that they can think up other data collection methods that better suit their own research "style."

In *Step 4,* learners analyze the data and explain the results or draw conclusions. In this step, too, each activity provides suggested ways of structuring the analysis and of presenting results. There is, however, as with all of the steps, a great deal of latitude in adapting the way in which this step is conducted.

Step 5 provides an opportunity for learners themselves to generate the target structure in its appropriate context. With some discourse analysis activities, this may not be appropriate. For example, if the research goal targets macro-level structures, such as the social forces that operate in the language classroom, then Step 5 is a point where learners generate language about the structure: they propose hypotheses, plan ways of validating their findings further, or discuss what was interesting or unexpected about the research findings.

Step 6 serves as a review in which learners summarize their findings. If in Step 5 learners themselves produced speech that included the target structure, then this step is the final stage of analysis, in which learners analyze the data they produced. They ask whether their own data about the target structure conform to their conclusions in Step 4—in other words, how their own learner-produced data compare to what they discovered in their earlier analysis.

The discourse analysis activities presented in this book encourage the instructor to act as coresearcher and facilitator rather than expert. However, teachers who are more comfortable with teacher-as-expert approaches may want to first do an activity themselves and/or research further the feature or structure under investigation

Findings are dependent on the data; thus, many of the activities have no one right or wrong conclusion. A primary goal of these discourse analysis activities is to stimulate student interest in language, to develop learners' confidence in their own abilities to "discover" truths about the structure of language, and to help raise learners' consciousness not only about the structure of language but also about their own linguistic strengths and weaknesses. My intent in presenting the activities in part 2 is primarily to have them serve as examples of the types of activities that can be used in the classroom. Ideally, language students and language teachers will become interested in and pursue topics beyond those presented in the activities in this book, developing their own research objectives and then designing and conducting original discourse analysis activities.

For Teachers: Discussion Questions

1. What are some of the reasons for bias against qualitative research? If you are familiar with quantitative research methodology, describe some of the advantages that this kind of research may have.
2. Think of one research question that would most appropriately use qualitative research methods, one research question that would most appropriately use quantitative research methods, and one that would most appropriately use a combination of these methods. Discuss your answers with others to get their perspectives.

3. As a language teacher, have you done anything that can be called qualitative research? An approach to answering this question is to think about whether you have systematically tried to describe, interpret, or change some language behavior or practice inside (or outside) the language classroom.
4. What have been your experiences with collaboration? Do you tend to feel comfortable working with others and sharing perspectives, or do you prefer to work independently?
5. Tape-record a short segment of speech. The context can be anything from a conversation in which you are participating to a more formal radio news program. Transcribe a minute or two of this talk. What problems do you encounter? What decisions do you need to make as you go? How long does it take you to do this transcription?

Suggested Readings and References

Bailey, K. M., and D. Nunan, eds. 1996. *Voices from the classroom: Qualitative research in second language education.* New York: Cambridge University Press.

Although the objective of this book is to describe what actually happens in language classrooms from the perspectives of teachers and researchers, the methodology used by these teachers and researchers is qualitative rather than quantitative. Thus, this book can serve as a "sampler" of qualitative research as well as a guide for people who want to conduct interpretive research in their own teaching and learning situations.

Briggs, C. L. 1986. *Learning how to ask: A sociolinguistic appraisal of the role of the interview in social science research.* New York: Cambridge University Press.

In this book, Briggs, trained in anthropological linguistics, reflects on his own research "blunders," and he thereby raises questions about interviewing procedures. He proposes techniques for designing, implementing, and analyzing interview-based research. Thus, this text is useful not only as a guide to interviewing techniques and approaches but also as a model of the kind of inquiry into methodology that is currently taking place in the social sciences.

Glesne, C., and A. Peshkin. 1992. *Becoming qualitative researchers: An introduction.* New York: Longman.

This readable book introduces the process of qualitative inquiry. It describes each stage of the research process, from research design to the reporting of research findings. Although it is extremely useful as a general introduction to qualitative research, it does not specifically address research in language studies, language acquisition, or language teaching.

Hatch, E. 1992. *Discourse and language education.* New York: Cambridge University Press.

This book was not intended as a how-to book in the same sense as the Glesne and Peshkin text (see the preceding listing), yet it can certainly provide a foundation in discourse analysis, the specific kind of qualitative research that the book is concerned with. In other words, the orientation of Hatch's book is that of a discourse analyst (studying systematicity in language) and of a language educator specifically (studying language learners' language). Thus, it is valuable in the narrower sense of providing exposure to the theoretical and methodological concerns of one kind of qualitative research.

AAAL (American Association for Applied Linguistics). 1996 Annual Conference Program Guide.

Auerbach, E. 1994. Participatory action research. In A. Cumming, ed., Alternatives in TESOL research: Descriptive, interpretive, and ideological orientations. *TESOL Quarterly* 28 (4): 693–97.

Bailey, K. M., and D. Nunan. 1996. *Voices from the language classroom: Qualitative research in second language education.* New York: Cambridge University Press.

Bogden, R., and S. K. Biklen. 1992. *Qualitative research for education: An introduction to theory and methods.* 2d ed. Boston: Allyn and Bacon.

Briggs, C. L. 1986. *Learning how to ask: A sociolinguistic appraisal of the role of the interview in social science research.* New York: Cambridge University Press.

Cazden, C. B. 1995. New ideas for research on classroom discourse. In "Research Issues": Methodological challenges in discourse analysis. *TESOL Quarterly* 29 (2): 384–87.

Chaudron, C. 1986. The interaction of quantitative and qualitative approaches to research: A view of the second language classroom. *TESOL Quarterly* 20 (4): 709–17.

Connor, U. 1994. Text analysis. In A. Cumming, ed., Alternatives in TESOL research: Descriptive, interpretive, and ideological orientations. *TESOL Quarterly* 28 (4): 682–84.

Cumming, A., ed. 1994. Alternatives in TESOL research: Descriptive, interpretive, and ideological orientations. *TESOL Quarterly* 28 (4): 673–703.

Davis, K. A. 1995. Qualitative theory and methods in applied linguistics research. *TESOL Quarterly* 29 (3): 427–53.

Eisner, E. W., and A. Peshkin, eds. 1990. *Qualitative inquiry in education: The continuing debate.* New York: Teachers College Press.

Erickson, F. 1977. Some approaches to inquiry in school/community ethnography. *Anthropology and Education Quarterly* 8:58–69.

Firth, A. 1995. On conversation analysis and foreign language data. Paper presented at the TESOL colloquium "Face-to-Face Interaction and SLL/A," Long Beach, CA.

Geertz, C. 1973. *The interpretation of cultures.* New York: Basic Books.

Glesne, C., and A. Peshkin. 1992. *Becoming qualitative researchers: An introduction.* New York: Longman.

Grimshaw, A. D. 1974. Data and data use in an analysis of communicative events. In R. Bauman and J. Sherzer, eds., *Explorations in the ethnography of speaking,* 419–24. New York: Cambridge University Press.

Heath, S. B. 1983. *Ways with words: Language, life, and work in communities and classrooms.* New York: Cambridge University Press.

Henning, G. 1986. Quantitative methods in language acquisition research. *TESOL Quarterly* 20 (4): 701–8.

Henze, R. C. 1995. Guides for the novice qualitative researcher. *TESOL Quarterly* 29 (3): 595–99.

Holliday, A. 1994. *Appropriate methodology and social context.* New York: Cambridge University Press.

Hornberger, N. H. 1994. Ethnography. In A. Cumming, ed., Alternatives in TESOL research: Descriptive, interpretive, and ideological orientations. *TESOL Quarterly* 28 (4): 688–90.

Larsen-Freeman, D., and M. Long. 1991. *An introduction to second language acquisition research.* New York: Longman.

Lazaraton, A. 1995. Qualitative research in applied linguistics research: A progress report. *TESOL Quarterly* 29 (3): 455–72.

Nunan, D. 1989. *Designing tasks for the communicative classroom.* New York: Cambridge University Press.

Peirce, B. N. 1995. Social identity, investment, and language learning. *TESOL Quarterly* 29 (1): 9–32.

Pennycook, A. 1989. The concept of method, interested knowledge, and the politics of language teaching. *TESOL Quarterly* 23 (4): 589–618.

Schiffrin, D. 1994. *Approaches to discourse.* Oxford: Blackwell.

Spada, N. 1994. Classroom interaction analysis. In A. Cumming, ed., Alternatives in TESOL research: Descriptive, interpretive, and ideological orientations. *TESOL Quarterly* 28 (4): 685–88.

Tarone, E. 1994. Analysis of learners' language. In A. Cumming, ed., Alternatives in TESOL research: Descriptive, interpretive, and ideological orientations. *TESOL Quarterly* 28 (4): 676–78.

Watson-Gegeo, K. A. 1988. Ethnography in ESL: Defining the essentials. *TESOL Quarterly* 22 (4): 575–92.

Wennerstrom, A. 1994. Intonational meaning in English discourse: A study of nonnative speakers. *Applied Linguistics* 15 (4): 399–420.

Wolfson, N. 1986. Research methodology and the question of validity. *TESOL Quarterly* 20 (4): 689–700.

Part 2
Activities

. . . .

Chapter 3
Ways of Speaking

. . . .

1. Discussion
2. Suggestions for Developing Original Activities
Sample Activities 1–14
For Teachers: Discussion Questions
Suggested Readings and References

Part 2 presents discourse analysis activities that instructors can use with their language students or that instructors themselves can use to explore spoken language. Chapters 3 and 4 begin with general introductions to the area under discussion—oral skills in this chapter and other traditionally taught skill areas (e.g., grammar, vocabulary) in chapter 4. In both chapters, I suggest ways to go about developing original activities and recommend further readings for readers who wish for more information on related topics.

The bulk of the two chapters in part 2 is devoted to a description of actual discourse analysis activities that have been used with English language students. Selected activities are accompanied by student-collected data (located in the appendixes), which serve both as examples of how language learners respond to using these activities and as evidence of the kind of learning that can take place.

The activities in this book are intended to help learners become aware of the patterns that operate in natural discourse. They are initially directed "outward": in this chapter, learners listen to and analyze data produced by others (usually native or "expert" speakers), making hypotheses about possible patterns. In terms of productive skills, the learners' findings can be used as topics of discussion and cross-cultural comparisons and as models used in planning and self-monitoring learners' own talk.

This awareness about learners' own oral skills can only be achieved through self-monitoring and self-evaluation. As with the skill of writing, in speaking, learners need first to produce language (in this case, the parallel is recorded speech, on audiotape or videotape) and then to analyze their language, to note areas of difficulty and patterns of error, to make conscious changes, and, ideally, to monitor progress in order to gain confidence in their own development. For years, teachers of writing have implemented such an approach (Kroll 1990), with the belief that consciousness about one's own skills can only contribute to increased proficiency. It is high time that spoken language be given the same kind of attention.

1. Discussion

The advent of technology in the past quarter century has allowed language researchers to tape-record spontaneous speech, a practice that has become a standard data-gathering method for sociolinguists, ethnographers, cultural anthropologists, and others interested in language use. Actual interactions by native speakers and by learners of a language can become frozen in time and thus can serve as objects of scrutiny. The technique of tape-recording spoken language data is compatible with an interest in language at the discourse level, although all levels of language are appropriate units of analysis, from the occurrence of a particular phonological feature or grammatical structure, to an entire speech act sequence and the bridging to another topic, to the ways of speaking that provide insight into people's attitudes and beliefs. However, when entire interactions are available as data, it is natural to move beyond the levels that interest most theoretical linguists—the sentence level (syntax), the word level (semantics), and the sound level (phonology). With masses of natural, spoken data available, it is appropriate to study greater chunks of discourse and to examine how and why items within this larger context are organized.

For researchers interested in spoken discourse, then, data consist of extended text. This is different from what may be used as data by a theoretical linguist—sentences generated by native speakers or by the researchers themselves, intended in part to serve as demonstrations of speakers' language competence. But by observing natural language spoken by actual users of the language, researchers can gain information not about what they think language is but about what it actually is and how it operates. Analyses need not be intuition based but are accountable to the data: they try to explain the data both sequentially (Why does X follow Y?) and distributionally (Why does X occur with Y and not with Z?) On an even broader level, what people think about is revealed in their ways of speaking—in their choice of topics as well as in the manner in which they express themselves, verbally and nonverbally.

Conversation

Conversation has been of primary interest to language researchers, since natural, unplanned, everyday conversation is the most commonly occurring and universal language "genre." In every language and culture, conversation is a speech activity in which all members of a community routinely participate. Conversation is thought to be the primary domain for language socialization and language development, yet it is also the most "unspecial" and unspecialized kind of communication: everyone learns how to make conversation, and everyone routinely makes conversation (with a few, very rare exceptions). The analysis of conversation is often thought to provide a foundation for discourse analysis in general, and even more importantly, it is believed that an understanding of the structures and processes of conversation is essential to an understanding of language.

Conversation analysts are interested in what is systematic about spontaneous, everyday conversation. Systematic features are exhibited as practices *in* conversation and as practices *of* conversation. Within a conversation, speakers can accomplish social functions: they can, for example, compliment, ask questions, give information, apologize, disagree, and make invitations.

In every language, there are also activities speakers do, for the most part unconsciously, that are systematic features of conversation: speakers take turns and observe the "rules" of turn taking specific to their speech community and language group, they repair inaccuracies of speech, and they indicate when they do and do not understand what an interlocutor is saying. Goffman (1976) refers to these features as "universal constraints" since they occur in all communication systems. "Social constraints"—which smooth interactions and allow participants to reveal their competence as speakers of a language and as members of a society—are also considered universal. Interestingly, most of these components have not drawn attention from language teachers, perhaps in part because they are largely unconscious practices and are thus not thought of as easily teachable. However, functions that speakers accomplish in conversation, called speech acts or language functions, have in fact been of interest to language teachers, since such functions are usually easily identifiable and formulaic and are therefore viewed as teachable and learnable.

Some conversation researchers separate the study of universal constraints (the practices *of* conversation) from the study of speech acts (the practices *in* conversation). Goffman (1981), for example, considers conversation to be by nature unplanned and aimless, noninstrumental except for phatic exchange and social participation. He describes conversation as the talk occurring when a small number of participants come together and settle into what they perceive to be a few moments cut off from (or carried on to the side of) instrumental tasks; a period of idling felt to be an end in itself, during which everyone is accorded the right to talk as well as to listen and without reference to a fixed schedule; everyone is accorded the status of someone whose overall evaluation of the subject matter at hand is to be encouraged and treated with respect; and no final agreement or synthesis is demanded, differences of opinion to be treated as unprejudicial to the continuing relationship of the participants. (Goffman 1981, 14 n. 8)

According to Goffman, then, speech acts might best be considered instrumental tasks that occur within conversation but do not themselves necessarily comprise conversation.

Conversation analysts are not the only researchers interested in conversation. Sociolinguists with broader interests are curious about how the conversational conventions, rules, and patterns of particular subcultures can be understood in the larger context of the society in which they occur; in other words, how do the conventions of conversation reflect the values and structure of the society in which they occur? Similarly, ethnographers and cultural anthropologists are interested in how conversation styles fit into and characterize the culture of particular groups or individuals. In contrast, speech event analysts explore conversation to see how utterances work together to perform functions.

Discourse analysts of various bents find the study of speech acts appealing since the sequences in which they occur, called speech events, are easily identifiable, with (usually) predictable beginnings, middles, and endings. For example, when a speaker of American English is about to invite a close friend to do something, there is usually a pre-invitation type question, such as "What are you doing Friday night?" It is clear to the listener in most cases that an invitation is about to follow, and if this is desired, the usual response is "Oh, nothing. Why?" The first speaker then describes possible plans (an implicit invitation) or possibly makes an explicit invitation. Invitation sequences, like other speech events, are relatively formulaic by nature.

In the late seventies, van Ek (1976) and a project of the Council of Europe took on the formidable task of analyzing speech events exhaustively, in order to better address learner needs. This functional-notional approach was taken up by a number of materials developers in the language-teaching field, since it was and still is believed that learners benefit from explicit instruction about the sociocultural appropriateness of various related utterances for accomplishing particular speech events in given settings (see, e.g., Tanka and Most 1990; Tillitt and Bruder 1985).

This interest in sociocultural factors reflects an interest in communicative competence (see chapter 1 for further discussion on this topic), which goes beyond sentence-level, accuracy-oriented approaches to teaching and takes into consideration other factors—the relationship of the speakers to each other, the formality of the setting (i.e., register), the ability of the learner to compensate for a lack of proficiency resulting in a perceived shortage of relevant vocabulary items or of grammatical structures. In fact, the notion of communicative competence as defined in Canale and Swain 1980 and Canale 1983 places at issue how the notion of competence is to be defined: are learners exhibiting competence if there is evidence in their spoken language of incomplete knowledge of the sociocultural rules of appropriateness, of the discourse norms, or of the strategies that ensure successful communication? Are they exhibiting competence if there is a great deal of grammatical inaccuracy in their spoken language at the level of syntax, pronunciation, and lexical choice?

These concerns and evidence from language learners whose learning processes appear to be fossilized have motivated a reassessment of classroom activities and procedures and, consequently, a return to greater attention to form (Celce-Murcia 1991; van Essen 1989; see also Yule and Tarone 1990, 179–82). A discourse-oriented approach to teaching speaking is compatible with the need to address form to a greater extent. Structure at both the micro and macro level can be brought to consciousness, and thus accuracy and appropriateness are issues at both levels.

While language teachers have addressed the macro aspect of conversational discourse, which focuses on the activities speakers do in conversation, few approaches focus on the more micro level features of conversation—the turn-taking system, for example (see Lynch 1996 and Yule 1996, both of which are exceptions in that they do suggest that turn taking can be addressed in the language classroom). Repair, a way of ensuring that communication is comprehensible and interpretable, is an exception: it is often taught as a type of macro-level speech event or as an information-gathering strategy. The goal of teaching repair is usually to employ a learner with a means of expressing a lack of comprehension and of requesting clarification—functions that are unquestionably of use to a language learner.

There are other aspects of repair that are rarely treated by language teachers. At the micro level, learners have an urgent need to initiate self-repair to ensure that they are being understood. In addition to that goal, self-repair and the use of "fillers" in conversation can help to ensure that speakers maintain their right to speak once they have gained the floor.

Beyond the issue of repair, there are many characteristics of conversation that may promote learning in language learners. When students are made aware of some of the micro mechanics of conversation that affect other people's perceptions of their language ability, their interest is piqued. This awareness can serve as a built-in motivation for learners to not only notice these practices but become more skilled at conversation themselves.

How and how much nonnative speakers participate in conversation affect judgments about their language competence, but these generalizations are not limited to nonnative speaker speech. For a friend or observer, how and when a speaker pauses or takes a breath before he or she speaks may be evidence about the speaker's personality, attitude, or verbal ability. Whether or not a speaker raises his or her voice to gain the floor or withdraws when there is competition to speak; how much a speaker hesitates or varies pitch; whether a conversation participant responds verbally and enthusiastically to other speakers' comments, maintains steady eye contact, or collaborates to help out another speaker by finishing his or her sentence—all this provides information not only about language skills but about who a person is and how that person thinks.

In such a verbally oriented language and culture as mainstream North America (excluding many individual exceptions and minorities who are oriented to silence), it is difficult to not link such "mannerisms" to personality. Interestingly, these mannerisms are actually conversation-based behaviors that every member of every language group practices as a conversation participant, although, naturally, they vary slightly from individual to individual and can be perceived in part as personal "style." Speakers are judged in part on their behavior as a conversation participant, rather than on content—on how they say something, rather than on what they are talking about. Interesting too is the fact that this basis for opinion forming on the part of listeners may be largely unconscious, but nevertheless, it may be helpful information for learners. Micro-level conversation behaviors can affect perceptions about personality. This may also be true in a learner's own language and culture: someone's conversational style may be the source of a personal reaction and/or an impression concerning personality.

Nonconversation Genres

Beyond the arguments for teaching conversation-related skills to language students are reasons for introducing other spoken language discourse structures. Learners of English are very likely to encounter the need to demonstrate some language competence in situations other than conversations in social settings. Speech events that are likely to occur within conversations (e.g., personal narratives) can also occur in genres associated with more formal settings. For the high number of nonnative speakers in academic or work environments, there are numerous occasions where the issue of register will affect how a speech event is conducted.

Some speech events may cross the boundary between formal and informal registers: one may or may not disagree with or complain to or apologize to a friend, for example, but it might be *necessary* to do any of these when in a more formal setting (e.g., with an employer or employee) or when in an academic setting (e.g., with an advisor or instructor). Usually intended for nonnative speakers in English-speaking colleges and universities, most functionally oriented language textbooks address the issues of social appropriateness and register (e.g., Bode and Lee 1987; Ferrer and Whalley 1990; Jones and Von Baeyer 1983).

There has been some attention given, too, to academic genres likely to be important to international teaching assistants (ITAs) in English-speaking universities and to visiting scholars in professional environments, such as conferences (see, e.g., textbooks for ITAs; Wennerstrom 1991 is an excellent source). Often included in activities designed for such learners are discussion leading and discussion participation, formal speech giving, and explaining or introducing concepts and responding to listeners' questions (which simulates a teacher-student or presenter-audience environment).

Recent work in the area of listening comprehension also emphasizes how important genre is in determining form. Listening to an academic lecture in a language not your own requires different skills than participating in a conversation (see Flowerdew 1994). This is in part due to the differences in the objective of the talk. Brown and Yule (1983) make the distinction between talk that is primarily transactional (where the goal is to convey information) and talk that is primarily interactional (where the goal is to establish and maintain social relationships). In transactional contexts, it is helpful, if not essential, to understand how information is structured and what features are important in the identification, deconstruction, and comprehension of this information.

As with conversation, it is possible in such academic genres to heighten consciousness of discourse practices at both the micro and the macro level. At the micro level, learners can be trained to alert themselves to discourse signaling cues in both the receptive and productive mode, as do ITAs, conference participants, and visiting scholars. Since it is believed that how learners hear English is related to how learners speak English, teachers of pronunciation, for example, often train learners to, first, identify intonation patterns in native speaker speech and, second, practice and produce these patterns in contextualized settings (Morley 1991).

At a more macro level, learners can be introduced to the practice of observing the ways in which discourse structures are associated with particular genres. For example, good lecturers and speech givers engage listeners early on, with introductions that include stories or examples relevant to the audience; they emphasize major points by presenting a number of perspectives or illustrations, by reiterating, and by incorporating vivid, timely, and/or useful explanations. Good discussion leaders are able to draw out individuals by bridging from previous participators' comments and by exploiting topics fully. These are examples of discourse features that language students can learn both to recognize and to use in their own speech.

Macro-Level Social Constructs

This chapter also includes sample activities that address constructs "larger than language"—for example, values, power relationships, and belief systems, revealed in and shaped by the ways people talk and the ways people write. Such structures are considered macro-level constructs, since they are not individual, identifiable constituents or even bundles of features that can be associated with certain genres or certain speech events. Rather, they are systems of thought and behavior that identify and shape particular cultures. These macro-level features relate to the wider definition of discourse as a cultural complex of signs and practices. Accordingly, classroom activities that explore these constructs examine how we live socially and also what factors contribute to regulating how we behave and what we believe.

Clearly, discourse activities at this macro level target constructs that are less discrete and more complex than those targeted by activities at the micro level. Research disciplines traditionally associated with such macro-level concerns are ethnography and cultural anthropology, both of which aim to create holistic descriptions that characterize the cultural values and structures of a society. This goal is not so different, actually, than that of research disciplines that concentrate on more micro-level features, since systematicity revealed by these features can also reveal truths about social contexts and, in fact, can invoke these contexts.

Although the sample activities presented in this chapter target structures or features at different levels, all are true to the goal of identifying system. All aim to raise researchers' consciousness about language and the forces that shape language. All use research tools associated with discourse analytic traditions of various disciplines.

Discourse Analysts Who Work with Spoken Language Data

For each sample activity presented in this chapter, a synopsis that orients the teacher to the academic discipline most likely to address the activity's topic is included. The discourse analysts most closely associated with the research objectives of the different activities in this chapter on spoken language include conversation analysts, sociolinguists, speech event analysts, and ethnographers. Two of the corresponding research disciplines—conversation analysis and speech event analysis—are narrower in scope than the others, targeting features considered to fall more toward the micro-level pole of the continuum. The remaining two disciplines—sociolinguistics and ethnography—are much broader, more inclusive, and more macro-level oriented.

Similar research objectives might be held and similar topics might be explored by other traditions not named here (e.g., cultural anthropology, communication theory). However, the four research types presented here are, I believe, most representative of the different discourse analytic traditions that explore spoken language. It is important to realize that the differences between traditions may be slight, depending on the research objective. In other words, the different disciplines are not always clearly distinctive.

Given those qualifications, the following researcher descriptions specify (1) the data typically used by the researchers under discussion, (2) the researchers' essential beliefs, and (3) the researchers' special interests. The descriptions are synopses that aim not at thoroughness but at essence. Learners and instructors who themselves design activities or who experiment with the sample activities in this book may find that they want to expand on these summaries.

Conversation analysts *typically use as data* videotapes and audiotapes of people interacting, supported by detailed transcripts. *They believe* that conversation can reveal truths about social contexts and that conversation invokes context. *They are interested in* the micro mechanics of conversation: sequencing, turn taking, repair.

Sociolinguists *typically use as data* language in use—observed or recorded communications. *They believe* that each community or subculture has its own unique set of conventions, rules, and patterns for the conduct of communication. *They are especially interested in* how these rules and patterns can be understood in the context of a general system that reflects the values and the structure of the society in which they occur.

Speech event analysts *typically use as data* the set of utterances, elicited or observed, that together perform a communicative function. *They believe* that research should result in a description of the speech setting, the participants, and the structure of the event, set in a template-like sequence. *They are especially interested in* the connection between function and form, and *they are also interested in* how speech act functions are realized in larger text units.

Ethnographers *typically use as data* interviews and participant and non-participant observations that occur in natural settings over a long period of time. *They believe* that cultural meanings are revealed by people's behavior, which can only be understood by incorporating the subjective perceptions and belief systems of the researcher. *They are especially interested in* developing descriptive and interpretive accounts that characterize the culture of a group or an individual.

More macro-level constructs, such as values, power and solidarity relationships (as in Tannen 1992), and belief systems, are revealed in and shaped by the ways people talk. Besides examining oral discourse, language researchers can also find rich sources for understanding cultural patterns in written texts. This issue is addressed in the macro-level oriented activities in this book's companion volume, *Discourse Analysis in the Language Classroom: Volume 2. The Written Language* (Riggenbach and Stephan forthcoming).

2. Suggestions for Developing Original Activities

An obvious area of application in the language classroom is for students to research how a particular speech event is negotiated, with the goal being to "discover" the components of that speech event. For example, what is the "formula" for a complimenting and thanking sequence, and how do such factors as age, gender, topic, and setting affect what is said and how it is said (Activity 7)? Or, when are complaints appropriate, and how can they be done sensitively and thus effectively (i.e., so that the problem is addressed)?

Recognizing the components of a particular speech event and understanding the sociolinguistic variables might be the final goal in a listening class, but in a course where speaking is the focus, it is the first step. Acting as a participant in the speech event—and producing the speech event in a linguistically accurate and sociolinguistically appropriate manner—is the obvious next step. Role plays and script writing are used fairly routinely in language classrooms to "practice" appropriate understanding of speech acts/events; other techniques are discussed in the sample activities in this chapter.

There also is a wealth of possibilities for creating classroom materials that have a more macro-level focus. Any topics that address the values, belief systems, or structure of a society are targeting macro-level discourse constructs. Characterizing the culture of a group need not be a massive undertaking; rather, activities can highlight pieces of what can contribute to a more holistic understanding of culture. For example, in Activity 14 learners view a full-length film that portrays a subculture not native to the learners, with one possibility that it be representative of the target language/culture. Learners focus on what is revealed about the film characters' belief systems in particular areas, which helps to narrow the otherwise formidable topic of culture. Almost any topic that is interesting to students can potentially be explored from a cross-cultural perspective or with the objective of understanding a society, even one's own, more holistically.

To explore more micro-oriented features, language learners first listen to language, analyzing actual language data. Next, they speak: they generate language themselves, using the data as a model for language that they produce or as the topic for further discussion. In activities that explore more macro-level constructs, learners first listen to the ways that topics are talked about or to what is revealed, through talk, about culture. The talk they then generate is a step in the analytic process: they discuss their findings, and they review their discoveries in light of their own cultural frameworks and personal orientations.

For most of the activities suggested in this book, then, the following model (as presented in chapter 2) will be useful.

Objective: The purpose of the activity.

Background: Research findings; information about the target structure.

Step 1: Predict Learners make predictions about the target structure.

Step 2: Plan Learners set up a research plan that will produce samples of the target structure.

Step 3: Collect data Learners observe and/or record the target structure in its discourse environment.

Step 4: Analyze Learners analyze the data and explain results/make conclusions.

Step 5: Generate Learners discuss the target structure or produce the target structure in its appropriate context.

Step 6: Review Learners summarize their findings or reanalyze the data that they produced, asking whether the data conform to their conclusions in Step 4.

Learner/Teacher Feedback: Samples of student comments, teachers' experiences, and/or student-gathered data.

Almost any communicative task that is addressed in a language textbook can be observed in its "native habitat" and may serve as the focus for a research project. In cases where a particular speech event rarely occurs naturally, predictably, or publicly, or in EFL settings where native speakers of English are not plentiful or accessible, elicitation techniques can be used. Working as speech event analysts and sociolinguists, learners can ask expert or advanced speakers to draw on their intuitions about acceptable native-like behavior in a given circumstance (see, e.g., research on refusals in Beebe, Takahashi, and Uliss-Weitz 1990, on requests in Kasper 1989, and on suggestions in Banerjee and Carrell 1988; also see an excellent overview on research in pragmatics in Turner 1996).

Student researchers can also conduct their research as ethnographers interested in describing culture and in observing how societal influences affect and shape behavior. Here, activities can be developed on the basis of what cultural constructs are likely to interest learners. The focus of these activities need not be the target language/culture. Rather, learners may want to explore diversity within their own culture. (See, e.g., Activity 13, which examines the values, beliefs, and structures of power held by language teachers and their administrators; this is an appropriate activity for foreign language settings and for the investigation of L1 as well as L2 classes.)

Learners can also use discourse analytic techniques to learn to associate structure with more formal genres. Rather than being the passive recipients of knowledge about the structure of a formal spoken argument, for example, or about the elements of a "successful" speech or lecture (Activity 11), students can discover for themselves what discourse features are commonly used with certain genres. Most activities in this book encourage students to develop their own research agenda within a topic, to allow them to pursue their own areas of interest.

Morrison (1989) suggests that students analyze news broadcasts to determine the links and connections between events and the ways in which certain rhetorical modes (e.g., cause and effect, comparison and contrast, and process—a chronologically ordered description of events) are structured. This project can be "individualized" by allowing students to collect data on current news of interest to them, and for a speaking activity this project could be taken a step further: students could act as reporters, imitating the rhetorical structures most appropriate for their own news stories, or they could create, produce, and act in their own television commercials, incorporating persuasive techniques they have observed in watching television commercials themselves (Activity 11A).

Wennerstrom (1991) requires international teaching assistants (ITAs) to clearly mark the transition points of their mini-lectures with appropriate word stress, contrastive stress, and pauses, which help to illustrate the organization of their talks. Next, the ITAs evaluate their speech to see whether or not they actually did mark these transition points effectively. This type of activity is similar to those that focus on speech events (Activity 7), in that learners are encouraged first to examine the ways in which certain types of utterances are associated with certain types of discourse and then to model what they hear and see. (See also Activity 8, which requires that learners first observe live discussions and then practice the language behavior they want to emulate.)

There are many characteristics of conversation that may also be good sources for materials development. Conversation activities could appropriately target any of the micro features of conversation: what speakers do to "gain the floor," what speakers do to maintain their turn of talk once they do have the floor (Activities 1 and 2), or how speakers express a lack of comprehension (Activity 4). Again, the goal of these activities is first to aid learners in understanding what native or proficient speakers of English do by generating discussion on possible patterns in the discourse and then to help learners to become aware of how their own practices of talk are similar or dissimilar to what they have noticed in observed native or proficient speakers' talk. Follow-up activities both reinforce areas in which learners find themselves strong and encourage learners to practice skills in which they find themselves weak.

Sample Activities 1–14

The activities in this chapter are organized according to where the target features fall on the continuum of language features and structures introduced in chapter 1, with more micro-level constituents presented first and broader macro-level structures presented last. (Chapter 4 focuses exclusively on micro-level features that are traditionally taught as part of oral skills: pronunciation, grammar, and vocabulary.)

Guide to Activities 1–14

Activity 1

Turn Taking   Conversation

Macro level   Micro level

Objective: This activity is designed to help heighten students' awareness about how turns in conversation are coordinated in English, specifically in the dialect of North American "standard" English. Ultimately the goal of this activity is to enable learners to participate in conversations with ease.

(Note: This is a core activity in that many of the following activities rely on how this assignment is conducted and on what is learned in this activity. Thus, instructors are encouraged to ensure that their students not overlook this particular activity.)

In this activity, your students will work primarily as **conversation analysts.**

Conversation analysts

- typically use as data videotapes and audiotapes of people interacting, supported by detailed transcripts.
- believe that conversation can reveal truths about social contexts and that conversation invokes context.
- are especially interested in the micro mechanics of conversation: sequencing, turn taking, repair.

Background: Many learners express frustration at not being able to "get a word in" when they are speaking with native speakers. In other words, they have difficulty claiming turns. Or, once the native speaker interlocutor has finally yielded a turn, the learner is not able or does not have time to say what she or he wants to say: the difficulty in this case is in maintaining the turn. Learners often believe that their language proficiency level causes these problems. This may be true in part, since words may not come easily and fluently to someone learning a new language. But the problem also may be due to conventions in the English turn-taking system that are different from a learner's native language.

For example, many learners feel that they are being interrupted if someone else talks at the same time they are talking; these occurrences—when some of one speaker's words are spoken at the same time as another's—are called *overlaps*.

In the following conversation, the beginning of the overlap is indicated by square brackets ([[) on separate lines. The participants in this conversation were a native speaker (NS) of English and a language learner (LL) from China.

1 NS: How long have you been in this country?
2 LL: Oh, almost three [months. Yeah. I came here . . .
3 NS: [Oh really? I thought . . . You said you just got
4   here. I thought maybe two or three weeks.
5 LL: No, three months. I came here in August, so . . .

The language learner (LL) answers the native speaker's (NS) question. But before she is completely finished, the NS's comments in response (in line 3) overlap with the LL's turn. The LL then yields the turn to the NS.

In some languages, overlaps are almost always considered socially inappropriate: speakers must wait until another speaker is silent before beginning a turn. (For discussions on differences in the turn-taking conventions of other languages, see Crago 1992; Barnlund 1989; Ramsey 1984; and Phillips 1983. Also see Dorn and Perez 1995, a study on how perceived power differentials can affect turn taking.) But in most dialects of American English, people want to avoid gaps, or silences, between turns. Except with family members or very close friends, long gaps between turns make people feel uncomfortable, and so they talk in a way that avoids such silences. Thus, short overlaps are completely "normal" and appropriate.

Sometimes, when a speaker seems to be having difficulty finding a word, another speaker in the conversation helps that speaker by providing words. In the following conversation, the NS, an American man, and the very proficient LL, a woman from China and the man's friend, are talking about the problems of giving parties. Notice how both speakers help each other out by providing words for each other. Ellipsis points (. . .) indicate a pause.

1 LL: But especially if I'm inviting people from . . . , for example, from
2   school, from work, and my old friends, and they don't know each
3   other; then I have got the added task of y'know
4 NS: Intro[duce—
5 LL: [uh—introducing one to another.
6 NS: Yeah.
7 LL: And you don't know whether they will mix and they will talk or
8   whether it will be a flop.
9 NS: Yeah, I know. I know. That's always . . .
10 LL: The fear.
11 NS: Yeah.

In line 4, the NS helps out the LL with the word "introducing." The LL continues her turn, in line 5, by overlapping the word that the NS supplies; in other words, she accepts the word that he has provided. Then, in line 10, she finishes the NS's sentence with the words "the fear." This example from a real conversation demonstrates that even native speakers sometimes search for words. Their speech is not perfectly fluent; they hesitate, make mistakes, and repeat themselves, which is normal in unplanned conversation.

Though overlaps are essential to smooth or fluent turn coordination, they have rarely been the focus of teaching units intended for students of English as a second or foreign language, even in conversation classes. Some researchers (e.g., see Brown and Yule 1983) feel that these turn-based conversation skills are difficult for nonnative speakers of English to learn. Yet few would argue against the claim that an increased awareness about what contributes to the "smoothness," or fluency, of conversation would be an advantage for learners.

Interestingly, pronunciation can also be perceived as a micro-level skill, since one aspect of pronunciation is phonetic accuracy: to be considered completely proficient and "native-like," nonnative speakers' speech must resemble unaccented, standard native speaker speech. This resemblance is unquestionably difficult for learners to acquire, yet pronunciation is a "skill area" that is traditionally taught. It is my opinion that a parallel focus on the micro skills that contribute to smooth turn taking is also a justifiable endeavor.

Step 1: Predict One way of preparing students for this project is to ask them to provide information about the turn-taking system in their own L1 (or in other languages they know). Although some of the features of the system may be largely unconscious, it is likely that learners have noticed some features about turn taking in English that clearly differ from those in their own languages. The following questions for students can activate schema and encourage cross-cultural comparisons.

1. In your native language (or other languages you know), is it acceptable for one speaker to overlap another speaker's turn? (An overlap occurs when one speaker starts a turn before another speaker has completely finished.)
2. If overlaps are inappropriate in your native language (or in other languages you know), how long must a gap be before another speaker can talk? (A gap is a silence between turns.) For example, can a speaker start up immediately after another has finished, or must he or she wait at least a second or two or more seconds before starting to speak?
3. What are some of the ways that you can tell when another speaker has finished or is about to finish a turn and is ready to yield the turn to another

speaker? Include nonverbal practices (such as eye contact) and other "clues" (such as changes in speed or tone of voice/intonation).

Step 2: Plan For this activity, students tape-record a fifteen-minute to twenty-minute conversation with a native speaker of their choice and then listen to the tape. In EFL settings, where native speakers of English are not abundant or available, learners can converse with more advanced or expert speakers of English—those who have lived abroad in English-speaking countries, for example.

After they record the conversation, they choose two short excerpts (about a minute each) and transcribe them: one excerpt should be an example of a "smooth," or successful, part of the conversation, where both speakers are participating and communicating; the other excerpt should be an example of a problematic point in the conversation. Each learner determines why he or she considers the second chosen point in the conversation problematic. Perhaps he or she had trouble "gaining the floor," or maybe there was a lack of comprehension.

Sometimes learners are hesitant to talk with native (or expert) speakers of English, especially on tape. But because this is such a valuable activity, a little encouragement—and perhaps a sample from an actual conversation between a native speaker and a nonnative speaker—is usually all it takes to convince learners to try it. It is also helpful for learners to have had previous experience hearing themselves on a video or audio recording.

For learners who do not know any native (or expert) speakers, it also might be useful to give learners suggestions about how to find conversation partners and how to approach them with requests for this assignment. (See the sample handout on turn taking in appendix 1.) To give relevant suggestions about how and where to encounter native speakers, instructors need to research the possibilities in their own institutions. In English language settings, some likely sources are classmates (for learners enrolled in other, non-ESL classes), roommates or floormates (for learners living in a dormitory or other student housing), conversation partner programs, tutors (from volunteer ESL tutoring programs), and host families.

For especially hesitant learners, this activity can be done with a partner, resulting in a three-way conversation between two nonnative speaker learners and a native (or expert) speaker. In this case, the conversation should be somewhat longer, and both learners should participate.

Students will need some practice in transcription for this activity; see the discussion in chapter 2 to be alerted to issues that may arise.

Step 3: Collect data Data collection involves tape-recording the conversation, choosing the two excerpts (examples of a successful and a problematic interaction), and transcribing the excerpts. This step can be assigned as homework.

Step 4: Analyze One format for analyzing data for this assignment involves group work. Individuals bring several copies of their transcripts and their tapes, cued up to either of the chosen excerpts—the successful or the problematic interaction. Instructors organize students into problem-solving groups of three to five students, each with a tape recorder available.

The group's task is to analyze one excerpt from each conversation and answer questions about them. For the "smooth," or successful, example, the group should answer the following questions.

1. What makes this part of the conversation successful?
2. Specifically, how does the turn coordination contribute to the smoothness of the interaction?
3. What do both speakers do to show cooperation, a willingness to listen, and an interest in talking, rather than competition for turns?

For the problematic interaction, the group should answer the following questions.

1. Do you agree that the interaction is problematic, or would you consider it successful? If you think it is an example of a problematic interaction, what makes it that way?
2. Specifically, how does the turn coordination reflect or contribute to the difficulty perceived by the speaker?
3. How could this problem have been solved? What could your classmate have done or said to make this a smooth and successful interaction rather than a problematic one?

Groups can then briefly describe the results of their analyses to the whole class in the form of a group report. Alternatively, analyses can be carried out individually, as homework. However, it is valuable and relevant for students to see the variety of problems and successes experienced by other learners; thus a group format is encouraged. Another way of involving larger groups is for the students to analyze data independently as homework and for the instructor or students to then bring in representative examples of the students' problems and successes for the benefit of the whole class. In large classes with overhead transparency projectors available, short excerpts displayed on transparencies can be presented and discussed by groups.

Additional questions appropriate for group discussion follow.

1. How can you predict when speakers are about to end their turns?
2. What are some of the ways speakers can claim turns?
3. When is it appropriate to yield a turn?

Step 5: Generate With this activity, the fact that the learner is one of the conversation participants has already ensured that they generate language themselves. But this activity can be particularly valuable if it is repeated at some later point, especially if learners are given opportunities to practice what they have learned. Additional Activity 1A may be useful for this purpose.

Additional Activity 1A—Claiming turns. In groups of three or more, assign at least one person to each of the following roles.

> Primary speaker—Tell a story or describe what you did yesterday/last weekend/at some event. Your job is to keep talking and make it difficult for other speakers to claim a turn. If someone else does claim a turn, your job is to claim another turn as quickly as possible.
>
> Listener—Your job is to claim a turn from the primary speaker as quickly and as often as possible, without being rude.
>
> Observer—Your job is to watch and listen to the interactions and take notes on what the primary speaker does to claim and maintain turns and on what the listener(s) did to claim a turn.

The instructor coordinates the activity by explaining these roles, by indicating when the conversation should start and finish, and by calling for feedback from the groups. Observers and conversation participants report their experiences to the class. Roles can be switched so that each student has both the challenge of being primary speaker and that of being listener.

Step 6: Review Learners have already analyzed their participation in a conversation, but this activity is most useful if there is more than one data collection opportunity (i.e., more than one conversation audiotaped or videotaped) and, accordingly, more than one data analysis. Since naturally occurring conversations are such a rich source for examining the features of turn taking, two or more opportunities to analyze conversation data do not make this activity redundant. Another useful follow-up analysis activity is Additional Activity 1B.

Additional Activity 1B—Predicting end-of-turns. The instructor selects an audiotaped conversation excerpt for the class to analyze in detail. An accompanying transcript would be helpful but is not necessary. It also might be useful if the conversation on the tape were between native speakers, so perhaps this tape could be data collected by the instructor rather than by the students.

The excerpt is played one turn of talk at a time. (There may not be "neat" divisions between turns in the case of overlaps or latches.) After one turn of talk is played, the tape is stopped, and the following questions are asked of the class.

1. Was the end of the turn predictable? If so, why?
2. How can you tell that the speaker was about to end the turn?

The class can make a list of some of the signals each speaker uses to show that he or she is ready to end a turn. Examples of such signals follow.

• The speaker has finished a complete thought.
• The turn consists of a complete sentence or phrase.
• The speaker has asked or answered a question.
• The speaker has finished telling a story.
• There is falling intonation, indicating the end of a sentence.
• There is rising intonation, indicating a response is expected.
• The speaker hesitates and/or slows down, indicating the desire to have a word provided by the other speaker or the desire to give the other person an opportunity to talk.

Depending on the excerpt used for this activity, this discussion may also evolve into a consideration of what signals show that the speaker was not ready to end a turn. For example, the speaker may hesitate after a point where there is obviously more information to come; he or she may say, "For example, . . ."; he or she may be listing things in a series ("I bought a shirt, a new ribbon for my printer, . . ."); or he or she may be listing steps in a process or story (". . . After that, . . ."). Another possibility is that the speaker may clearly demonstrate competition for the turn if another speaker attempts to talk: the speaker's volume may increase, or he or she may hurry through the end of a sentence and start another without falling intonation.

Learner/Teacher Feedback: See the data samples in appendix 2, which are examples of student-collected conversation data. The two excerpts, originally transcribed by students (but then modified for this text in the interests of accuracy and easier reading), demonstrate two conversation areas that learners often find problematic. In Transcript 1, the student was concerned with comprehension: she expressed frustration at not understanding the native speaker and not being able to immediately clear up the problems. She also was irritated that she could not come up with a particular word that she needed. However, on closer examination of this problematic excerpt, the student felt encouraged and even successful, since she was able to negotiate meaning—to understand and to make herself understood. Her group also came up with suggestions for getting clarification more quickly and for ensuring comprehension on the part of the interlocutor.

Transcript 2 is an example of a problem clearly related to turn taking. Here the student posed the problem as follows: "I wanted to finish telling about how birthdays are celebrated in China, but she [the NS] wouldn't let me finish." Using turn-taking terminology, the question was, How could the language student have reclaimed her turn? Group members offered useful suggestions for ways that the learner might have done this.

This conversation activity has been used successfully with low-intermediate as well as advanced speakers and in foreign language settings as well as in North America. Learners find the transcription process itself useful and are usually interested in looking at what happens "below the surface" of a conversation, especially when they are one of the conversation participants. Many factors contribute to how much learners invest themselves in the analysis process, and some groups are more enthusiastic than others (e.g., an advanced conversation class in an ESL setting may find this activity fascinating and useful; a lower-level EFL listening-speaking class may prefer more traditional structured activities, such as audiotaped excerpts of talk, accompanied by discussion questions).

One important factor that contributes to this activity's success is the teacher's interest. Teachers who do this activity for the first time sometimes express frustration at the "lack of control" they have in structuring the activity, since the data are student collected and the problem-solving task is student driven. Thus, some teachers find it helpful to introduce this activity with data samples that they have collected and transcribed previously, since they can then support their explanations of various turn types with authentic data.

Activity 2

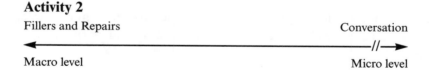

Fillers and Repairs   Conversation

Macro level   Micro level

Objective: This activity is designed to help increase students' awareness about some of the ways a turn of talk can be maintained in order to "buy time" to self-correct. Ultimately the goal of this activity is to enable learners to become competent at maintaining their turn long enough to ensure that they have said what they want to say and that they are understood by listeners.

In this activity, your students will work primarily as **conversation analysts.**

Conversation analysts

- typically use as data videotapes and audiotapes of people interacting, supported by detailed transcripts.
- believe that conversation can reveal truths about social contexts and that conversation invokes context.
- are especially interested in the micro mechanics of conversation: sequencing, turn taking, repair.

Background: Many learners express frustration at not being able to maintain a turn of talk long enough to say what they intend to say. This is in part due to proficiency level, since words may not come easily and fluently to someone learning a new language. But the problem also may be due to a lack of knowledge about strategies that can be used to lengthen a turn of talk and to self-correct.

For this activity, it is enlightening for learners to analyze natural, unplanned native speaker speech, since they can then have it demonstrated to them that it is perfectly normal for native speakers to search for words, hesitate, make vocabulary and grammar mistakes, and repeat themselves. As with the turn-taking activity (Activity 1), if native speakers are not readily available, speech from a speaker considered expert or proficient in English (e.g., someone who has lived in an English-speaking country) would work. Or it may be appropriate to audiotape or videotape talk from a radio or television show; informal contexts, such as talk shows, sitcoms, or "relaxed" interviews, would be most appropriate, since more formal, read or rehearsed talks are likely to contain few or no repairs.

Step 1: Predict The following questions for students can stimulate interest in the topic and encourage reflection about conventions in learners' own languages.

1. In your native language (or in other languages you know), how, other than silence, do speakers show that they are searching for a word? Are there particular sounds or words that speakers use to maintain turns while trying to find the right way to say something? (These sounds or words are called *fillers* or *filled pauses*, since they are used to fill up conversational space and time.) Are there accompanying nonverbal signals?
2. What can you predict, or what have you observed, about the way people use fillers in English?
3. In your own native language (or in other languages you know), how do

speakers correct their own speech? Do they use particular phrases that mean something like "What I meant to say is . . ." or "No, that's not the word I wanted"? (Such phrases are called *repairs,* since a speaker uses them to fix, or repair, his or her own speech so that it is more accurate— either grammatically or semantically—in terms of meaning.)

4. What can you predict, or what have you observed, about the way people self-repair in English?

Step 2: Plan For this activity, students can use tape recordings they made for the turn-taking activity (Activity 1), focusing on the native (or expert) speaker's speech rather than on their own. Or they can work in research teams and observe native speakers speaking in informal, unplanned contexts, analyzing, for example, explanations (rather than a formal lecture) by an instructor, native speakers talking to each other, or even television or radio interviews, especially those in which the interviewees are not actors or professional speakers. It will be helpful to tape-record data if possible, since this will allow a more detailed and accurate analysis.

Students are examining native (or expert) speaker speech for examples of "flaws": vocabulary and grammar errors, repetitions, hesitations, fillers, and repairs. They can anticipate what they will see and hear by preparing a data collection chart like the following (modified according to student interests).

Data Collection Chart for Activity 2
Fillers and Repairs

Speaker:
Setting/Context:

Examples of Problems	**Examples of Repairs** (Was the problem corrected? How?)
Errors (specify—what was the error?):	
Repetitions (specify—what was repeated? how often?):	
Hesitations (specify—silences or fillers, and if fillers, what were they— sounds, words, laughter?):	

If there are topics that students are particularly curious about, they might also want to develop survey questions for native speakers. Sample survey questions follow.

1. What do you do or say when you want to change what you have just said and make yourself clearer?
2. Suppose you are in a conversation with someone and you know that they want to talk next. If you have not finished what you are trying to say or have not said it exactly right, what do you do or say?
3. What do you do when you cannot think of the right word?

Step 3: Collect data Ideally, learners audiotape or videotape their data. One way to ensure reliability of findings is for learners to fill in a data collection chart once during the original "listen" (as the speaker is producing the language) and once after (when analyzing the language on tape). This is also an appropriate activity for groups, since listening for repairs requires focused attention. The point, though, is not necessarily for listeners to hear every single case of repair but for them to begin to identify the kinds of things a speaker says and does when the words or ideas are not automatic, for one reason or another.

If survey questions are given (e.g., "What do you do when . . . ?"), then another step in the data collection process is to take careful notes on their responses or, better yet, to audiotape them.

Step 4: Analyze One format for analyzing data for this assignment involves group work and the pooling of data. Examples of problems and repairs can be compiled on a list. A note taker, whose job it is to write down examples provided by individuals or groups, could be assigned. Alternatively, the instructor or students might want to play excerpts that contain especially interesting or unusual examples of repairs, fillers, or inaccuracies.

Step 5: Generate A discussion of the following questions for students can be a useful way to present the results of the analysis.

1. Does there seem to be a "standard"—one kind of repair or one kind of filler that many speakers use?
2. Or does how a person uses repairs and fillers seem more individual and idiosyncratic?
3. How do the observed strategies for repairing speech in English compare with strategies in your native language?

Another way to integrate the analysis is for learners to work on turn maintenance and repair in their own speech. However, students should be warned that these can be difficult strategies to master. For certain personality types especially, native or nonnative, it can be a challenge to overcome the urge to withdraw when someone else is clearly making a move to speak. Sometimes it is easier to simply give up when it is difficult to say what is really intended. But the rewards for trying are increasing confidence that it is possible to express oneself adequately.

There are ways to encourage conscious generation of speech that "buys time"—speech that incorporates repairs and turn-maintenance devices. One method is to assign students to keep in their research notebook a "short list" of fillers and repair markers that they feel comfortable with—such phrases as "You know" as well as short "meaningless" fillers, such as "umm." The research notebook is the appropriate place for a reminder to repeat previous words and phrases in order to buy time, using short repair markers, such as "I mean," as well as longer phrases, such as "What I really mean to say is . . ." Students should practice these whenever possible if they find it helpful.

A good format for practicing repairs and turn maintenance is an oral dialogue journal. Learners talk spontaneously on an audiotape about a topic assigned by the teacher or about a topic of choice, and the instructor or another student responds briefly on tape to the content of the talk (thus creating a taped "dialogue"), optionally including some feedback about the speaker's use of fillers and repair markers. Another option is for students to have a conversation in pairs, with the goal being to leave as few silences and turn-claiming points as possible. Finally, the follow-up activity discussed in Additional Activity 1A is a possible format for practicing such turn-maintenance strategies.

Step 6: Review If learners audiotaped their own speech in either of the formats suggested in Step 5—the oral dialogue journal or the pair conversations—or in any context where they are required to speak for an extended period of time (i.e., more than a comment or two), they can then analyze their speech, looking specifically for time- and space-filling devices and a lack of long silences. Another method of analysis is to employ an observer in a small group of three or four students (see Additional Activity 1A) who provides feedback to speakers on their avoidance of silence and their use of fillers and repair markers.

Learner/Teacher Feedback: Learning to "buy time" in conversation is a skill that takes time to improve, in part because it is difficult to maintain consciousness about self-repair, and also because automaticity is so closely linked with the development of language proficiency. Thus, it is advisable to practice conscious self-repair often. If it is practiced often, progress can be observable. Learners who have analyzed samples of their speech over a span of time, rather than as a one-shot exercise, have expressed the most satisfaction with this activity.

Perhaps the most valuable aspect of this activity, however, is not the progress that learners may (or may not) observe in their own ability to self-repair. Rather, it is the consciousness that learners develop about native speaker speech being less than perfect. Many learners are surprised by the lack of smoothness in casual speech by native speakers. Other "revelations" for learners are that even native speakers sometimes search for words and/or say things they do not mean and that native speakers in informal settings do not always speak accurately in the prescriptive sense (i.e., that in informal conversation, grammatical "rules" appropriate for formal written English are suspended).

Activity 3
Listener Responses/Backchannels   Conversation,
Social and Academic Settings

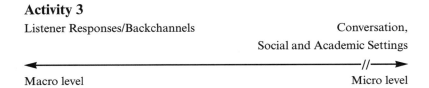

Macro level   Micro level

Objective: This activity is designed to increase learners' consciousness about the active role of the listener in a conversation.

In this activity, your students will work primarily as **conversation analysts.**

Conversation analysts

- typically use as data videotapes and audiotapes of people interacting, supported by detailed transcripts.
- believe that conversation can reveal truths about social contexts and that conversation invokes context.
- are especially interested in the micro mechanics of conversation: sequencing, turn taking, repair.

Background: Conversation-based studies reveal that languages have different traditions of how speakers respond to listeners—how they show understanding of the speaker's words and meanings and how they show that they are willing to allow the speaker to continue talking (see, e.g., Tao and Thompson 1991; White 1989; Phillips 1983). In other words, different languages/cultures have different ways of expressing these necessary turn-taking "mechanics."

How actively a listener responds can be the basis for judgment on the part of other conversation participants. North Americans typically yield turns and show understanding by nodding their heads, maintaining eye contact, and occasionally backchanneling verbally—using the *continuers* "yeah" or "mm-hm" (so called because they indicate that they are allowing the speaker to continue with his or her turn). Bavelas (forthcoming) shows that listeners also tend to "match" the speaker's emotional tone, by means of facial expressions, gesture synchronicity, and verbal comments that disclose attitudes of sympathy or camaraderie, such as "Oh really?" and "That's awful." These usually occur at moments of marked intensity, often, during the telling of a story, when major events occur in the complicating action.

If listeners do not backchannel, show changes in facial expression, or nod, they are often either perceived as bored or suspected of not comprehending. In fact, studies by Hawkins (1984) and Riggenbach (1991) show that nonnative speakers who backchannel frequently and appropriately are sometimes judged to be more fluent or proficient than they really may be. In other words, even when they may not comprehend what is being said, their backchanneling indicates to speakers that they do.

Body language also conveys information about a listener's response to the talk or to the speaker. Tannen (1984) notes that body language can be very important in communicating information between listener and speaker: information about interest level, attitude toward the interlocutor, feelings about the topic or content of the talk, or the willingness to continue the conversation. Physical proximity (how far away or how close together the interlocutors are standing or sitting), eye contact, facial expressions, synchronized gestures, and physical alignment (how directly interlocutors sit or stand in relation to each other, as opposed to twisting away from each other, or how harmoniously or disharmoniously their arms and legs "line up" with each other) can all provide information about effect. Thus, a recognition by learners of the many ways that listener responses convey information can be both useful and interesting.

Step 1: Predict To stimulate thinking about backchanneling behavior, learners can consider the following questions about how listeners respond to speakers in their L1 (or in other languages they know).

1. How do people show that they are understanding the speaker and also willing to let the speaker continue talking? Are there particular sounds or words that are commonly used? Are eye contact and other nonverbal signals used?
2. How does the way understanding is conveyed change with different participants in conversation (family members, close friends, professional col-

leagues)? How does the age and gender of the participants affect the kinds of responses listeners make to speakers?

3. How does the interaction change with different settings (in a classroom discussion, at a classroom lecture, at a party, on the street, on the telephone compared to face-to-face)?

4. What other nonverbal cues (such as body language) can give conversation participants information about each other?

Step 2: Plan This kind of activity is appropriate for individuals or research teams. Learners will need to observe native or expert speakers when they are in the process of listening rather than speaking. Thus, working in teams can provide reliability checks on the observations that learners make. In addition, learners may be interested in observing listener responses in different settings, and thus it would be appropriate to have each member of a research team assigned to observe in a different setting. In EFL settings where native speakers are not plentiful or accessible, television shows or films made in English-speaking countries are an alternative context for observations. As always, however, the more authentic (i.e., the less scripted) the source, the better.

To supplement observations, learners may be interested in brief surveys of native/expert speakers of English and of speakers of their own L1. They might survey, for example, whether there are specific listener responses that are annoying or distancing (too little or too much eye contact, too frequent or too little backchanneling, etc.).

Step 3: Collect data One method of obtaining data is videotaping actual interactions, since nonverbal information is so essential as a component of appropriate (and inappropriate) listener responses, and since material could be made available for analysis by others besides the data collector. However, since people are sometimes initially uncomfortable around video equipment, unrecorded face-to-face observations have the advantage of not interfering with the naturalness of the interactions.

Learners should make detailed notes on exactly how listeners respond to speakers in various settings and with various participants. Observers should also ground their impressions in observed phenomena. For example, why specifically did they feel that a conversation participant was bored, rude, or engaged in the conversation? If there is the opportunity to interview conversation participants to get further evidence about attitude or effect, this could be interesting supplementary data.

In taking notes, observers should, as usual, include information about the setting and the participants (age, gender, relationship to each other, etc., if known). In addition, the following aspects of the interaction should be described: (1) particular sounds or words that are commonly used to show that the listener understands the speaker and is willing to let the speaker continue talking, (2) the nature and amount of eye contact, and (3) other non-verbal signals. These could be recorded on a form designed specifically for this assignment, although in this case, since the goal of the activity is to obtain as rich a description as possible, it might be advisable to take notes in a more open-ended, free-form format.

Observers should also be mindful of the fact that in conversations, the speaker and listener sometimes shift roles very quickly: the speaker yields the turn and becomes the listener, a third participant may then claim the turn and become the speaker, and so on. Thus, more information can probably be gained if the observer is a nonparticipant, removed from the temporal demands of the turn-taking cycle.

Step 4: Analyze Learners determine what patterns, if any, were observed in this activity and whether particular sounds, gestures, and physical reactions seemed to demonstrate "active" listening in the interactions observed. Evidence can come from how well the interaction "moved forward" or progressed, or, from the opposite perspective, observers might have noticed interactions where the listener appeared either bored or anxious to speak, thus curtailing the forward "movement" of the interaction. In these cases, learners determine what specifically the speaker did or said that gave the observer (and possibly the speaker too) this impression.

Step 5: Generate Research groups can report on their findings, which may naturally involve a discussion of the results, especially if there were varying results or unusual cases. An interesting way to present information on atypical cases is a role play that mimics the interaction, since exaggerated gestures or unusual strategies for claiming (as opposed to yielding) turns can be effectively demonstrated visually. Videotapes of authentic interactions are ideal for group discussions. However, as discussed earlier, video equipment can cause some discomfort and may interfere with the naturalness of interactions if speakers are unaccustomed to being recorded.

Another method for generating language or language-related behavior is to actually practice listener responses, the target structures. A good format for doing this is presented in Additional Activity 3A.

Additional Activity 3A—Practicing listener responses. In groups of three or more, assign at least one person to each of the following roles.

> Primary speaker—Tell a story or describe what you did yesterday/last weekend/at some event. Your job is to keep talking and to respond as naturally as possible to the listener. This may mean that you stop talking or change the subject if the listener appears bored or does not seem

to understand you. Or it may mean that you relinquish the turn to the listener if it is clear that he or she wants to speak.

Listener—Your job is to respond to the speaker as naturally and politely as possible. If you have something to say or you want to react to something the speaker says, take a turn when it is appropriate. If you do not have anything to say and you want to react, show the speaker you are listening, comprehending, or not comprehending with appropriate backchanneling behavior.

Observer—Your job is to watch and listen to the interactions and take notes on what the listener does and says. If the speaker changes, keep focusing on the participant who is not doing the talking.

The instructor coordinates the activity by explaining these roles, by indicating when the conversation should start and finish, and by calling for feedback from the groups. Observers and conversation participants report their experiences to the class. Roles can be switched so that each student has both the challenge of being primary speaker and that of being listener.

Step 6: Review If learners participated in Additional Activity 3A, the results can serve as data for further analysis: The observers can report on what the listeners did or said, and the primary speakers can supplement this report with information about their reactions: for example, whether they got the sense that the listener was bored/interested/enthusiastic and whether they felt that the listeners were eager or overly eager to talk and, if so, how this affected how soon the speakers relinquished their turns. This information can serve as useful feedback for learners on their own listening behavior.

An interesting twist on this activity is to observe the ways in which speakers work to ensure comprehension. The following activity suggests a format for gathering these data.

Additional Activity 3B—Ensuring comprehension. Learners observe speakers in various settings for the ways in which they check to see if listeners are comprehending what they are saying. In their research notebook, they collect a list of phrases speakers use for this purpose, making sure to record information about the setting and participants. In such settings as an informal classroom, the means for ensuring comprehension may be very explicit, whereas in a conversation, this may be done entirely nonverbally. Teachers often directly ask students, "Are you following? Everything clear so far?" But in a conversation, an interlocutor may simply notice that her listener looks puzzled; thus a repair would follow.

Learners can explore what kinds of differences there are in comprehension-checking behavior in formal versus informal settings, along with the following questions: What phrases or strategies seem most successful and least successful in determining whether listeners are able to understand or follow the speaker? Which phrases or strategies do learners feel more comfortable using in various settings?

The "short list" of phrases used to ensure comprehension can be kept in a handy, easily accessible place in learners' research notebooks, along with or near the list of self-repair prompts from Activity 2.

Learner/Teacher Feedback: Possibly the most valuable aspect of this activity is a heightened consciousness about the active role of the listener. In addition, appropriate backchanneling/listener responses may differ from culture to culture, and this fact alone may serve as the basis for interesting discussion.

It is also helpful for learners to notice what they do or do not do as listeners in a conversation and how this might be perceived by their interlocutors. Finally, shifting the perspective back to the speaker, as in Additional Activity 3B, can help learners understand what may motivate frequent comprehension checks from the speaker or, on the contrary, what signals the listener is giving to move the interaction forward without the need for comprehension checks.

Activity 4
Initiating Repairs

Conversation, Academic Settings

Macro level   Micro level

Objective: This activity is designed to, first, increase learners' awareness about strategies for ensuring understanding of another person's speech and, second, enable learners to become competent at expressing a lack of comprehension and/or a need for clarification, thus initiating repairs.

In this activity, your students will work primarily as **speech event analysts.**

Speech event analysts

- typically use as data the set of utterances, elicited or observed, that together perform a communicative function.
- believe that research should result in a description of the speech setting, the participants, and the structure of the event, set in a template-like sequence.
- are especially interested in the connection between function and form and in how speech act functions are realized in larger text units.

Background: As is evident in many ESL/EFL textbooks designed to improve students' oral skills, understanding others and being understood by others can be a challenge for learners of a language. Most instructors and language theorists believe that it is possible to teach learners strategies that help make it clear to their interlocutors that they must clarify, repeat, or simplify their utterances so that they can be better understood. In addition, it is sometimes helpful if speakers themselves are aware of ways they can incorporate comprehension checks into their talk to ensure that their interlocutors understand them.

Step 1: Predict One way of preparing students for this project is to ask them to provide information about how to ask for clarification and express lack of comprehension in their L1 (or in other languages they know). The resulting discussion should stimulate thinking about the different factors involved (e.g., how settings and participants may affect the interaction). The following questions for students can activate schema and encourage cross-cultural comparisons.

1. In other languages/cultures with which you are familiar, how do people let other speakers know that they do not understand what they are saying? Include nonverbal practices (confused looks, changes in eye contact) as well as verbal practices. (These are called *repair initiations,* since a listener is getting the speaker to fix, or repair, his or her speech so that is clearer to the listener.)
2. How do these methods change with different participants (teachers compared to family members or close friends)? Does the age and gender of the participants affect the interaction, and if so, how?
3. How does the interaction change with different settings (classroom compared to a casual conversation at home)?
4. Is it sometimes rude to initiate repairs? If so, what are the circumstances?

Step 2: Plan For this activity, students can use tape recordings they made for the turn-taking activity (Activity 1), looking for repair initiations in either speaker's speech, or they can work in research teams and observe instances of requests for repair in contexts that interest them—certain settings or certain types of participants.

Students can anticipate what they will see and hear by creating a data collection chart like the following.

Data Collection Chart for Activity 4
Signaling Understanding or Lack of Understanding

Participants:
Setting/Context:

Examples of Repair Initiations (How did the person indicate that he/she did not understand?)

Nonverbal signals:

Words/phrases:

Questions:

Other ways that showed
lack of understanding:

Students may also consider other methods for getting information about how repairs are initiated. They may want to directly ask native (or expert) speakers how they indicate that they do not understand what another speaker is saying, that they need clarification or more information, or that they want the speaker to repeat what he or she said. Another source for learners of English is an ESL/EFL textbook on speaking, since many of these more recently published books include lists of phrases useful for initiating repairs.

Step 3: Collect data Videotaped data are preferred, since the nonverbal signals that people use to indicate lack of understanding would then be visible. In many cases, however, this is not feasible or available. Observations of the interaction can provide most of the same information, especially if they are supplemented by audiotapes.

Thorough observations without audiotapes or videotapes can be sources of reliable data, especially if learners work in groups and have the opportunity to do practice observations beforehand. To provide this practice, the instructor can role-play an interaction with someone who is not a member of the class; in this interaction there can be a deliberate misunderstanding and a repair initiation (a puzzled look, a question such as "Huh?" or "Could you repeat that?", or a comment such as "I didn't get what you said about . . ."). The ideal method of practicing would involve a videotaped interaction that the class as a whole could view and review, make notes on, and discuss in terms of their perceptions and the similarities and differences in what they noted.

If survey questions are given to native or expert speakers in Step 2, then another step in the data collection process is for students to take careful notes on interviewees' responses or, ideally, to audiotape these short interviews.

Step 4: Analyze Learners compile their findings, including information about setting and participants and about verbal and nonverbal practices. This information can be recorded on one large chart, or a note taker can be assigned to compile individually collected or team-collected data. One of the outcomes of this step will be a list of phrases and strategies used to initiate repairs, including information from the interviews. Learners will want to consider this question: Are certain strategies for initiating repair appropriate in some settings and not in others?

Step 5: Generate There are several options for presenting the results of the analysis and for generating repair initiations. Student groups can report on their findings. Alternatively, if students have already compiled their findings, a large group discussion on the results would be appropriate. Learners will discover that different types of repair initiations will get different results. For example, "Huh?" does not locate the point at which the listener is experiencing difficulty in comprehension; this would also be appropriate only in informal settings with participants who have established a casual relationship (e.g., friends and most family members). A list of repair strategies appropriate for different settings could be recorded in the students' research notebooks.

Or a student group can present their results in the form of a role play, thus generating repair initiations themselves. Role plays can be scripted by students and rehearsed beforehand if this makes them more comfortable; ideally these would be videotaped so that they can serve as the basis for further analysis (Step 6).

Learners can elect to specify the setting and participants before or after each role play, with the role play modeling a socially and linguistically appropriate interaction. Alternatively, students may perform the role play and let the audience guess the participants and setting; this is especially valuable if other groups in the class worked on this same project.

Step 6: Review The teacher may want to test students by providing an utterance and describing the problem the listener has in comprehending the utterance. Examples might be that the listener did not hear some of the words, did not know the meaning of one particular word, did not understand the entire utterance, or needs clarification in the form of an example or illustration. Students then are asked to demonstrate appropriate and timely repair initiations, either individually or in teams. This can also be turned into a whole group project by allowing the "audience" to evaluate the adequacy of the demonstration.

If learners audiotaped their role plays in Step 5, they can then evaluate these. Their job in this case is to determine whether or not the speech that they have produced conforms to the generalizations they made about what constitutes an appropriate repair initiation.

Learner/Teacher Feedback: Students report that they find this activity useful. Low-intermediate students expand their repertoire for negotiating meaning, thus clarifying input and developing strategies that aid their listening comprehension. Advanced students of English interested in more efficient communication have examined how different kinds of prompts can help to focus the repair. Learners at all levels appreciate seeing how repairs come about in real language interactions, which makes the goal of effective repair initiations more tangible.

Activity 5

Openings   Conversation

Macro level   Micro level

Objective: This activity is designed to help heighten students' consciousness about how conversations are begun, or "opened." Ultimately the goal of this activity is to provide learners with options for producing openings that are socially appropriate and linguistically accurate and for responding to native speaker openings naturally and straightforwardly.

In this activity, your students will work primarily as **sociolinguists.**

Sociolinguists

- typically use as data language in use—observed or recorded communications.
- believe that each community or subculture has its own unique set of conventions, rules, and patterns for the conduct of communication.
- are especially interested in how these rules and patterns can be understood in the context of a general system that reflects the values and the structure of the society in which they occur.

Background: People in different cultures have different ways of greeting each other and of opening conversations. Social settings and the nature of people's relationships help to determine what openings and greetings are appropriate.

Step 1: Predict One way of preparing students for this project is to ask them to provide information about how openings are done in their L1 (or in other languages they know). The resulting discussion should stimulate thinking about the different factors involved (e.g., how settings and participants affect the interaction). The following questions for students can help to activate schema and encourage cross-cultural comparisons.

1. How do people greet each other in languages/cultures with which you are familiar? Include nonverbal practices (hugging, kissing, handshakes, physical distances that people maintain, eye contact, etc.) as well as verbal practices.
2. How does this interaction change with different participants (family members, close friends, professional colleagues)? How does the age and gender of the participants affect the interaction?
3. How does the interaction change with different settings (in the classroom, at a party, on the street, on the telephone compared to face-to-face)?

Step 2: Plan This kind of activity is appropriate for research teams, since individuals may be particularly interested in observing openings in certain settings or with certain types of participants. In such group work, learners pool their data. Students can anticipate what they will see and hear with a data collection chart like the following (modified according to student needs). The chart can also be a way for students to divide up tasks if they are working as teams.

Data Collection Chart for Activity 5
Openings

	Verbal Interactions	**Nonverbal Interactions**
Participants		
age (approximate):		
gender:		
relationship:		
Setting:		

Step 3: Collect data Either students can be asked to conduct this step as homework, or class time can be used, depending on course needs and on where and when the class meets (i.e., the availability of potential interactions for observations). If possible, it is helpful if the students are given an opportunity to practice their observation and note taking before actually collecting data, since this can alert them to what they might expect and to how quick and thorough they may need to be. To do this, the instructor can role-play an opening with someone who is not a member of the class; the ideal method of practicing would involve a videotaped interaction that the class as a whole could view and review and then discuss in terms of the similarities and differences in what they took notes on.

This activity is suitable for teamwork, since observers may be alerted to different aspects of an interaction and thus may contribute different perspectives that can serve as a check on reliability. Another way to assign different responsibilities to team members is to have different observers work in different sites: one person can plant themselves at a table in a coffee shop; another may watch how a supermarket cashier greets (or does not greet) his or her customer; another may "eavesdrop" on callers at a busy telephone booth.

Step 4: Analyze Learners compile their findings, including information about setting and participants and about verbal and nonverbal practices. This information can be recorded on one large chart, or one note taker can be assigned to compile individually collected or team-collected data.

Step 5: Generate There are several options for presenting the results of the analysis and for generating openings. If students worked in teams, each team can compile their results into a group report and present it to the rest of the class. If other groups worked on the same project with differing results, this can lead to a discussion on possible contributing factors.

Or a student group can present their results in the form of a role play, thus generating closings themselves. Role plays can be scripted by students and rehearsed beforehand if this helps them accurately represent their results. Role plays can be set up deductively (where the setting and participants are identified before the role play) or inductively (where the audience makes guesses about the participants and setting after the role play is performed). The latter setup is especially valuable if other groups in the class conducted a similar project.

Finally, the teacher may want to evaluate students by specifying setting and participants and then asking students to demonstrate appropriate interactions in an oral performance test; this can also be done as a whole group project by allowing the "audience" to evaluate the adequacy of the demonstration.

Step 6: Review This step of the process is especially appropriate if learners themselves have generated openings, either in a role play or as "answers" to stimuli provided by the teacher in a testlike oral performance. In this case, learners and their instructor are in effect evaluating whether or not the speech that they produce conforms to the generalizations that they made about openings after analyzing their observed data.

Learner/Teacher Feedback: After doing this activity, learners express both surprise and relief at how routine and how casual openings usually are in English, especially in comparison to languages and cultures where this act can be quite complex because of the influence that interlocutors' age, relationship, and position has on how openings should be conducted (see, e.g., Noguchi 1987, for more information about Japanese specifically).

Activity 6

Closings   Conversation

Macro level   Micro level

Objective: This activity helps learners understand the "mechanics" of how conversations are ended, or "closed." Ultimately the goal of this activity, similar to that of Activity 5, is to provide learners with options for producing closings that are socially appropriate and linguistically accurate and for recognizing and responding naturally to native speaker attempts to close a conversation.

In this activity, your students will work primarily as **sociolinguists.**

Sociolinguists

• typically use as data language in use—observed or recorded communications.
• believe that each community or subculture has its own unique set of conventions, rules, and patterns for the conduct of communication.
• are especially interested in how these rules and patterns can be understood in the context of a general system that reflects the values and the structure of the society in which they occur.

Background: Closings in American English are more complex than openings. Many people, native speakers included, are not aware of what have been called "preclosings"—signals that the speaker wants or intends to end the conversation soon. Some examples are an interlocutor breaking eye contact to glance at his or her watch, the use of the discourse marker "Well . . ." as a break from the previous topic, and a brief explanation about a pressing engagement ("Oh, I've got a class in a few minutes"). Abrupt endings to a conversation without any of these preclosing signals are usually considered rude in American English. Thus, one of the challenges for the language researcher is to "tune in" to preclosing signals and, ultimately, to be able to produce these as a prelude to an actual closing.

Step 1: Predict As with the openings activity (Activity 5), one way of preparing students for this project is to ask them to provide information about how closings are done in their L1 (or in other languages they know). They should then anticipate the different factors involved (e.g., how settings and participants affect the interaction). The following questions for students can encourage this kind of cross-cultural comparison and can activate schema.

1. How do people end a conversation in other languages/cultures with which you are familiar? Include nonverbal practices (hugging, kissing, handshakes, eye contact, etc.) as well as verbal practices.
2. Is it necessary to signal before the closing that it is time to end the conversation, or is it appropriate to simply stop the conversation? (This signal that the conversation will end soon is referred to as a *preclosing.*)
3. How does the interaction change with different participants (family members, close friends, professional colleagues)? How does the age and gender of the participants affect the interaction?
4. How does the interaction change with different settings (in the classroom, at a party, on the street, on the telephone compared to face-to-face)?
5. What can you predict, or what have you observed, about the way closings are done in English? For example, how can you tell if a native speaker wants to end the conversation, and what is meant by "Let's get together sometime"?

Step 2: Plan If individuals have particular areas of interest, this activity is appropriate for research teams. For example, one person in the team may want to focus on preclosing signals, while another may be interested in the actual closing comments and behavior. Or certain participant combinations (e.g., student-teacher) or certain settings may interest learners, and observations could then be divided up accordingly. If topics are pursued independently, learners then pool their data.

In foreign language settings, where a pool of native speakers may not be readily available for observations, students can observe closings between characters on American, British, or Australian-made television shows or movies. Though scripted, these interactions may resemble authentic interactions closely enough to offer evidence of contrast in cross-cultural comparisons. Closings in contexts other than casual conversation might be evident in television or radio talk shows in English, although there is no guarantee that a closing will be heard in its entirety or at all. Legutke and Thomas (1991) use international airports as the setting for learner research like this. However, it is likely that what may be most easily observed in an airport are acts of leave-taking between people intimate with each other (friends and family members) rather than the nuances involved in preclosing and closing that occur in more extended, casual conversations with participants less intimately involved with each other.

Students can anticipate what they will see and hear and can divide up tasks by recording their observations on a data collection chart like the following (modified according to student needs).

Data Collection Chart for Activity 6
Closings

	Verbal Interactions	**Nonverbal Interactions**
Preclosing Signals:		
Closing Signals:		
Participants		
age (approximate):		
gender:		
relationship:		
Setting:		

Alternatively, there may be topics that students are particularly curious about, which may or may not occur during the course of their observations. Therefore, learners might also want to develop survey questions for native (or expert) speakers. Examples of survey questions follow.

1. How do you feel if someone ends the conversation without any warning (e.g., they just say, "I gotta go. Goodbye," and leave)?

2. If you say, "We should get together sometime," do you really mean it or are you just being polite?

3. If you really have to end the conversation but the other person keeps talking, how do you let the person know, without offending him or her, that you must stop?

Step 3: Collect data As in Activity 5, students may elect to conduct this activity as a team, especially if there is only limited access to native speakers and to television shows or movies in English. This activity is suitable for teamwork, since it is more challenging to observe closings than openings: when they occur is not so predictable as openings, and the nuances of preclosing require that the observer be quite close in distance to the interaction, if not one of the participants.

In another possible method for collecting data, the learner participates in a conversation as naturally as possible, allowing the closing to unfold. This method can be tricky and may affect reliability, since the learner-participant is trying to take part naturally in a conversation yet is also aware of the target structure under focus. Thus, having a team member who functions as observer of, rather than fully participating in, the conversation is especially helpful, since the learner-participant then has the freedom to talk naturally.

Assigning different responsibilities to team members can be effective, with observers working in different sites: one person can listen to how lectures are "closed" by professors and lecturers in academic settings; another might listen to telephone conversations (unfortunately, though, only one end of the conversation can be heard, so some information would be lost); others could watch closings in a television show or movie. In some situations it is likely that interviewing native or expert speakers will be the most productive method of obtaining indirect data about closings.

Step 4: Analyze As in Activity 5, learners can decide how best to compile their findings. Information about setting and participants and about verbal and nonverbal practices can be recorded on one large chart, or a note taker can be assigned to compile individually collected or team-collected data.

If speakers were interviewed rather than, or in addition to, being observed, responses to questions should also be compiled. One person could be assigned to write responses to questions on a blackboard or large piece of paper, or students could individually write down their responses on the paper or blackboard.

Step 5: Generate As in Activity 5, there are several options for presenting the results of the analysis and for practicing preclosings and closings. Students can first compile their results into a group report that they present to the rest of the class. If other groups working on the same project had different results, a discussion about the possible contributing factors is likely to evolve.

Groups can present their results in the form of a role play, scripted or spontaneous, thus generating the preclosings and closings themselves and demonstrating what they consider to be a socially and linguistically appropriate interaction. The setting and participants can be specified before each role play. Alternatively, the "actors" may prefer to let the audience guess who the participants represent and where the interaction probably occurred. An interesting twist on this activity is for the instructor to play the role of an uncooperative interlocutor who refuses to "take the hint" offered by the learner's preclosing signals. A simulated (or actual) telephone conversation is an appropriate and authentic context for such a role play. This activity can evolve into a valuable discussion of what steps an interlocutor must take when preclosing signals are ignored.

Step 6: Review The teacher may want to evaluate students by specifying setting and participants and then asking students to demonstrate appropriate interactions in an oral performance test. This can also be done as a whole group project by allowing the "audience" to evaluate how appropriate the demonstration was both socially and linguistically.

Learner/Teacher Feedback: For nonnative speakers, one of the most puzzling components of closings is the token invitation "Let's get together sometime." (Note that this is not generalizable to all native English-speaking contexts.) Learners who are new to U.S. culture often take this literally and, in response to this "invitation," attempt to schedule an appointment or date, which is most likely met with bewilderment on the part of the "inviter." Thus, understanding that this closing component is part of a formula, just as certain expressions may be in other languages and cultures, is helpful.

Similarly, learners usually are glad to be alerted to common preclosing signals and find knowledge of them useful both as listeners and as speakers. Most learners have concerns about appearing rude to their interlocutors; many admit that they would rather allow the speaker to continue ad nauseam than to "make a break" and cut the conversation off. Thus, it can be a relief to learn what preclosing signals are appropriate and also likely to be noticed. Since awkwardness in closing a conversation may well be "foreign" to speakers of other languages, preclosing signals and closings may need to be practiced in simulations, with a speaker who does not show any indication of stopping talking.

Activity 7

Speech Events

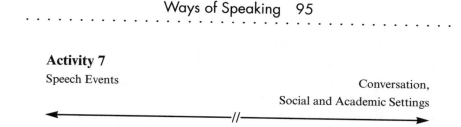

Conversation,
Social and Academic Settings

Macro level

Micro level

Objective: This activity is designed to increase learners' awareness about how particular speech events are negotiated, with the goal being to "discover" the components of those speech events—the individual utterances and speech acts—and to note the factors that affect them. Ultimately the objective of this activity is for learners to understand and participate effectively in speech events they are likely to encounter.

(Note: The instructor may choose either to have the class focus on one speech event at a time or to allow research teams to pursue different speech events as research topics and then to pool results. If the instructor chooses the former option, a large part of a speaking course could be spent on speech event analysis and practice; see the textbooks cited in section 1 earlier in this chapter for examples of how entire courses are organized around speech events.)

In this activity, your students will work primarily as **speech event analysts.**

Speech event analysts

- typically use as data the set of utterances, elicited or observed, that together perform a communicative function.
- believe that research should result in a description of the speech setting, the participants, and the structure of the event, set in a template-like sequence.
- are especially interested in the connection between function and form and in how speech act functions are realized in larger text units.

Background: Many speech events in English have relatively predictable "formulas," which are affected by such factors as setting, age and gender of participants, and nature of topic (e.g., how serious the problem is in the case of a complaint or apology or how personal a compliment or invitation is). Other speech events are more complex and not necessarily reducible to a formula.

In the late 1970s and early 1980s, the Council of Europe thoroughly examined various speech acts or "language functions" that nonnative speakers were likely to encounter (see, e.g., van Ek 1976). This research revealed that some complex speech events are composed of several discrete speech acts and a number of possible utterances that can accomplish particular functions. In addition, register was found to be an important factor in determining the specific components of a speech event. Notional-functional approaches to language teaching, so popular in the 1980s, emerged from this research effort that viewed language in part as a tool for accomplishing real-life functions.

Some speech events may cross the boundary between the formal and informal registers: one may or may not complain or apologize to a friend, for example, but it might be *necessary* to do so in a more formal setting (e.g., with an employer or employee) or in an academic setting (e.g., with an advisor or instructor). Some other language functions often associated with more formal or academic settings are treated in Activity 8.

Step 1: Predict Some speech events that occur within conversations and that would therefore be suitable research topics for this activity are

> invitations
> compliments
> requests
> offers
> suggestions
> apologies
> complaints

Students can prepare for this project by considering how a particular speech event is structured in their L1 (or in other languages they know). This stimulates thinking about the different factors involved (e.g., how settings and participants affect the interaction). For most speech events (invitations, compliments, requests, offers, suggestions, apologies, complaints, etc.), the following questions for students are an appropriate way of eliciting discussion on cross-cultural differences and similarities.

1. How do people perform this speech event in other languages/cultures with which you are familiar? Is there a "typical" interaction? For example, does the interaction involve a certain kind of question or comment followed by a certain kind of response? Include accompanying nonverbal practices as well as verbal practices.
2. How does this interaction change with different participants (family members, close friends, professional colleagues)? How does the age and gender of the participants affect the interaction?
3. How does the interaction change with different settings (in the classroom, at a party, on the street, on the telephone compared to face-to-face)?

4. What can you predict, or what have you observed, about the way this speech event is performed in English?

Step 2: Plan Almost any communicative task that is addressed in a language textbook on speaking can be observed in its "native habitat" and may serve as the speech event under study. However, in cases where a particular speech event rarely occurs naturally, predictably, or publicly, or in EFL settings where native speakers of English are not plentiful or accessible, elicitation techniques can be used; learners can ask expert or advanced speakers to draw on their intuitions about acceptable native-like behavior in a given circumstance.

Complaints are not easily observed, for example, since they often are planned ahead of time and performed quite privately, occurring "live" between two people only—the one who is lodging the complaint and the one to whom the complaint is directed. Thus, for this particular speech event, elicitation techniques may be a more effective means of obtaining data than observations would be.

Students might design short prompts intended to elicit complaints. Examples follow.

1. On a test you took, the instructor added your points incorrectly. You were given seventy-five points (a letter grade of C) when you really should have gotten eighty-five points (a B). What do you do and say?
2. Since your friend was going to buy tickets for an upcoming concert, she offered to get yours for you. Not only did she get tickets for the wrong day, but she also kept the change (over ten dollars). What do you do and say?

Students may also consider other methods for obtaining information about the speech event they are researching. Fictional films or television programs (e.g., sitcoms or soap operas), even in overseas settings, may be appropriate sources for observing certain speech events, such as compliments, requests, offers, or invitations. If there are topics that students are particularly curious about, they might want to develop survey questions for native speakers. The analysis of compliments, for example, may generate questions like the following.

How do you feel if you tell a friend that you like her haircut and she says, "I hate it. It's too short"?

Another source for learners of English might be ESL/EFL textbooks on speaking, since many of these more recently published books include lists of phrases useful for a range of language functions/speech acts.

If it is possible to tape-record data, as it would be if responses are elicited rather than "live," it is preferable to do so, since a tape recording will allow a more detailed and accurate analysis. Or students can record their observations on a data collection chart, designed according to what learners anticipate about the speech event they are studying. A data collection chart should, as usual, leave room for information on participants and setting. For elicited information that is not tape-recorded, as much detail as possible should be provided about the respondent's comments. In situations where data are collected solely by observation and note taking—where it is not possible or feasible to use recording equipment (audio or video)—it is preferable that learners work in teams and do some practice observations/note taking to increase the reliability of their findings.

Step 3: Collect data If audiotaped or videotaped conversation data are available or if television or radio programs are the data source, learners listen to or view this material with the objective of locating speech events that may naturally occur in the course of the interactions—compliments, requests, and invitations, for example.

If learners are eliciting responses to prompts they have developed, ideally they have recorded these responses on audiotape. In the absence of recording equipment, some of the details of elicited responses are lost. However, this is acceptable if the "rules" of social appropriateness are the primary focus. The gist of the responses can be observed, especially if learners have by now started to develop skill at note taking.

The most indirect method of collecting data on speech events is to elicit written responses to prompts prepared by students. This may be an appropriate method of identifying the components of a speech event, especially if the goal is simply knowledge of the speech event "norms" in English. Gathering written data is least desirable in a class focusing on oral skills, since the opportunity to actually practice listening and speaking would be lost.

Step 4: Analyze For each speech event learners are examining, the primary task for learners is to determine whether there is a "typical" interaction. And since register is such an influential factor in how some speech events unfold (or whether they occur at all), learners would need to hypothesize how different participants and settings affect the "formula" of the speech event. Students might here return to the questions posed under Step 1.

Step 5: Generate An interesting way to present the results of the analysis is for students to prepare a teaching handout that they would use if they were responsible for teaching other nonnative speakers about the ways that a speech event can be appropriately conducted in English. For models, learners can use ESL/EFL textbooks organized by language functions/speech events. Textbooks often include short dialogues that demonstrate a particular speech, including dialogues that are adapted or completely rewritten to show how register alters the speech event. Such dialogues could be performed in a role play to demonstrate the co-occurring nonverbal features and generate the target language—language appropriate for one particular speech event.

Step 6: Review Textbooks typically contain lists of phrases useful for a particular speech event, including information about register. For example, the following list was generated by learners who were examining how suggestions are made in English. As part of the review step of this project, the list was compiled from native speaker responses to different prompts that the learners designed.

Student-Generated List for Activity 7
Suggestions

Is it possible that if you (indirect suggestion/
solution to problem) then . . . ?   More formal

Maybe it would be helpful if . . .

Do you think it would be possible to . . . ?

Perhaps you could . . .

You might . . .

Why don't you . . .

You should . . .   Less formal

The ordering of the list evolved after the learners participated in much discussion on the topic of politeness. In this particular case, learners worked in teams on different speech events and compiled their findings into lists of appropriate phrases organized by register, model dialogues, helpful "pointers," and practice activities—descriptions of settings and prompts designed to elicit the speech event (see appendix 3). Each student then collected these results together into a notebook, with one "chapter" on each different speech event studied. Thus, each student had a learner-generated "textbook" on informal speech events.

Finally, the teacher may want to test students by specifying setting and participants and then asking students to demonstrate appropriate interactions. It is especially interesting and entertaining to do this as a whole group project in which the "audience" evaluates how appropriate the interaction was. Such a format is likely to evolve into a discussion on how speech events compare across languages/cultures.

An interesting spin on this activity is for the instructor to play the role of an uncooperative interlocutor who refuses to follow the sequence "formula." This can evolve into a valuable discussion of what steps an interlocutor can take when signals are ignored or not noticed.

Learner/Teacher Feedback: This is an inherently interesting activity for learners of all levels and language backgrounds. Different learners may be drawn to different aspects of the analysis. Some may want practical information on particular speech events that they are most likely to need or encounter in their target-language settings. Some may be interested in determining what "sounds better"—the grammatical accuracy and stylistic choices associated with phrases used in a particular speech event. Others may be curious about the ways that a speech event differs from their own language, which may reveal deeper, more macro-level discourse structures related to cultural values and cultural ways of thinking. Almost without exception, though, there is something for everyone in this activity.

Activity 8

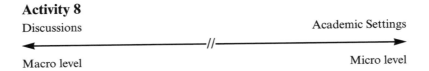

Discussions   Academic Settings

Macro level   Micro level

Objective: This activity is designed to heighten students' awareness about what contributes to a successful, well-balanced discussion. Ultimately the objective is for learners to participate in discussions competently and successfully and to learn some strategies for good discussion leading.

(Note: This activity focuses on more formal, academic discussions; see Additional Activity 8A for suggestions about how to adapt this activity for more informal settings.)

In this activity, your students will work primarily as **speech event analysts.**

Speech event analysts

- typically use as data the set of utterances, elicited or observed, that together perform a communicative function.
- believe that research should result in a description of the speech setting, the participants, and the structure of the event, set in a template-like sequence.
- are especially interested in the connection between function and form and in how speech act functions are realized in larger text units.

Background: There are many ways to contribute to a discussion. Participants can ask questions, state their opinions, and provide feedback on other people's contributions. They can give information, make conclusions, clarify, and draw other participants out. Different individuals may be comfortable with only certain kinds of contributions, and good discussion leaders recognize that all kinds of contributions are valid and valuable.

Step 1: Predict Learners brainstorm about the activities that are performed in a discussion. Questions for consideration follow.

1. What are some of the activities that discussion participants do? Make a list.
2. Specifically, how do they accomplish these activities? What do they do and say? After each activity in the list made in response to the preceding question, give an example of how the activity is accomplished.
3. If there is an appointed discussion leader, what does this person do differently than the other discussion participants?
4. What are the qualities of a "good" discussion? What are the qualities of a "poor" discussion? (Opinions may differ!)
5. What are some of the differences between informal discussions (e.g., those that may occur in conversation between friends) and formal, planned discussions (e.g., a panel discussion)?

Step 2: Plan For this activity, learners will observe a discussion in an informal, academic setting or a more formal setting (e.g., a political discussion on the radio or television or a planned panel discussion at a conference). For students in a university or college, there will be many opportunities for these kinds of observations. In EFL settings or nonacademic settings, learners will need to rely on discussions that are aired as part of a television or radio show.

Based on what they expect to see and hear, learners can prepare a data collection chart like the following (adapted depending on student needs).

Data Collection Chart for Activity 8
Discussions

Setting:

Participants

    number:

    relationship/hierarchy (Is there an appointed discussion leader?):

    seating format (make a quick sketch—use another sheet of paper if necessary):

Discussion Strategies

    What does the discussion leader do to promote discussion?

Discussion Leader's Remarks (What did she/he say?)	**Discussion Leader's Function** (What happened?)
1.	
2.	
3.	

What do the discussion participants do to contribute to the discussion?

Discussion Participant's Remarks (What did she/he say?)	**Discussion Participant's Function** (What happened?)
1.	
2.	
3.	

Additional notes (on impressions regarding effectiveness, individual contributions, etc.):

If learners work in groups, tasks can be specified beforehand, with certain individuals focusing on certain activities and the language that is used to accomplish these (e.g., one person can examine how people give or ask for opinions; another may look for the ways in which people are "nominated" to speak). Alternatively, different learners may want to look at specific participants (asking, e.g., how "good" participants claim turns or maintain turns—see Activity 1 for more information on this topic).

Or learners may want to look at the "movement" of the discussion in general. In this case, their sketch of the seating format on the data collection chart can be enlarged to serve as a discussion flowchart. The following student sample represents the first six turns of talk at a graduate seminar in sociology. There are one appointed discussion leader (DL) and eight participants (A through H). Arrows are used to show who speaks next (e.g., after DL's initial question, C spoke, followed by DL, then H, then back to C, then another comment by DL). The tallies indicate the number of turns for each speaker.

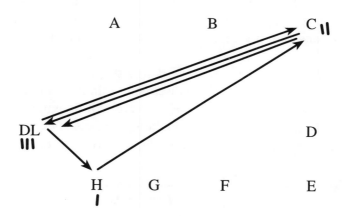

Since tracing the movement of a discussion can be quite complex and thus quite messy to keep track of, a good suggestion is to break this task into shorter samplings—three- to five-minute segments. This kind of observation is most reliable if supplemented by videotaping or if separate observers can collaborate and compile their results.

Step 3: Collect data Learners observe a discussion and make detailed notes, filling out information on their data collection chart, tracing the movement of the discussion on their discussion flowchart, or elaborating with specific details on features that interested them (particular comments, certain individuals' performance, unexpected topic changes, etc.). It is advantageous if the observed discussion(s) can be videotaped, since observations can then be double-checked with the original interaction, thus increasing the reliability of the findings. Audiotapes are also helpful in allowing more specific analyses, although visual and nonverbal cues important to the discussion would obviously not be available on them for review.

Step 4: Analysis An interesting way to approach the data is for learners to rate the discussion they observe on a ten-point scale (1 = poor; 10 = excellent). They should be prepared to support their rating with specific evidence about what makes the discussion good or poor. This can be a provocative direction for the analysis, since it inevitably leads to a discussion of what criteria are considered valuable in enhancing a discussion, and since opinions may vary quite markedly. If the discussion was taped, the instructor or students might want to play excerpts that contain interesting examples that illustrate their opinions and that demonstrate how different activities are carried out.

This activity lends itself to group work and the pooling of data. Revealing the structure or framework of the discussion is important, and an appropriate task is to compile a list of the different types of activities being performed by the discussion participants, including the specifics of how these jobs are carried out. The following list is adapted from one class's compiled list.

Student-Generated List for Activity 8
Discussions

What Discussion Participants Do (functions)	**How They Do It** (phrases used)
1. Give opinions	I think that . . . I believe that . . . In my opinion . . .
2. Agree	I agree with . . . Yeah, that's how I feel.
3. Disagree	I disagree. I think that . . . But I don't believe that's accurate.

4. Ask for information

But isn't it true that . . . ?
(in a discussion about birth control policies
and overpopulation):
    What's the population of . . . ?

5. Give information

(answer questions posed)
(offer facts vs. opinions):
    . . . has over eight hundred million people.
(cite source/recent statistics)

6. Nominate other speakers

Do you agree with me?
What do you think, (name)?
(turn to another speaker and
make eye contact)

7. Give feedback to others

Excellent point.
But isn't that a little off the track?

8. Clarify/ask for clarification

That's not what I meant.
Let's get this straight. Do you
mean that . . . ?

What Discussion Leaders Do
(functions)

How They Do It
(phrases used)

1. Encourage people to participate

Do you agree with that, (name)?
(Name), what do you think?

2. Manage turns

Could you expand on that, please?
(cutting a speaker off)
    I understand what you're saying, but I'd
    like to hear what someone else has to say
    now.
    Thanks, thanks. Let's hear from
    someone else.

3. Provide feedback to participants

Thanks for your comment, (name).
Good point.

4. Summarize/paraphrase/
draw conclusions

So you're saying that . . . ?
So, it seems that the consensus so far
is that . . .
I'm interested in (name)'s comment that . . .

If some learners were interested in the movement of the discussion and collected data on a discussion flowchart, this information should be related to the previous findings. For example, how did discussants who actively participated claim or maintain their turns? If the discussion leader took a less active role and participated infrequently, how did this affect the "shape" the discussion took?

Step 5: Generate Analysis of the data will necessitate talking about individual or group results and is thus a useful method of generating discussion on the topic. Students might also want to role-play particularly effective strategies for giving their opinions, reclaiming their turn, and so on.

However, the most efficient way of generating data from all students is to give a discussion-leading assignment. In a large class, it may be helpful to have two or more students leading each discussion (either assigning them different roles or having them be responsible for specific parts of the discussion—e.g., one person leads the first ten minutes; another leads the second ten minutes); it may also work to have two or more discussions taking place at one time. Audiotaping and/or videotaping the discussion is desirable.

To simulate an actual discussion in an academic setting, discussion participants should have the opportunity for some kind of topic preparation beforehand. For example, discussion leaders might provide the participants with a short (one- to two-paragraph) summary sheet that provides general information about the topic and that poses some initial questions, intended to stimulate thinking on the issues. A controversial topic that does not require specialized knowledge is most appropriate for a mixed group of students with different educational backgrounds and interests.

Step 6: Review Since it is difficult to maintain perspective about one's own participation in a discussion, both as a participant and as a facilitator, peer evaluation is advised for at least part of the analysis. Learners can observe each other, using either of the data collection formats generated in earlier steps to note the movement of the discussion and the frequency of individual participation, the kinds of activities performed by discussion leaders and participants, and information on how these were performed (including nonverbal participation—nodding to indicate agreement, eye contact to nominate another speaker, etc.).

A tape of the discussion can supply the peer evaluator with additional information, and it can be especially useful data for self-analysis, which will most likely support the peer evaluator's observation with specific examples of how an activity was accomplished.

Additional Activity 8A—Talk show host. Learners videotape or audio-tape a television talk show, of which there are many to choose from in North America. As with the academic discussion, learners analyze the types of activities being performed by the talk show host and the discussion partici-pants. How specifically do the talk show host and the participants give and ask for opinions, agree and disagree, and give and ask for information? How does the talk show host nominate speakers, provide feedback, clarify, para-phrase, and summarize?

After the analysis of the discussion, there are several options. Ideally, stu-dents opt to organize their own talk shows in which they take turns acting as the talk show host. They can choose the topic, preferably a controversial one or one related to some current event of interest to them; they can invite guest speakers or themselves assume the roles or identities of the discussion partic-ipants; and they can later evaluate or rate each other's or their own perfor-mance as a talk show host. Videotaping the discussion is clearly an advan-tage. (Additional Activity 8A is adapted from Asplin 1995.)

Learner/Teacher Feedback: With one group of students, there was some ini-tial resistance to analyzing academic discussions ("Too boring!" was one of the comments), though the talk show host activity did not provoke the same reaction. After the fact, however, these learners admitted that the focus on academic discussions was useful, especially for graduate students or for those who were preparing to be full-time students. They came away from this activ-ity with some consciousness about the ways in which they themselves con-tribute to discussions, the activities they can do to strengthen their participa-tion, and the skills they have and need to lead discussions.

Activity 9

Storytelling   Conversation

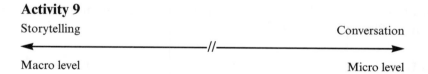

Macro level   Micro level

Objective: This activity is designed to provide learners with information about narratives and narrative structure. Another goal is for learners to be able to tell stories in a natural and appropriate manner.

In this activity, your students will work primarily as **sociolinguists.**

Sociolinguists

- typically use as data language in use—observed or recorded communications.
- believe that each community or subculture has its own unique set of conventions, rules, and patterns for the conduct of communication.
- are especially interested in how these rules and patterns can be understood in the context of a general system that reflects the values and the structure of the society in which they occur.

Background: Language researchers who have formally studied the oral narrative describe the specific components present in a typical narrative in English (e.g., see Labov and Waletsky 1967; Bauman 1986; Toolan 1988). If these are reduced to what is most essential for a complete and successfully told story, they include (1) introductory information that orients the listener in terms of time and place (the "who," "what," and "where" of the story); (2) the complicating action, or main acts, of the story; (3) the resolution, or climax, of the story (what finally happened); and often, but not always, (4) some kind of concluding or evaluative comment (How did the speaker feel? How was she or he affected by these acts?), which usually serves to link the story to the next topic or next speaker.

A more macro-level approach to viewing narrative is to consider the function of narratives in different languages and different situations. For example, in some settings narratives are used to teach something to the listeners. In other contexts, it might be appropriate to tell a story to diffuse an argument or prove a point. In some cultures, there are certain forums specifically for storytelling, and good storytellers are respected and revered (e.g., see Bauman 1986; Young 1987; Stahl 1989).

Step 1: Predict Students can prepare for this project by providing information about stories in their L1 (or in other languages they know). Questions for discussion follow.

1. When do people tell stories in other languages/cultures with which you are familiar? Can you think of people who are known as good storytellers? Why are they considered good storytellers? What makes a story "good"? Are there certain parts or components of the story that must be present? Or is good storytelling determined by the speaker's personal "style"?
2. How does the storytelling format change in an informal setting (e.g., in conversation, such as when you tell family members or close friends about something that happened to you)?

3. What can you predict, or what have you observed, about the way stories are told in English in unplanned conversations? What is different about storytelling in other contexts?

Step 2: Plan Learners can decide what kinds of narratives they are interested in examining—elicited or spontaneous. In students' conversation data (collected in Activity 1), there may be examples of spontaneous narratives that occurred in the process of unplanned conversations. It is much easier, however, to elicit narratives, especially if there are suggested topics that will stimulate speakers to tell their account of something significant that happened to them.

To prepare to collect data, students can work in small groups, or, if the instructor prefers, the whole class can brainstorm for topics that will be used to elicit stories from native or expert speakers. Examples of general topics that may be appropriate for this activity are happy and memorable acts (when you first met/dated your partner, when you first learned you were going to go overseas, the birth of a child), memorable events (something that changed your life), and an embarrassing/exciting/terrifying moment. An example of a more specific topic is a mistake your parents made with you or, if you are a parent, a mistake you made with your children. Since learners are responsible for choosing a topic, they can decide if a topic is either too personal or too general and thus not personal enough.

Students may also consider other methods for obtaining spontaneously occurring narrative data. Fictional films or television programs (e.g., sitcoms or soap operas), even in overseas settings, may be appropriate sources for observing extemporaneous storytelling in conversation, although it should be taken into account that these are scripted and may not resemble unplanned narratives very closely. In the United States, National Public Radio stations air programs during which stories are likely to emerge—more informal, unplanned stories in the course of interviews on such programs as *Fresh Air* and on entertainment radio shows, such as *Car Talk* or Garrison Keillor's *Prairie Home Companion;* scripted, prewritten stories about topics of national interest in news shows, such as *All Things Considered.* Finally, church sermons and public talks or lectures may be contexts in which stories are likely to emerge.

Step 3: Collect data It is preferable to tape-record narratives, since this will allow a more detailed and accurate analysis. In some contexts it may not be feasible to tape-record spontaneously told stories: in face-to-face interactions, it could be awkward and distracting to the speaker if the conversation must halt in order to begin recording; stories that emerge in radio and television programs are not always clearly marked to indicate the beginning, and thus the introductory material may be lost.

When tape-recording is not available or desirable, learners should be encouraged to work in teams to increase the reliability of their findings. It is helpful if learners first get some practice in listening for narratives as they occur in the context of conversation or another activity. In addition, to hone observation skills, learners should take notes, reconstruct the story, and listen to feedback from other students on what they might have missed or misrepresented.

Step 4: Analyze Students can work in small or large groups to share their tape-recorded stories, analyzing them for components they consider essential. In some cases, depending on interest, it might be appropriate to transcribe stories or parts of stories, which will allow an examination of the data in greater detail.

If learners have a collection of narratives as their database for this activity, there are several options for analysis. Narratives can be categorized in terms of their function (e.g., did they serve as illustrations? as accounts or descriptions?) or the genre that situates them (e.g., did they occur in the course of the conversation? as a "work of art" in a theater performance? as part of a church sermon?). Would it have been possible or appropriate to convey the information from the story in another, nonnarrative format?

Narratives can also be ranked in terms of their entertainment value, effectiveness, length, or amount of detail. Is there enough/too much information provided? What makes the story weak, strong, good, or boring? Do all learners agree on these characterizations or rankings? If not, why not?

Regardless of the database used or the first sweep made at analysis, a question appropriate for whole group discussion is, What are the essential components for a successful oral narrative? There is no one "correct" answer to this question; there may be differences of opinion about this question as well as about which narrative is the best/most successful. However, learners should be sure to analyze their reactions to a particular narrative and to give reasons for their opinions.

Step 5: Generate If narratives were elicited and/or audiotaped, making sense of the narratives in the data sample and deciding which analytical perspective is most useful or productive can serve as the basis for generating talk about narratives. A group discussion is a useful format for discussing findings. Differences of opinion are likely to emerge, since storytelling conventions may vary in different languages and cultures, and since individual topic and style preferences may be quite different.

If data were not audiotaped or videotaped, then a natural way to produce the data is by means of story retelling. Learners who worked in teams can first compile their data and then make sure that in their reconstruction of the story no essential components are missed. This step, of course, again questions what determines whether a component is essential or not and where that line "ends" and an overtelling, with too much detail, begins.

Finally, learners can tell their own real-life stories, working in pairs or small groups to elicit and tape-record narratives from each other. The topics generated in Step 2 might be appropriate, or new topics may emerge from the stories learners have collected.

Step 6: Review The analysis of learners' own narratives is appropriately done as homework, individually or in pairs. With this activity, pair work/peer evaluation tends to provide some perspective, since individual self-monitoring analyses may be approached in an overly critical manner. It is helpful if the focus of this analysis is on what components were included in the narrative (rather than what components were missing) and on what ways the story was successfully told (rather than on what was "wrong" with it). With this orientation, peer evaluation may be helpful in providing positive feedback.

Additional Activity 9A—Planned narratives. As a final follow-up activity, learners can retell their stories, incorporating suggested improvements. Or "new" stories, also planned in advance, can be told. If stories are shared, one at a time, with the whole group, the instructor may want to have students vote on the top two or three stories (in specific student-generated categories, if desired—the funniest, the most common experience, the story most well told, etc.). An anonymous, written poll is a good way to get this information from class members. The "winners'" stories should be carefully reanalyzed, with learners providing specific evidence about what discourse features contributed to the stories' strength.

Additional Activity 9B—Written narratives. Learners retell their stories in writing. Without any information about the differences in writing and speaking, this activity can serve as an introduction to Activity 10, which is also cross-modal (and it can serve as a bridge to the forthcoming companion volume on written language research activities). This activity is most effectively done if learners first make written versions of their taped stories, then transcribe these taped stories. They can trade their data sets—the spoken and written versions of the same story—with their classmates, with the goal being to start noticing some of the features specific to each modality and to develop a list that describes the differences between them.

Learner/Teacher Feedback: First, students always appreciate hearing each other's stories. Determining which student-told stories are "best" can be validating to good storytellers yet not diminishing to those whose stories were not considered best. Even without a story competition, learners remark that learning more about others in the class through hearing their stories is valuable and interesting.

Regarding native and expert speaker stories, more advanced learners have expressed surprise at the breadth and range of the narrative. Students find that stories can be told for a variety of reasons and in a variety of contexts and that the label "story" can be applied to lots of activities that "happen" in conversation or other genres, even activities quite different in form, length, and function—e.g., a description of the events of the day; a three-utterance retelling of a dream; a fifteen-minute, step-by-step radio mystery; a how-to explanation of a recipe.

Activity 10

Style   Writing/Fiction, Informal Settings

Macro level   Micro level

Objective: This activity examines how an individual's speaking style can be "translated" into written language. (Thus, it is different than most of the activities in this unit, with the exception of Additional Activity 10B, in that it examines relationships between writing and speaking; it is also different in that it targets both micro- and macro-level structures.) A goal of this activity is to develop in learners a sense of how features characteristic of speaking are represented in writing and also of how these features can convey information about fictional characters' personality and their spoken language "style."

In this activity, your students will work primarily as **stylisticians.**

(Note: Since this activity involves written text, it involves an area of research usually associated with writing.)

Stylisticians

- typically use as data written texts, often those that are perceived as literature.
- believe that research should result in an explanation of how the linguistic conventions of phonetics/phonology, semantics, and syntax are used in writing to create specific intended effects and impressions in the reader.
- are especially interested in the range of features in a written text that appear to be significant or important (i.e., if the features were altered, the text would "feel" different to the reader).

Background: Stylistics is the study of style. One of the primary goals of this discipline of study is to examine the ways in which literary texts use linguistic conventions in the areas of phonetics/phonology, semantics, and syntax to create certain intended effects in the reader (and sometimes in the listener, even though the tradition in the discipline of stylistics is to focus primarily on written language). For example, phonetic features, such as rhythm, stress, and rhyme, are carefully exploited in well-crafted poems, where wordiness or lengthiness is often not valued. A stylistic examination of the vocabulary used in scientific reports will reveal that the use of field-specific jargon is an accepted practice in such works. And in the area of syntax, stylisticians are interested in patterns of sentence formation: word order that deviates in some way from what is expected can seem quite striking.

These linguistic conventions are often exploited by writers, who intentionally or unconsciously "imitate" spoken language in their portrayal of their characters in dialogue with each other. For example, characters' dialects are revealed by their choices of words and by their conformity or lack of conformity to prescriptive standards of grammar and pronunciation. Written characters' personalities are further developed by their manner of speaking as revealed by hesitations, by patterns of interruptions, or even by passivity in responding to others (i.e., an inability or refusal to initiate turns and/or a lack of backchanneling or response to the speaker).

Step 1: Predict How is speaking style represented in written speech? What do writers do to show something about their characters' style or personality? In this step of the activity, student researchers form a discussion group to talk about these questions. Although it is natural to talk about a topic in general terms at first, learners should be encouraged to start to develop lists of the specific activities writers do with language to show that their characters are talking and of the specific features of language that convey information, through characters' speaking style, about these "speakers'" backgrounds, personalities, and attitudes.

If the discussion to this point has been only about English, encourage students to think about how fictional characters' speaking style is portrayed in languages other than English. Do there seem to be differences in the written fiction of different languages?

Step 2: Plan In this step, student researchers find evidence for the activities they talked about in the discussion. In other words, they find examples of the specific features in a particular written text (a) that show that a fictional character is speaking and (b) that give readers information about that particular character's background, personality, and emotions/ attitudes.

Research teams can divide duties, with each team member collecting data from different sources. The teams will look for examples of speaking style in fiction of various types: novels, short stories in magazines, even cartoons. Learners can examine fiction in both English and other languages with which they are familiar. Decisions to make are about the number of examples learners want to collect and about the range of sources.

Step 3: Collect data Access to a photocopier makes this step easy, since learners can then copy short passages that are examples of a fictional character speaking. Or they can copy down these examples by hand; in this case, in the interest of time and efficiency, they may want to write down only those quotations that clearly show that the character is talking—passages that are differentiated clearly from the written prose about the character. Useful examples to write down are those that give a lot of information about the fictional "speaker"—emotional state, dialect and normal way of speaking (as represented by grammar and pronunciation, or accent), and attitudes about others (as represented by manner of interaction—hesitations, interruptions, amount of talking the speaker does, etc.).

Step 4: Analyze The question addressed in this analysis is, What are the ways that writers (a) show that a fictional character is speaking and (b) give readers information about that particular character's background, personality, and emotions/attitudes? For this step, learners can work alone and pool their results or can pool their data and work together. The result should be a list of specific examples of the linguistic features writers use to accomplish these tasks. The following list is an example of one way this analysis could be structured.

Data Analysis for Activity 10
Speaking Style

Examples of Speaker's Grammar	**Data Source** (novel? story? etc.)
1.	
2.	
3.	
etc.	

Examples of Speaker's Pronunciation/Accent	Data Source (novel? story? etc.)
1.	
2.	
3.	
etc.	

Examples of Speaker's Word Choice	Data Source (novel? story? etc.)
1.	
2.	
3.	
etc.	

The learners and instructor then review their findings in a whole group discussion. Are there certain activities writers always do to show that their characters are talking? In other words, what are the activities that are most typically done?

An example opinion question is, What are the activities that seem to be the most effective? In other words, what are the "best" ways to tell readers something about fictional characters' speaking style and thus to give information about these characters' background and about their personality or emotional characteristics?

Step 5: Generate This is an opportunity for student researchers to try out some of the writing techniques they have learned. Rather than create a fictional character out of the blue, though, learners base their written creations on a real person. Thus, the first step is for students to interview someone who they consider interesting or who has had interesting experiences. This might be someone who is considered a "character" in some way, perhaps because of strong personality characteristics (e.g., they might be unusually outgoing or adventuresome). Or it might be someone who likes to tell stories or whose life has been different in some way from the interviewer (e.g., maybe the person is very old and has seen many changes during her or his lifetime). Students audiotape or videotape this interview, which will most likely evolve into a storytelling session (rather than a question-and-answer interview).

This interview need not be in English, since part of the objective is to "translate" spoken language into written language. If all of the members of the class (and the instructor) share a language and do not live in an English-speaking country, then it might be interesting to conduct this step in the shared language. However, since there are likely to be different conventions in different languages, it is important to translate the foreign language version into English and then to compare and contrast the two versions. Naturally this can be useful in classes where students speak a common native language and where skills in both speaking and writing are targeted.

In "translating" the interview into writing, learners first need to find a section of the speaker's talk that is complete in some sense—perhaps a story that the speaker tells, with a beginning and ending, or a description that gives some background information. If there is a limited amount of time for this activity, learners should aim for one or two written pages that "characterize" something about the speaker, which can give readers information about the kind of person the speaker is, the mood the speaker is in, or the attitudes and emotions the speaker is experiencing about the topic of talk.

Because detailed transcriptions (like those done for Activities 1–4) can be difficult to read, the written version does not need to be a direct transcription (and it cannot be if the goal is to produce an English version of an interview conducted in a language other than English). The writer is the editor too, and the goal of the written version is to capture something of the flavor of the character who is speaking. In the interest of doing this, sentences, phrases, and words can be deleted; words or phrases that help to develop the character of the speaker can be added (e.g., the slang expressions a speaker uses can give information about the speaker's age-group and circle of friends); and words can be spelled phonetically to show how the speaker is talking—or how the speaker might talk if he or she used English (e.g., the use of "gonna" instead of "going to" can show that the speaker is relaxed or in a casual situation).

Step 6: Analyze In this step, learners share their written products with each other and then discuss their reactions as readers. After reading a piece, what do they know about the character who is speaking (i.e., the person who was interviewed). Was the character "successfully" portrayed in writing? What other specific things could the writer/interviewer do to the written version to give more information about the person and to develop the person's character more fully? Readers can give suggestions for ways to edit the piece so that it is more effective.

This step is best done if readers of the piece are also able to listen to the initial, tape-recorded interview. (For this, the excerpt used as the basis of the written piece is adequate, rather than the whole interview.) Thus, it is logical for the writer to collaborate with a reader who knows the speaker's L1, so that the reader is better able to make judgments about whether the written version is authentic sounding in that it captures something of the style of the speaker.

Learner/Teacher Feedback: Though this activity might sound daunting to instructors who have paid little attention to the differences between speaking and writing, it is actually quite straightforward. Works of fiction in any genre can provide examples of the conventions used to express speaking style, and some of these conventions are easily adopted or imitated. For example, italicized words can be used to show that the word is stressed (or yelled); in cartoons, underlining and capitalizing words show this.

This activity can be great fun for all types of learners, since it is a fairly straightforward way to experiment with writing style for those with an interest in this. Yet it is also engaging for the learners who are simply absorbed in the stories and characters of the speakers they interviewed. Thus, capturing something about the flavor of these speakers can be motivating in itself and entertaining. An added benefit is that the activity results in a collection of student-written character portrayals, many of these excellently done (see the sample portrayal in appendix 4).

Activity 11

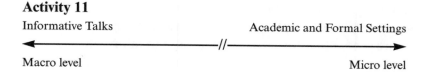

Informative Talks · · · · · · · · · · · · · · · Academic and Formal Settings

Macro level · · · · · · · · · · · · · · · Micro level

Objective: The goal of this activity is to instruct learners about the many purposes of informative talks, the ways in which informative talks can be structured, and the importance of supporting material. Ultimately, the objective is for learners themselves to plan and deliver short informative talks.

In this activity, your students will work primarily as **speech event analysts.**

Speech event analysts

- typically use as data the set of utterances, elicited or observed, that together perform a communicative function.
- believe that research should result in a description of the speech setting, the participants, and the structure of the event, set in a template-like sequence.
- are especially interested in the connection between function and form and in how speech act functions are realized in larger text units.

Background: Informative speaking, the kind of talk associated with academic lectures and news reports, seeks to increase the knowledge and understanding of an audience. Most good informative speeches and reports have clearly defined purpose statements, which point out what the speaker's objective is. Good informative talks also contain a reason for the audience to want to listen to and learn from the speech, logical organization and clearly emphasized main points, and effective supporting evidence.

Step 1: Predict The following questions for students can help to stimulate thinking about the structure of informative talks.

1. Introductions to lectures often start out with statements that indicate what the speaker's goal is or what the audience will be able to do after hearing the speech (e.g., "After hearing my lecture, you will be able to list the three main causes of . . ."; "Today I am going to describe the situation surrounding . . ."). What other key verbs might be used in informative purpose statements? (Possibilities might be *analyze* and *compare.*)
2. Besides stating the purpose, what are some of the other functions that introductions to informative talks accomplish?
3. What are some of the ways that important points are emphasized?
4. Supporting material is used in informative talks to develop ideas by clarifying and by making the talk interesting and memorable. Providing examples and detailed descriptions are two ways of using supporting material. What are some other forms of support used in informative talks?
5. What can you predict, or what have you observed, about the effect of the setting on informative talks? For example, how are short television news reports different from hour-long academic lectures?

Step 2: Plan Part of the planning will involve locating a talk that is of interest to students. Learners will need to decide what kind of informative talk best suits their purposes. On a North American college campus, there are likely to be plenty of opportunities for students to attend live talks on a variety of topics. In other settings and non-English-speaking countries, learners may need to rely on radio or television news programs.

For this project, students will observe/listen to and later analyze an informative report. As usual, it is preferable to audiotape or videotape talks, so that learners can be specific in their analyses. Students may also consider other ways of supplementing their data about informative talks; for example, they can consult a textbook on public speaking or interview people they consider good at giving talks or lecturing.

Step 3: Collect data In teams or individually, learners observe and listen to a talk. Videotaping is the ideal data collection method, since the entire event, including the accompanying nonverbal information, is then available for viewing. Audiotaping is of course acceptable for recording radio talks, but in the case of live performances or televised talks, student researchers who audiotape their data should pay attention to and take notes on the paralinguistic features.

This activity is most successful if there is opportunity for review (i.e., if the talk has been audiotaped or videotaped), since this allows closer examination of the more micro-level structures, such as references to supporting evidence and transitions to major points. If taping is not possible, the activity is still potentially useful, especially with the collaboration of students who work in research teams. Members of the research teams could focus on different features, with some, for example, looking at the introduction and the "purpose statement," others examining how main points are emphasized, others observing the use of transitions or supporting material, and so on.

Step 4: Analyze Analyses will result in answers to the questions in Step 1. The analyses can be supplemented with a rating of the lecture observed. For this, learners use a ten-point scale (1 = poor; 10 = excellent) and prepare to support their rating with specific evidence about what made the talk good or poor. Data can be analyzed in small groups, individually, or, if a tape of the informative report is especially interesting and clear, as a whole group. Students can compile their results into a learner-designed evaluation sheet that outlines the important components of an informative report. This can then later be used to analyze learner-produced data (in Step 6).

Step 5: Generate All learners should have the opportunity to develop and deliver an informative report, but time constraints and course objectives must be considered in determining the length of the talks. Topic selection should be discussed; the instructor may want to preapprove student-chosen topics to ensure that they are not too narrow or specialized or too general and unfocused. Talks should be videotaped so that nonverbal factors can be considered, but if this is not possible, audiotaping will suffice.

If the issue of naturalness of speech has not come up, it might be helpful to address this topic before learners begin preparing for their talks, since one of the differences between more informal settings (e.g., a daily academic lecture) and more formal settings (e.g., a televised news report) is spontaneity: the former is usually somewhat ad-lib; the latter is read, memorized, and/or rehearsed. The instructor and students might want to decide together which format is preferred for this assignment. An appropriate compromise may be that learners prepare an outline from which to speak and that they rehearse (but not memorize) their talk beforehand.

Step 6: Review Since it is difficult to maintain perspective about the success of one's own talk, peer evaluation is advised for at least part of the analysis. Learners can observe and evaluate each other, using the sheet they generated in Step 4, which notes the important components of an informative report. Observers can also take notes on the content of the talk, which can help to demonstrate to the speaker whether the organization of the talk was clear to listeners and whether the main points were emphasized adequately. Finally, observers should give some attention to delivery, noting nonverbal aspects (eye contact, posture, use of gestures) and auditory aspects (volume, rate, word stress, and use of pauses).

Another successfully used format of evaluation is immediate oral feedback on the talk from two different observers, limiting their comments to one positive observation (What was one of the primary strengths of the talk?) and one critical/constructive comment (What is one area that was weak or needs further work?). These short oral comments are helpful to other members of the audience in preparing their own talks and can be followed up with the more thorough written analyses that the evaluation form and the outline will provide.

A tape of the talk can supply the peer evaluator with additional information, and it can be especially useful data for self-analysis. Learners should transcribe at least a portion of their own talk, to verify the peer evaluators' observations and to monitor micro-level features (see chapter 4 for activities targeting micro skills, such as grammar and pronunciation).

To more specifically focus the kind of talk students analyze and to shift the topic to a tone that is more informal and more in tune with popular culture, Additional Activity 11A may be useful.

Additional Activity 11A—Persuasion. Learners are often interested in the fine line between talks that are clearly informative and those that move into the arena of persuasive talks. Persuasion is the act of motivating someone, through talk (usually), to change a particular belief, attitude, or behavior. Communication specialists and speech writers generally believe that two of the factors that contribute to a successful persuasive talk are the speaker's sensitivity to audience (since the audience must believe in the seriousness of the problem) and the audience's perception of the logic of the argument. However, the act of persuasion can take many forms and does not necessitate a formal register. Television commercials are a prime example of attempts to persuade. Television commercials can run the range of registers from serious, formal, logical arguments to informal, multimedia appeals to humor or basic instincts.

For this activity, students will observe/listen to, record, and analyze a television commercial. Two essential questions appropriate as a way of framing the analysis follow.

1. How does (or doesn't) the television commercial exhibit audience sensitivity?
2. What form does the persuasive attempt take?

Since audiences may vary from each other in terms of age, gender, educational background, ethnicity, political beliefs, and/or jobs or professions, learners need to determine who specifically the commercial is targeting. In terms of audience appeal, the following questions are relevant: Is there a problem from the audience's point of view? How does the problem relate to the audience? Does the problem actually require a change?

The different types of persuasive strategies, or appeals, used in persuasive talks are (1) credibility-based appeals, which rely on the audience's acceptance of the speaker and his or her sources of information as accurate; (2) logical appeals, which depend on the audience's perception of the speaker's argument as sound and reasonable; and (3) emotional appeals, which stimulate audience reaction by tapping into common feelings of fear, anger, pride, or pity.

The two topics of audience appeal and persuasive strategy provide plenty of food for thought. Accompanied by videotapes of the television commercials under analysis, these topics can stimulate classroom discussion that is likely to evolve into a more general discussion on popular culture and cultural values, which can serve as a nice lead-in to Activity 12 on attitudes and assumptions. An additional step in this activity is for students to prepare, videotape, view, and analyze a commercial collectively.

Learner/Teacher Feedback: The nature of a particular class can greatly affect the success of this activity. In classes composed primarily of international teaching assistants (ITAs), for example, evaluating and developing informative talks is an important goal. Groups less concerned with formal academic genres (e.g., general conversation classes) have expressed great enthusiasm for Additional Activity 11A. With videotapes of the actual television commercials, this additional activity can get a bit outrageous. Teachers, be prepared!

Activity 12

Attitudes and Assumptions   Conversation, Informal Daily Interactions

Macro level   Micro level

Objective: This activity targets some of the larger, macro-level social and affective forces that operate in every social encounter. It is designed to heighten awareness about what is happening "below the surface" in typical day-to-day interactions that learners have outside of the classroom.

In this activity, your students will work primarily as **ethnographers.**

Ethnographers

- typically use as data interviews and participant and nonparticipant observations that occur in natural settings over a long period of time.
- believe that cultural meanings are revealed by people's behavior, which can only be understood by incorporating the subjective perceptions and belief systems of the researcher.
- are especially interested in developing descriptive and interpretive accounts that characterize the culture of a group or an individual.

Background: In applied linguistics literature, schema theory is most often used in the context of discussions about reading. Reading theorists and materials designers often encourage teachers to consider that the act of reading involves not only the ability to decode text—to understand words and to make sense of the grammar—but decoding on a less tangible, macro level: when we read, we make assumptions based on what we know about the topic or related topics, on our experience with the subject matter as social and emotional beings, and even on our associations with the genre (we approach reading a newspaper differently than we approach the reading of a poem).

In oral language, what we bring to a "spoken text" is even more complex, due primarily to two factors: time and the far greater range of nonlinguistic information available—the visual and auditory information and, in face-to-face interactions, the social setting and the relationship between speaker and listener. In authentic oral interactions, we do not have the leisure to analyze and reanalyze what has been said, as we can when we are reading. In face-to-face interactions, our own involvement as not just listeners but potential speakers affects the rate of interaction and how an interaction is negotiated between interlocutors. But unless we are working with tapes or transcripts of a spoken interaction, comprehension must take place immediately or very close to the time that the words are spoken.

There are many sources of interest that we could turn our attention to. Recently, in the field of teaching English language, there has been interest in the social and affective forces that underlie a learner's language-learning experience, both inside and outside the classroom. Thus, this activity asks students to focus on encounters in English that they have outside of the classroom. (In non-English-speaking environments, this activity could be redesigned to investigate nonstudent community members' attitudes toward the learner/student of English.)

Learners are encouraged to observe how they are feeling, what they are thinking, and what assumptions they have about the speaker—her or his role and position and her or his reaction to the learner. What conclusions do they make about the encounter as a whole? Exploring these issues is useful since students can develop an awareness of assumptions that might limit or influence their language-learning experience and, more generally, their experience in and with the target culture. This activity is also useful as a way in which learners can meaningfully engage with and notice their similarities with each other. Peirce (1994) employs such observation as a way for immigrant women to collectively process experiences they have with their new target culture.

Step 1: Predict Some of the questions that follow are intended for people whose contact with native speakers is at least somewhat limited (i.e., students who conduct most of their interactions outside of the classroom in their native languages rather than English).

1. What encounters will you, students of English, have outside of the classroom? For example:

   • Do you use the telephone to get information?
   • Do your daily errands (going to the bank, the doctor, etc.) involve using English?
   • How often do you speak in English outside of the classroom each day or each week?

2. What is your experience speaking English? After an interaction in English, do you usually feel a particular way? For example:

   • Do you feel excited because you communicated successfully?
   • Do you feel frustrated because you had difficulty understanding or expressing yourself?

3. After an interaction in English, what do you think about the person you are talking to?

   • Do you think they have a certain attitude about you? (Do you think they have an opinion about you? Are they behaving in a certain manner?)
   • Do you have any reactions to the person you are talking to? (Do you feel happy because you feel the person behaved with respect and understanding? Do you feel angry because you feel misunderstood?)

If students regularly converse in English with friends or family members and spend most of their social time speaking in English, some of the preceding questions might not be so relevant to them. If this is the case, the focus of the activity can be changed to investigate attitudes that people have toward the student/learner. For example, is the learner considered a good or poor student? Why? Is the student's teacher/program of learning respected? Why or why not? Any questions that explore contextual factors that may affect the student's learning are relevant and can be examined.

Step 2: Plan Students' data will consist of notes they write about the interactions they have in English, so they need to be alert to situations when they can expect to interact in English. Students should keep their research notebooks handy in case they have time immediately following interactions to note their observations. It is also helpful if learners are able to save some time each night to write about their interactions further.

Step 3: Collect data Situations in which learners are able to reflect on their encounters immediately afterward (if they have the time and space) are ideal in the sense that the experiences are fresh in their minds. Immediately after encounters is a good time for them to write down the words that were spoken as best as they can remember (in short encounters) and, for interactions that are face-to-face, the physical things that they noticed. For example, how close were the interactants standing? Did the learner notice or react to any of the speaker's physical characteristics—facial expressions, what the person was wearing, and so on?

If students are not able to think about their experiences until later, they should try to recall the facts about the interactions. It may help for students to try to be conscious about whether they are writing about facts or feelings/impressions.

Step 4: Analyze Students read over their notes. About each statement they have made, they ask themselves whether they were writing about facts or feelings/impressions.

Next, they sum up the interaction, making two or three comments each in the areas of language, social situation, and emotional context.

They should answer the following questions about language.

1. Did you understand the speaker's words and meaning? Did the speaker understand you? How do you know?
2. If there were difficulties, can you "locate" them? For example, were you not able to understand or think of a particular word, did you say something "wrong," was the speaker's accent hard to understand, or did the speaker speak too quickly or quietly?

In terms of social situation, they should answer the following questions.

1. What was your perception of the speaker's role or position? How did you—speaker and listener—relate to each other in terms of social position? How might this encounter have been different with two native speakers of your L1?
2. How important was the physical setting of the encounter? For example, if you had been somewhere else, would something different have happened?
3. What message did the visual facts give to you? For example, did you react to what the person was wearing or to his or her physical characteristics? Do you tend to make assumptions based on what a person wears? on physical appearance (e.g., hairstyle, makeup, etc.)? on how close to you a person stands? (Most people do!)

In the area of emotional context, they should answer the following questions.

1. How did you feel before/after/during the encounter? Why?
2. Does this feeling affect your language-learning experience? Does it encourage you to learn? Does it make you feel discouraged or apathetic?

Step 5: Generate This step of the project might best take the form of a short report in which learners describe the situation and summarize what they have discovered about the social situation or about their personal reactions. If students and the classroom instructor all speak the same first language, they might consider reporting the results in their native language.

Step 6: Review After students hear their classmates' reports, they discuss their experiences. Were their similarities in their accounts and conclusions? Based on what learners found out from each other, are they able to make more general statements or to give advice? For example:

- In situations like this, you should always . . . . and you should probably . . . . because . . . .

Or were learners' experiences quite different from each other, due to personality, personal reaction, or past experiences? If this is the case, they might not be able to come up with observations that correspond to "social truths" that appear to operate as underlying factors common to everyone's experience. Rather, they may come up with some discoveries about themselves and their tendencies to react in particular ways. For example:

- In situations like this, I tend to assume . . . . because . . . .
- I tend to react . . . . because . . . .
- It's helpful to be aware of this pattern of mine because . . . . (Comments about the student's language-learning experience would be relevant.)

Learner/Teacher Feedback: Students who did this activity "out of context" in the sense that it was the only activity they did from this book reacted quite differently than students who did the activity as one in a series of participatory, research-oriented activities. Students in the former group were initially hesitant about reporting in detail their encounters and talking openly about their processing reactions (Zimmermann 1995), while the latter group plunged into the activity wholeheartedly, freely offering advice, reporting on similar experiences and reactions, and making generalizations. As with any of these activities, the cohesiveness of a particular class and their and the teacher's experience or lack of experience with student-generated and student-run activities certainly influence how smoothly an activity is conducted and how well received it is initially.

Activity 13

Language Classroom Research   Academic Settings

Macro level   Micro level

Objective: This activity targets the educational values that operate within the language classroom. Specifically, learners are taught skills that assist them in ascertaining what assumptions about effective language learning are held by language teachers in the classrooms they observe.

In this activity, your students will work primarily as **ethnographers.**

Ethnographers

- typically use as data interviews and participant and nonparticipant observations that occur in natural settings over a long period of time.
- believe that cultural meanings are revealed by people's behavior, which can only be understood by incorporating the subjective perceptions and belief systems of the researcher.
- are especially interested in developing descriptive and interpretive accounts that characterize the culture of a group or an individual.

Background: The topic of assumptions operating within a language classroom can be useful for language students, since many may not have thought about how their own beliefs and educational "models" can potentially conflict with or complement those operating as part of the institutional framework or those held by the teacher.

This activity is especially appropriate if the language learning setting is an English-speaking country or in foreign language settings in which instructors are not natives of the culture and language.

Holliday (1994) points out that the communicative approach to teaching, widely believed to be valid and effective, may actually be inappropriate in many foreign language settings—for example, where classroom size prohibits working in small groups; where a focus on oral, rather than written, communication is incompatible with student goals and needs; and where the use of only English may simply not be justifiable.

Since students of any discipline in any setting are, in a sense, socialized to adapt to the values of the classroom, this activity is designed to raise learners' awareness about just what those values are. In addition, learners are introduced to the notion of the power structures that operate "behind the scenes"—the program and institutional constraints and the cultural and educational background that may affect how individual teachers conduct their classes.

Step 1: Predict For comparative purposes, learners are first asked to think about the assumptions underlying the educational models used in teaching their L1 or in other educational settings learners have participated in. (Instructors can contribute their perspectives, too, using their own language-learning experiences as baseline data.) Example questions for students follow.

1. What were the objectives, both stated and implied, of the language courses you took? If you can remember activities or exercises that were "prototypes" in the sense that they were regularly used over the course of a particular class, what were the smaller-scale objectives of such typical activities? For example, were students supposed to do or accomplish something—such as solving a problem or coming to a consensus? Or, rather, was the goal to practice using a word, a sound (a phoneme), or a grammatical structure in order to attain accuracy?
2. How were the language classes you took conducted? Learners can approach this question by examining the following different categories:

   • the role of the teacher and the role of the student—Would you characterize the teacher-student relationship as formal or informal? What "codes of behavior" were there for students—how were they required to behave in the presence of their teacher? Was the position of teacher considered an honorable one or "just another job"? Was the teacher clearly the expert?

- the type and format of the classroom activity—What was a typical language learning activity? How does this relate to the teacher's or institution's attitude about how language is best learned? What was the typical format for a language learning activity: lecture, small group, individual study? What size was the typical class?
- the use of the target language—How much of the lesson was conducted in the target language? Was accuracy emphasized? Were there tasks or activities that focused on communication and thus de-emphasized accuracy? Were students encouraged or discouraged to speak in their native language?

3. How was "good language learning" exhibited in the classes you took? Who were considered the best students, and what did they do that was better than or different from the others? What type of classroom behavior was encouraged or discouraged?

These questions can help elicit short descriptions of the educational models that appeared to be valued in those particular classroom settings. An additional question goes a step deeper: Where did this model come from? If, for example, it fits with the "traditional" educational model of that setting or that country, why is or was that model valued? Are there other "institutions" (e.g., family, religions) in that setting that hold similar values?

Finally, it is important that, in answering these questions, learners give some attention to what happens behind the scenes. For example, what institutional and program constraints were operating to influence teacher decision making? Were teachers required to answer to their administrators, and if so, how closely were their actions controlled and/or followed? Or were teachers able to exercise a great deal of independence in how they conducted their own classes? Did they have input into curriculum development, syllabus design, and course and program evaluation?

Step 2: Plan Learners will observe a language class, not necessarily an ESL/EFL class, but possibly a class in their L1 or in another language of interest to them. Since some teachers do not feel comfortable being observed, it is important that students reassure the teacher that the observation is not a critique but an information-gathering session. As with any classroom observations, real names need not be used when learners discuss their findings. In fact, in urban or academic settings where there are a number of language classes available for observation, it might be wise for students to conduct their research in classes not likely to be recognized by most students.

For this activity, it is advantageous to form research teams to pool observations and thus increase the reliability of findings. Observers should describe the classroom environment and the types of activities conducted; they should make notes on explicit comments, both by teachers and by students, that may serve as evidence of their perceptions about student-teacher relationships, about the objectives of the class and the lesson, about how language is best learned, and about what information is useful for students. (For example: When does the teacher give positive feedback? When do students ask for clarification or more information? Does the teacher make statements like "You need to know this because . . ."?)

In situations where teachers under observation are receptive and open to the learners' research, learners may opt to follow up the observation with interviews. This step is essential if learners want information about the influences that are not discernible in the observation—the political and social forces that affect how a program or institution is organized and thus how an individual course fits into this broader picture.

It is important to remember that what happens in the language classroom may not always be wholly representative of a teacher's attitude toward language teaching. Institutional and program constraints may greatly affect how teachers pace and organize their classes. Interview questions addressing this issue, then, might illuminate such a situation. For example, learners might want to ask teachers, "If you had the freedom to change this class so that it would more perfectly suit your style or your students' needs, what would you do differently?" The questions posed in Step 1 might also be useful for learners as they develop interview questions.

An interview is helpful, but not essential, in addressing questions that focus on an instructor's belief about language learning and language teaching. Questions can probe this topic directly (e.g., "In your opinion, what kind of activity is most helpful to students—one that focuses on accuracy or one that focuses on successful communication?"). Or learners may want to be less direct, locating specific practices they have observed in the more general context of the topic of effective teaching (e.g., "I noticed that some students made grammar mistakes when they were talking about . . . but that you didn't correct them. Can you tell me why you chose not to correct their errors?").

It is important to remember that a way into the underlying beliefs and attitudes is to listen carefully to how something is talked about. Sociolinguists, cultural anthropologists, and ethnographers believe that social contexts create and are created by language and thus that how people talk about things can reveal deeper concerns.

. . . .

Step 3: Collect data Videotaping or audiotaping the classroom session is optional in this activity, since the goal is primarily to determine underlying attitudes about effective language teaching and learning. In other words, the micro features of an interaction (specifically how something is said or done) are not as crucial as the macro features of a communication (what is said or done and, on an even deeper level, just why it is said or done—what attitudes or behind-the-scenes structures motivate it).

A data collection chart that anticipates relevant actions is a helpful tool for researchers. Learners can modify a chart like the following one to suit their needs and interests. After the initial descriptive information, the following chart reserves the right side of the page for comments/reactions, while the left side is for factual descriptions. However, some learners may want to save any analyses-related comments for a later time.

Data Collection Chart for Activity 13
Classroom Observation

General Descriptive Information

Language:

Level:

Number of students:

Students' native language(s):

Class setup (describe and/or sketch):

Activity/Task Analysis (Fill out for each different activity.)

Description   Comments

Objectives (Stated directly?):

Language goal or functional goal:

Materials:

Learner groupings/format:

Classroom Interaction

Description	Comments
Ratio of teacher vs. student talk:	
Teacher's use of target language:	
Teacher's use of native language(s):	
Student involvement/class atmosphere (give specific examples that illustrate):	
Error correction, feedback, and praise:	

With teachers who seem especially receptive to this student project, learners may want to schedule an interview that follows their observations. The interview questions should be prepared before the student observations, and they should directly or indirectly target teachers' attitudes about effective learning and effective teaching as well as the program and institutional constraints that influence how the particular classes are organized and conducted.

Step 4: Analyze Learners pool their classroom observation notes, first simply describing what they saw and then interpreting these actions in the context of the (observed) instructors' beliefs about effective teaching and successful learning. Learners should discuss any discrepancies in their interpretations of events, making sure that their accounts are grounded in evidence. In other words, theories about what is revealed in a certain action, comment, or interaction should be based on actual events.

Learners can frame their analyses around some of the questions posed in Step 1. The goal is to uncover some of the assumptions that individual language teachers have about what comprises effective language teaching and, accordingly, how successful language learning is demonstrated. Again, it is helpful to remember that teachers' behavior in some situations might reveal instead what their administrators' attitudes are about effective language teaching. Interview data on this subject can help to reveal the effect these forces may have on individual teachers and their classes.

Analyses should minimally treat the following topics: according to the teacher and/or judging from what learners observed, (1) the role of the teacher and the role of the students, (2) the role and use of the target language versus the native language(s) of the students, and (3) the type and format of classroom activity that appears to be best suited for teaching and learning, as exhibited in the kinds of activities employed and the teacher's responses and feedback to students. In some cases this may be very skill specific: a teacher of reading, for example, may use very different types of activities than that same teacher would use in a grammar class.

In cases where instructors were interviewed, analyses should also treat the topic of power: Who is ultimately responsible for making decisions about curriculum development and about syllabus and course design? How closely must an individual teacher respond to these decisions?

Step 5: Generate After pooling interview responses (when available) and observation notes, learners then discuss their interpretations in their research groups. This step can easily move into a whole group discussion that can both investigate competing interpretations of the same data (addressing possible "unseen" factors, such as institutional and program constraints) and examine differing results emerging from different data sets—different classrooms, different teachers.

This is also the appropriate stage for learners to compile descriptive paradigms associated with the language classes they observed. Completing the following statement on a chart is a good method for doing this, since conclusions would then be visible to the entire group. It also "neutralizes" the kinds of teaching that were observed: one method is not necessarily better, in other words, but may be more appropriate and more in line with an individual teacher's (and his or her administrator's) goals.

Conclusions: The teacher I observed (or his/her program planner/administrator/curriculum designer) believes that a good language-teaching activity should . . . . since language is best learned . . . . In addition she/he (or they) believe . . . . (state additional beliefs about use of target or native language/amount of interaction/etc.) since . . . .

Step 6: Review This final step allows learners the opportunity to reflect on their own beliefs about language teaching and to discuss the ways in which their beliefs may be similar to or different from those observed in the situation analyzed in their research. Learners themselves can compile a chart similar to the one in Step 5, this time stating their own opinions.

I believe that a good language-teaching activity should . . . . since language is best learned . . . . In addition, I believe . . . . since . . . .

An additional final step in this activity is for students to go back further, if possible, to the source of their beliefs. For example, Chinese students from Taiwan may prefer teaching approaches that resemble the grammar-translation method, simply because this is the way they were taught and are most comfortable with. Or, from a more macro perspective, the influences of Confucianism on educational methods may be noted and discussed.

Learner/Teacher Feedback: Students have been generally receptive to this assignment, in some cases because of their curiosity about language teaching methods different than what they are used to. Some students were in fact surprised by how strongly they identified with their home country's traditional views on language teaching; or more accurately perhaps, they were surprised at how strongly and unconsciously they had been affected by the models they were exposed to in their early education. Learners who are training to be teachers or are themselves already teachers may have two different and incompatible beliefs depending on whether they are operating from the student perspective or the teacher perspective.

Most of the learners who have done this activity as one of many of these kinds of language research assignments are, by this point (and fortunately!), strong supporters of the learner-as-researcher concept. One student completed the descriptive statement in Step 6 as follows: I believe that a good language-teaching activity should "get the learner involved," since language is best learned "if you're curious about the language and culture." In addition, I believe "that you learn best if you can decide on what is interesting to you, not just the teacher decides," since "you need to be responsible for your own learning." This student's statement is testimony enough for this activity.

Activity 14

Belief Systems   Film, Social Settings

Macro level   Micro level

Objective: This activity encourages learners to explore some of the cultural, social, and psychological values that appear to be operating in the lives of the fictional characters they view in a film. By treating the film as data that they must then describe, analyze, and understand in terms of perceived norms of that culture, learners gain hands-on experience in deciphering cultural constructs.

In this activity, your students will work primarily as **ethnographers.**

Ethnographers

- typically use as data interviews and participant and nonparticipant observations that occur in natural settings over a long period of time.
- believe that cultural meanings are revealed by people's behavior, which can only be understood by incorporating the subjective perceptions and belief systems of the researcher.
- are especially interested in developing descriptive and interpretive accounts that characterize the culture of a group or an individual.

Background: Although many students of foreign or second language are immersed in cultures nonnative to them, few are given tools for exploring these cultures to make sense of them and to view them as coherent and holistic systems. For the purposes of this discussion, culture is defined as the set of characteristic customs, behaviors, beliefs, and language that marks a sociologically definable group of individuals. Introductory books on culture often categorize areas or belief systems that are universals, in the sense that groups that make up particular cultures generally share similar points of view. A list of these areas/belief systems is provided in Step 1.

Step 1: Predict Learners first familiarize themselves with the following different topic areas that together form a set of belief systems that members of a culture or subculture share.

1. worldview/philosophy—beliefs about God, spirits, animals, luck, life after death
2. relationship with family—attitudes and beliefs about old people, parents, ancestors, children
3. relationship with others—attitudes about the value of equality, humanitarianism, honesty
4. relationship with society—moral and ethical beliefs, as well as attitudes about freedom, emotions, work and play, time
5. relationship with self—beliefs about what defines success, power, material well-being; attitudes about individualism
6. relationship with land and animals

   Learners then make statements about their own culture—the culture they identify with, which usually is a particular country or group of people (e.g., "Zimbabwean people believe that . . .") although it could also be an identifiable subculture (e.g., "Shona people [as opposed to other Zimbabwean subcultures] believe that . . .").

In a multilingual/multicultural classroom, making statements about one's own culture can be done as a game. Learners write down three statements about any of the topic areas listed earlier in this step ("We believe that . . ."), the teacher collects these statements and reads them aloud, and the other students must guess what culture (usually country) is being described. In monolingual settings, learners read their statements to each other to see if others agree with their generalizations. They may not, and if they do not, it is likely that the learners are referring to subcultures that may be distinct from each other in certain ways.

Step 2: Plan In research teams, learners view a film (or videotape) of their choice, preferably, but not necessarily, in their target language, and ideally representative of some aspects of contemporary culture. These suggested guidelines are not set in stone, but since part of the point of this activity is to treat as data the film that learners view, the act of not identifying fully as a member of the culture can help learners attain a more objective researcher status.

Learners first find out what they can about the film they are about to view, asking for recommendations and descriptions from friends and reading movie reviews, synopses, or even scripts. Based on what they have heard or read, they then make predictions about the values and beliefs systems of the characters in the film, using the list in Step 1. In making their predictions, students can consider questions like the following.

- What do you think that (a main character) believes about success?
- What do you think are, for her or him, the signs of success?
- What do you think her or his attitude is toward old people? toward children?

Each research group assigns a note taker to record their predictions. After the learners have viewed the film, it will be interesting for learners to note how many of their predictions were "off" and how many were "on."

It is helpful to remind learners that how people talk about things can reveal deeper concerns. For some films, having access to the videotape for repeated viewing or even to the soundtrack (an audiotape) or a script can allow for more careful listening to the ways that the characters talk about things. For films where language variety is an issue, this may be very important. For example, characters in a particular film may reveal attitudes toward each other that differ depending on the language variety used. This could be an important clue regarding group membership, which may reveal a socially or politically motivated value held by members of a culture (who are represented by the films' characters). Listening for such attitudes or values as they are revealed in characters' ways of speaking would be, in this case, an important part of analyzing the data.

Step 3: Collect data This step involves simply viewing the film. Note taking is an option, although it is a rare person who can break up his or her movie-viewing experience with note taking, especially in a theater (as opposed to a video) setting.

In a case where the issue of social class and language variety seems to be important, or where attitudes and values may be detected in the way people talk to or about each other, data collection should also involve some attention to language on a more micro level. Students should consider questions like the following, for example.

- What words provide information about a character's status or social class?
- Can accents be characterized?
- Does the grammar used by characters identify them as belonging to a particular class or "group"?

Learners should, at the minimum, take notes on the language features that appear to have significance, and ideally, they should have access to a tape or script of the film that they can review later.

Step 4: Analyze The overall goal of this activity is for the learner to penetrate the culture represented in the film and to identify some of the belief systems that the film's characters seem to be operating under. A systematic way to go about this is to go through the list presented in Step 1. Some of the categories in the list may not be relevant, given a particular film, so learners should focus on the areas that elicit the most discussion, which are also likely to be the most relevant areas.

These areas may in fact be the dominant themes of the film. Although there are differing opinions of exactly what themes are and certainly on the themes of any particular film, one test for theme is to ask: What are the characters' greatest concerns? What is the intended message of this film? What did we (or what were we supposed to) learn from this film? These questions will elicit discussion, especially if viewers identified with the characters, themes, and/or story lines of the films they viewed.

Step 5: Generate After research teams have met and discussed their films, it is appropriate for the whole group to meet. One member from each group can report on the film they viewed, limiting this report to a brief description of the plot, the values or belief systems held by the main characters, and the dominant themes that each group identified in their postviewing discussion.

An advantage of groups watching the same film is that different opinions are likely to emerge about the values and belief systems of the characters and about the dominant themes.

Learners should be reminded that it is appropriate to ground their opinions in evidence from the film itself. For example, they should be able to complete a statement like the following: "I believe that (the character) really did have respect for his parents, since (episode that supports this opinion)."

If dialect or language variety emerges as an issue in a film, learners should give some attention to how characters talk and should use the characters' actual words, phrases, and sentences as evidence for opinions on the values and belief systems this language reveals. For language-related topics, those groups who had access to videotapes, audiotapes, or scripts will have an advantage in discussing their film and in presenting actual data that supports their points of view.

Step 6: Review This step is an opportunity for learners to reflect on their own belief systems and to compare and contrast their culture with the culture represented in the films they viewed and/or heard about from other class members. Students who want practice in more formal presentation skills might prefer to present this information in the form of a short informative report (see Activity 11 for suggested guidelines on how to go about this). The teacher and students might together want to negotiate on the amount of class time each report should take, which would help learners determine how to limit their topics (probably to a few major points from the list of areas/belief systems). Alternatively, such cultural comparison makes for an interesting class discussion.

An interesting follow-up activity (Additional Activity 14A) asks learners to further explore topics that emerged in discussions on belief systems.

Additional Activity 14A—Interviews. Learners either individually or in groups prepare questions on topics of interest to them, with interview subjects chosen on the basis of accessibility and on subjects' knowledge of or experience with other cultures. Accessibility may be an issue in foreign language settings where native speakers of English simply may not be available to interview.

However, nativeness (being native to the target language/culture) is not necessarily a desirable characteristic for an interviewee in this activity. Some learners may prefer to conduct an interview in their own native language with someone who has lived overseas or has had either extensive experience with or knowledge of another culture. Others may want to conduct short interviews with a range of people who represent different subcultures.

The interview topics need not be directly related to themes in the films learners viewed; rather, they may be topics that have emerged in the discussion of the film, or they may simply be topics of personal interest to individuals or research teams. A sampling of the topics learners have pursued and of some of the related questions they have developed are presented here.

One research team was interested in the topic of family. In order to interview a diverse sampling of people (in a North American college campus setting), they worked to develop questions that were simple but that got to the core of the issues they wanted to address. For example: Who is in a family? Who decides this, or is it decided for them? Who has the authority in the family? Do different family members have different rights and responsibilities, and if so, what are they? What is the purpose of a family? How is a family viewed by people outside of the family? Learners in this particular group were surprised at the variety of family "types," some far removed from the traditional, nuclear family. Students were especially surprised to find that many of the interview subjects considered their pets part of their family.

This topic itself—family pets—was the chosen topic for another pair of students who were fascinated by the relationship Americans had with their pets. Another group, this one in an urban university in Malaysia, where the native population is quite diverse, explored the topic of communication with the following questions: Who or what can be communicated with—God, animals, plants, the dead? What forms do these communications take?

Also related to communication was a topic chosen by another group of students, who asked, What kind of communication is most valued? This topic emerged after Japanese and non-Japanese English language learners in a U.S. university viewed a Japanese film (with subtitles) where one of the major issues was conflict between ways of communicating. The film's characters who had lived in the West valued verbal directness; the Japanese characters who were considered more traditional valued the ability to discern others' thoughts and emotions without the need for words. One of the primary goals of the group who pursued this topic further was to establish opinions about what kinds of communication are found to be most appropriate and most valued among different cultures.

Learner/Teacher Feedback: Students are typically enthusiastic about this activity, initially because they choose a film of interest to them rather than having a film chosen for them. The topic of a culture's belief systems, especially when driven by data (the film), never fails to elicit discussion and is appropriate for students in lower levels as well as more advanced students and in foreign language settings as well as target language settings. It is possible, however, that in some language programs there may be some resistance to analyzing culture and making cross-cultural comparisons. One student commented: "I'm sick of culture. Our [ESL] teachers are always making us do activities about culture." Fortunately, though, this reaction to the activity does not seem to be common or enduring. Since the follow-up activity is based solely on topics that students generate, the interest level for it is high.

The list of topic areas/belief systems in Step 1 is helpful in structuring this activity and in focusing the analysis. When I attempted this activity without the list, the discussion, though lively, evolved into a free-for-all. This may be appropriate in some situations, though many teachers and students prefer a more structured approach.

Concluding Notes

It is my hope that teachers who have read this sampling of activities will experiment with these "tried and trusted" activities in their language classes. But more importantly, these activities can serve as ideas for teachers who would like to develop activities of their own.

Chapter 4 also presents spoken language discourse analysis activities, but it differs from this chapter in that it focuses on the micro skills that are traditionally "taught" in the oral skills classroom as spoken language subskills: pronunciation (including rhythm and intonation), grammar, and vocabulary.

For Teachers: Discussion Questions

1. How can all of the classroom activities presented in this section be said to use oral discourse as their database? Can one definition of discourse be used to organize and incorporate all of the activities? Or is it more helpful to think of each activity as responding to and emerging from a different definition of discourse?
2. Consider the four types of research (presented in this chapter) that work with oral data: conversation analysis, sociolinguistics, speech event analysis, and ethnography. What are some beliefs and goals that researchers from these disciplines share? Where might their interests diverge?
3. What are the advantages of working with videotaped or audiotaped data? In what situations or with what types of activities might it be more appropriate to simply observe interactions or communications as they occur?
4. The activities in this book are organized according to how the structures under focus relate to points on a continuum, with micro-oriented features on one end of the scale and macro-oriented constructs on the other. Choose one sample activity and argue its designation on the continuum from a different point of view. For example, Activity 1, on turn taking, is designated as focusing on micro-level skills: how might this activity be perceived as more oriented to the macro level?

5. In the last two steps of each activity, learners generate language and review their data. Sometimes learners themselves produce data samples that they then review and analyze. Other times the language they generate is in the form of a discussion and the review phase of the process is an overview of what learners have discovered from the activity. For Activities 11–14, in which the last two steps take the latter form, can you suggest ways that learners could incorporate self-monitoring of their own learner-generated speech samples?

Suggested Readings and References

Anderson, A., and T. Lynch. 1988. *Listening.* New York: Oxford University Press.

Like the other books in this excellent series, Language Teaching: A Scheme for Teacher Education (e.g., Bygate's *Speaking,* also summarized here in the suggested readings), this book provides a theoretical perspective, demonstrates links between theory and practice, and suggests activities for teachers that can be helpful both in developing course materials and in increasing awareness. This book thoroughly discusses research findings about language comprehension yet is grounded in its many useful practical examples of listening materials and its discussions that talk about what is involved in developing, piloting, and revising these materials. Thus, this book can serve as an excellent resource for teachers interested in designing listening comprehension materials.

Brown, G., and G. Yule. 1983. *Teaching the spoken language: An approach based on the analysis of conversational English.* New York: Cambridge University Press.

This text serves as an excellent introduction to the nature of spoken language and the ways that it differs from written language. It is accessible to students new to these studies and is well supported with examples of authentic spoken language samples. Perhaps the most appealing feature of this book is the presentation of principles and techniques for teaching oral skills and listening comprehension.

Bygate, M. 1987. *Speaking.* New York: Oxford University Press.

This book is both a theoretical and practical treatment of the speaking skill specifically, with one section devoted to differences between speech and writing. It considers, first, the complexity of "subskills" involved in the act of speaking and, second, the principal types of activities and exercises used to teach speaking. A final section of the book encourages language teachers to take the initiative to explore further what learners are (and are not) accomplishing in the course of their oral classroom activities. Thus, this book is useful as a comprehensive source of ideas not only on how to teach speaking but also on ways in which teachers may approach the analysis of discourse and increase their effectiveness as instructors.

Flowerdew, J., ed. 1994. *Academic listening: Research perspectives.* New York: Cambridge University Press.

This book is a thorough analysis of recent work in the area of listening comprehension, specifically focusing on academic lectures. How listeners process information is one of the topics treated; another investigates the features of lecture discourse. Though this book is particularly strong because of the range of research perspectives represented, pedagogical implications are discussed, too. Thus, this book may be useful for language teachers who seek information about the skill of academic listening.

Hatch, E. 1992. *Discourse and language education.* New York: Cambridge University Press.

Although this entire book is an excellent source of information on how communication is structured, the first four chapters are especially relevant for those with an interest in the structure of spoken discourse specifically. Chapter 1 describes the structure of communication systems, while chapter 2 demonstrates the ways in which these communication components are expressed in specific languages. Chapter 3 examines how "script theory" explains the organization of communication. Chapter 4 takes a slightly different perspective toward analyzing the content of communication, using speech act theory and speech act analysis. Thus, these four chapters provide an excellent foundation in how discourse analysts from various backgrounds understand spoken language.

Wennerstrom, A. 1991. *Techniques for teachers: A guide for nonnative speakers of English.* Ann Arbor: University of Michigan Press.

This book, developed as a core text for an ITA training course, is designed to expose foreign teaching professionals to different aspects of teaching and to explain common patterns of speech (e.g., word stress, contrastive stress, and pauses). Learners analyze the speech of native speakers who demonstrate on an accompanying video speech patterns and teaching techniques, they practice incorporating what they have learned into their own speech, and they perform a short teaching activity that integrates these new skills. Learners are encouraged to audiotape or videotape all short activities, with opportunities for structured follow-up evaluation. Thus, this book incorporates discourse analysis of speech from two perspectives: that of the listener, analyzing native speaker examples; and that of the speaker, analyzing his or her own speech.

Yule, G., and W. Gregory. 1989. Survey interviews for interactive language learning. *English Language Teaching Journal* 13 (2): 142–49.

> This article presents an example of a highly flexible activity for language students that allows them the opportunity to focus on the way spoken language is structured. Possible topics of study include the cooperative maintenance of turn taking, backchannels and other "participation indicators," and repair strategies, such as clarification requests and confirmation checks. This article, then, suggests ways in which discourse analytic techniques can be used by students in instructional contexts for the development of their oral skills.

Anderson, A., and T. Lynch. 1988. *Listening.* New York: Oxford University Press.

Asplin, W. 1995. Course materials. University of Washington ESL Center/downtown program, Seattle.

Banerjee, J., and P. Carrell. 1988. Tuck in your shirt, you squid: Suggestions in ESL. *Language Learning* 38 (3): 313–64.

Barnlund, D. C. 1989. *Communicative styles of Japanese and Americans: Images and realities.* Belmont, CA: Wadsworth.

Bauman, R. 1986. *Story, performance, and event: Contextual studies of the oral narrative.* New York: Cambridge University Press.

Bavelas, J. Forthcoming. Nonverbal aspects of fluency. In H. Riggenbach, ed., *Perspectives on fluency.* Ann Arbor: University of Michigan Press.

Beebe, L., T. Takahashi, and R. Uliss-Weitz. 1990. Pragmatic transfer in ESL refusals. In R. Scarcella, E. Andersen, and S. Krashen, eds., *Developing communicative competence in a second language,* 55–74. New York: Newbury House.

Bode, S., and S. Lee. 1987. *Overheard and understood.* Belmont, CA: Wadsworth.

Brown, G., and G. Yule. 1983. *Teaching the spoken language: An approach based on the analysis of conversational English.* New York: Cambridge University Press.

Canale, M. 1983. From communicative competence to communicative language pedagogy. In J. C. Richards and R. W. Schmidt, eds., *Language and communication.* New York: Longman.

Canale, M., and M. Swain. 1980. Theoretical bases of communicative approaches to second language teaching and testing. *Applied Linguistics* 1:1–47.

Celce-Murcia, M. 1991. Grammar pedagogy in second and foreign language teaching. *TESOL Quarterly* 25 (3): 459–80.

Crago, M. 1992. Communicative interaction and second language acquisition: An Inuit example. *TESOL Quarterly* 26 (3): 487–506.

Dorn, S., and T. Perez. 1995. Look who's talking: Language students as conversation negotiators. Course paper for English 578: Research in Second Language Acquisition, University of Washington M.A. TESOL program, Seattle.

Ferrer, J., and E. Whalley. 1990. *Mosaic II: A listening/speaking skills book.* New York: McGraw-Hill.

Flowerdew, J., ed. 1994. *Academic listening: Research perspectives.* New York: Cambridge University Press.

Goffman, E. 1981. *Forms of talk.* Philadelphia: University of Pennsylvania Press.

Goffman, E. 1976. Replies and responses. *Language in Society* 5 (3): 254–313.

Hawkins, B. 1984. Is an appropriate response always so appropriate? In S. Gass and C. Madden, eds., *Input in second language acquisition,* 162–78. New York: Newbury House.

Holliday, A. 1994. *Appropriate methodology and social context.* New York: Cambridge University Press.

Jones, L., and C. Von Baeyer. 1983. *Functions of American English: Communication activities for the classroom.* New York: Cambridge University Press.

Kasper, G. 1989. Variation in interlanguage speech act realization. In S. Gass et al., eds., *Variation in second language acquisition: Discourse and pragmatics,* 37–58. Clevedon, UK: Multilingual Matters.

Kroll, B., ed. 1990. *Second language writing: Issues and options.* New York: Cambridge University Press.

Labov, W., and J. Waletzky. 1967. Narrative analysis. In J. Helm, ed., *Essays on the verbal and visual arts,* 12–44. Seattle: University of Washington Press.

Legutke, M., and H. Thomas 1991. *Process and experience in the language classroom.* New York: Longman.

Lynch, T. 1996. *Communication in the language classroom.* New York: Oxford University Press.

Morley, J. 1991. The pronunciation component in teaching English to speakers of other languages. *TESOL Quarterly* 25 (3): 481–520.

Morrison, B. 1989. Using news broadcasts for authentic listening comprehension. *English Language Teaching Journal* 43 (1): 14–18.

Noguchi, R. 1987. The dynamics of rule conflict in English and Japanese conversation. *International Review of Applied Linguistics* 25:15–24.

Peirce, B. N. 1994. Using diaries in second language acquisition. *English Quarterly* 26 (3): 22–29.

Phillips, S. 1983. *The invisible culture: Communication in classroom and community on the Warm Springs Indian Reservation.* New York: Longman.

Ramsey, S. 1984. Double vision: Nonverbal behavior East and West. In A. Wolfgang, ed., *Nonverbal behavior: Perspectives, applications, intercultural insight,* 139–70. Lewiston, NY: Hogrefe.

Riggenbach, H. 1991. Towards an understanding of fluency: A microanalysis of nonnative speaker conversations. *Discourse Processes* 14:423–41.

Riggenbach, H., and L. Stephan. Forthcoming. *Discourse Analysis in the Language Classroom: Volume 2. The Written Language.* Ann Arbor: University of Michigan Press.

Stahl, S. D. 1989. *Literary folkloristics and the personal narrative.* Bloomington: Indiana University Press.

Tanka, J., and P. Most. 1990. *Interactions I: A listening/speaking skills book.* New York: McGraw-Hill.

Tannen, D. 1992. Rethinking power and solidarity in gender and dominance. In C. Kramsch and S. McConnell-Ginet, eds., *Text and context: Cross-disciplinary perspectives on language study,* 135–47. Lexington, MA. Heath.

Tannen, D. 1984. *Conversational style: Analyzing talk among friends.* Norwood, NJ: Ablex.

Tao, H., and S. Thompson. 1991. English backchannels in Mandarin conversations: A case study of superstratum pragmatic "interference." *Journal of Pragmatics* 16 (3): 209–23.

Tillitt, B., and M. Bruder. 1985. *Speaking naturally.* New York: Cambridge University Press.

Toolan, M. 1988. *Narrative: A critical linguistic introduction.* London: Routledge.

Turner, K. 1996. The principal principles of pragmatic inference: Politeness. *Language Teaching* 29 (1): 1–13.

van Ek, J. A. 1976. *The threshold level for modern language learning in schools.* New York: Longman.

van Essen, A. 1989. Grammar: Its place in foreign language education. *Der fremdsprachliche unterricht* 96:4–10.

Wennerstrom, A. 1991. *Techniques for teachers: A guide for nonnative speakers of English.* Ann Arbor: University of Michigan Press.

White, S. 1989. Backchannels across cultures: A study of Americans and Japanese. *Language in Society* 18:59–76.

Young, K. G. 1987. *Taleworlds and story realms: The phenomenology of narrative.* Boston: Martinus Nijhoff.

Yule, G. 1996. *Pragmatics.* New York: Oxford University Press.

Yule, G., and E. Tarone. 1990. Eliciting the performance of strategic competence. In R. Scarcella, E. Andersen, and S. Krashen, eds., *Developing communicative competence in a second language,* 179–94. New York: Newbury House.

Zimmermann, G. 1995. Course paper for English 574: Research in Second Language Acquisition. University of Washington M.A. TESOL program, Seattle.

Chapter 4
Micro Skills: Pronunciation, Grammar, and Vocabulary

In this chapter, the focus is on the spoken language micro skills that are traditionally treated in the ESOL classroom: pronunciation, grammar, and vocabulary. Here one goal is to enhance learners' own productive skills and their sense of what, in their own oral language, needs to be strengthened, whereas in the previous chapter there was more of an emphasis on raising learners' consciousness about data produced by native or expert speakers and in identifying norms or patterns.

A short discussion introduces the chapter. This is followed by suggestions on ways to go about developing original activities. Similar to chapter 3, the bulk of this chapter is devoted to an explanation of actual discourse analysis activities that have been used with English language students. Following the sample activities are recommendations for further readings for those who wish for more information on related topics.

1. Discussion

Pronunciation, grammar, and vocabulary are believed to be "subskills" related to speaking. The discourse analysis activities in this chapter focus on these three "areas." Besides its exclusive focus on these micro skills, this chapter differs in another way from the previous one in that learners here examine their own speech for accuracy. To explore more micro-oriented features, learners first listen by analyzing actual language data or by eliciting information from interviewees. Next, they speak: they generate language themselves, and they examine the self-produced data for accuracy. They determine whether their own usage conforms to the patterns, features, or "rules" they have observed or hypothesized.

Although the discourse analysis activities in this chapter focus on constituents considered more toward the micro pole of the continuum of language features and structures presented in chapter 1, these features, like those targeted in the activities in chapter 3, are best focused on in a greater discourse context rather than at the word or sentence level. For many years—many centuries, even, according to Rutherford (1987)—it was the norm in language teaching to present and practice grammatical structures in isolation or at the phrase or sentence level, with little regard for the ways in which form, meaning, and function interacted. Similarly, pronunciation practice often involved the mechanical repetition of words that included the targeted phonemes. And for years, the traditional way—if not the only way—of "learning" vocabulary was to memorize words and their corresponding definitions. To use words, structures, and sounds meaningfully, and at the same time accurately, in real communication was rarely either a consideration or an objective.

Accumulating evidence suggests that it may be necessary for learners to focus on accuracy of form in order to prevent fossilization (Larsen-Freeman and Long 1990; Pienemann 1984). Thus many instructors now advocate explicit attention to accuracy of form, but via an inductive, discourse-based approach (Ellis 1995; Celce-Murcia 1991). There is an emerging interest in teaching form by using techniques that encourage students to operate in the role of language researcher: learners examine sounds, words, and structures as they naturally appear in both written and spoken discourse, and they inductively develop hypotheses about the rules regarding these structures. Developing and nurturing learners' awareness of the patterns and regularities of language is believed to be beneficial, since it can contribute to learners' ability to use language that is both linguistically accurate and socially appropriate (Connor 1996, 1991; Celce-Murcia 1991).

One way of heightening awareness about language is to allow students to act in the role of discourse analysts/language researchers so that they can make observations about language and discover evidence of patterns and "rules" for themselves. Rather than being the passive recipients of the explanations and the often mechanical exercises provided in textbooks, learners can have a more active involvement in their learning process. They can choose materials that will be useful to them, targeting the areas of grammar, pronunciation, and vocabulary that they want to work on. They can be involved with the design of exercises and activities that they find most challenging and interesting, and in this way, they engage meaningfully with language

Many advocates of the communicative approach to teaching language have de-emphasized accuracy, since one of the underlying assumptions of this approach is that the mastery of meaning is of primary importance. The Natural Approach, a teaching method popular in the 1980s, actually rejected a focus on form altogether as a valid use of classroom time (Krashen and Terrell 1983). Negotiation as a way of facilitating speaking skills was deemed of greater importance than attention to form. However, along with evidence of fossilization in language learners, there now appears to be a greater awareness of the ways in which form, meaning, and function interact. Accuracy and meaning need not be incompatible or independent pursuits; linguistic competence is viewed as one element that can contribute to an overall communicative competence. In other words, it is now understood that learners can focus on accuracy of form while at the same time communicating meaningfully (Larsen-Freeman 1991).

Concentrating on form is not necessarily equivalent to an explicit teaching of grammar. For example, many language teachers and researchers now believe that vocabulary needs to be explicitly taught (e.g., Sokmen 1992; Seal 1991; Nation 1990; McCarthy 1990; Fox 1987; Carter and McCarthy 1988). Vocabulary teaching is believed to be something that should not always be subordinated to other skill areas or learned "by absorption" in the natural course of communicating in the target language. Rather, there are discourse-based vocabulary skills that students can observe and practice.

In the same way, skills associated with pronunciation are believed to be more effectively "learned" if they are explicitly "taught" (Celce-Murcia, Brinton, and Goodwin 1996; Wennerstrom 1994). For example, prosodic features, such as intonation, rhythm, and stress, are not always automatically acquired by most adult learners of a language and must be targeted as micro-skills that can contribute to an overall proficiency. Thus, linguistic accuracy can be realized at different levels and with features other than morphosyntax. Discourse analysis activities that focus on micro-level structures are an appropriate way of doing this.

Grammar

What do discourse analysis activities have to offer in the area of grammar? First, spoken English, which is the focus of this book, is notably different than written English. Examining a detailed transcript for the first time, while listening carefully to audiotaped speech, can be both a shock and a revelation. Adult native speakers often do not use complete, fully formed sentences; they rephrase and repair their utterances; they cut themselves or each other off in midsentence or midphrase; they do not always obey the rules of prescriptive standard English grammar. A number of studies address ways in which spoken language differs syntactically from written language (e.g., Ford 1993; Horowitz and Samuels 1987; Kroll and Vann 1981; Ochs 1979). Conversation analysis is in fact a type of discourse analysis whose exclusive terrain is the study of spontaneous spoken language. However, only a few grammar textbooks for ESOL students explicitly address the ways that form is affected by context (e.g., Badalamenti and Stanchina 1997; Riggenbach and Samuda 1997; Thewlis 1997; Frodesen and Eyring 1997). One way to develop in learners an awareness of such usage variables is to use discourse analysis activities. Learners can focus on particular grammatical structures in natural speech and observe how what is actually said may or may not conform to the prescriptive rules presented in textbooks. In addition, they can examine how their own usage corresponds to these rules, set goals for themselves, design meaningful practice activities, and keep track of progress they make.

Second, the choice of grammatical structures may differ in different contexts. The syntax of a formal, prepared informative speech delivered to an academic audience is likely to resemble writing: sentences are dense and complex. Different settings can shape the form an utterance takes: a request may take the form of an imperative in one setting ("Close the window"), a question that uses a modal in one setting ("Could you close the window, please?"), a seemingly unrelated statement in another ("I'm freezing"). Observing how grammar corresponds with the situation and setting can be done using a discourse analysis approach. Students can observe grammatical structures (e.g., verb tenses, the passive voice, article usage) as they appear in authentic spoken discourse, and they can then make hypotheses about why particular grammatical choices were made instead of others, which can ultimately lead to an outlining of the "rules" that determine these choices.

Vocabulary

Discourse analysis activities are also suitable for vocabulary development. Nation (1990) makes a distinction between increasing learners' vocabulary and establishing learners' vocabulary. Increasing vocabulary involves selectively introducing learners to new words; establishing vocabulary involves building on this vocabulary by using words in meaningful contexts. As Sokmen (1992) points out, simply memorizing lists of words or even learning words in context does not guarantee retention—or in Nation's words, this does not ensure that particular vocabulary words are "established." Rather, words need to be organized and associated in ways that are meaningful to individual learners. Working with words that naturally appear in spoken discourse is a potentially rich approach.

Deciding what words to target and how to approach "learning" are decisions worthy of consideration. Students attending university classes will need a substantial receptive vocabulary to understand lectures and read books and articles, but a large productive vocabulary may not be necessary, especially if most social interactions occur in the students' L1. If students primarily want to converse in the target language, it will be less important to become familiar with a large number of words than to know how to use meaningfully a smaller number of core words, especially since even highly educated native speakers tend to use a fairly unsophisticated vocabulary in conversation with peers and intimates (Goffman 1981). Discourse analysis activities designed by learners themselves generate tailor-made vocabulary studies. Learners can concentrate on high frequency words or specialized vocabulary that they determine is useful to them. Alternatively, they can focus on words that cause particular difficulty for them.

Students can observe the vocabulary that is used in a certain setting and notice how usage may differ in other settings. For example, the words used in a conversation may be notably different than those used in an academic lecture. More specifically, vocabulary usage in a discussion in an introductory course in women's studies will contrast markedly with the vocabulary used in a graduate-level lecture in mechanical engineering. Authentic spoken language data collected by students can be used in a discourse analysis activity in which students make hypotheses about why particular vocabulary choices were made instead of others.

In addition, noticing what words native or expert speakers use can be enlightening to learners who assume that native speaker speech is "perfect." As with grammar, vocabulary usage in informal settings may break the rules in terms of standard, formal, "news announcer" English. Vocabulary may vary widely according to who the interlocutors are and what the setting is. Speakers' dialects not only affect their choice of words in specific settings but also contribute to the nature of their established receptive vocabularies.

Pronunciation

Dialect also plays a part in how words are pronounced. This aspect of pronunciation, then, can also be explored through discourse analysis activities: learners can collect audiotaped speech from speakers of different dialects of English and systematically compare the pronunciation of specific words and the sounds in words. This kind of activity is helpful for raising consciousness about the notion of standard English, namely, that considerations of power and status figure into the determination of what is "standard" among the many varieties of English.

Also included in the study of pronunciation is the phenomenon of "fast" English. Nonnative speakers of English are initially surprised when they are first exposed to natural English spoken by native speakers. In speech, words are not discrete or separated from each other; they are normally linked together, often in one clause-length "stream" of words. Compared to informal speech, formal speech calls for more full words and for fewer contractions and ellipses (dropped words or sounds). Discourse analysis activities can encourage students to examine these features of pronunciation. In addition, learners can explore how their own pronunciation corresponds to these features. Then, to target these features in their own speech, learners can design meaningful practice activities.

2. Suggestions for Developing Original Activities

When targeting micro-level rather than macro-level features, it is helpful to think of the individual constituents that contribute to the subskills of pronunciation, grammar, and vocabulary. Determining what students need and want to learn is, of course, an important preliminary step in designing activities. Once a syllabus has been planned—or, better yet, negotiated with input from students—language textbooks on pronunciation, grammar, and vocabulary can serve as useful sources of ideas for developing discourse analysis activities. Anything that is "taught" as a unit in most textbooks can also serve as the basis for a language research activity.

In developing activities, it is always helpful to keep in mind students' general needs and interests in the spoken language. For example, how much do learners intend and/or want to interact with native speakers or with speakers of other languages whose common language is English? In other words, how important is it for learners to develop speaking, as opposed to listening, skills? In situations in which a learner's peers are mostly native speakers of the learner's mother tongue, the amount of time in an English-speaking country is short, or there is little integrative motivation (as in Gardner and Lambert 1972), it is often more beneficial for learners to focus on developing their receptive skills. Thus, discourse analysis activities that target listening rather than speaking may be more useful.

What do students need and want to listen to? Students may need to understand academic lectures and may benefit from listening for vocabulary that marks transition points in the lecture (Activity 25). Or it may be important for learners to converse with native speakers, in which case it can be helpful to develop an awareness of some of the features of fast English: for example, in casual English, speakers link words together (Activity 17) and take other "shortcuts" that increase their rates of speech (Activity 16). For students needing to develop an extensive vocabulary, audiotapes of spoken language interactions can provide rich data for exploring new words and can provide the basis for developing skills that encourage long-term retention of these new words (Activity 23).

Learners' hobbies, fields of study, and interests may provide information about the kinds of discourse analysis activities that would be useful. Learning vocabulary specific to specialized "areas" that learners determine can be a worthwhile activity (Activity 24).

If greater accuracy in learners' own speech is an objective, discourse analysis activities can be developed that help heighten learners' awareness about the features of grammar, pronunciation, and vocabulary that they need to work on (Activities 18, 22, and 26). It may also be helpful for accuracy-oriented learners to conduct research on particular grammatical structures, in order for them to develop some consciousness about the fact that native speakers do not always follow the rules of standard prescriptive English (Activities 20 and 21).

In doing these activities, learners have a more active involvement in their learning process, rather than being the passive recipients of the explanations and the often mechanical exercises provided in textbooks. They determine what spoken language contexts are most interesting and relevant to them and, based on this, develop their own activities. They find real-life examples of the sounds and features that are sometimes targeted in pronunciation classes, the structures that are presented in grammar classes, and the words that are "taught" in vocabulary classes.

Sample Activities 15–26

Guide to Activities

Sample Activities 15–18: Pronunciation

Activity 15

Word Stress and Pauses   Spoken Language

◄──────────────────────────────────────//──►

Macro level   Micro level

Objective: This activity is the first of four designed to introduce learners to the analysis of their own speech for accuracy in terms of pronunciation, one of the more conventional "subskills" of speaking. Specifically, this activity examines word stress and the use of pauses in native speaker speech and learners' own speech. Ultimately the goal of this activity is to enable learners to use stress and pauses more effectively.

Background: To emphasize important words in a sentence, speakers of English use "stress"—louder, longer, or higher-pitched words compared to other words in a sentence. Hagen and Grogran (1991) call the most emphasized word in a sentence the information focus, since words that are stressed are usually the words that contain the important information for the listener.

Typically the most stressed word in a sentence is a content word (a noun, a verb, an adjective, or an adverb) as opposed to a function word (a preposition, a conjunction, or an article). (For a more comprehensive treatment of the topic of content versus function words, see Hagen and Grogan 1991, chapters 8 and 9.) However, any word in a sentence can be emphasized if that word is important. It is important when it contains new information, when it contrasts with another word, or when it has a special meaning.

Stressing a word is one way to show that a word is important. Another way is to pause before and after the important word. However, this practice—pausing to show that a word is important—is more typical of formal, planned speech than of informal, unplanned speech, such as conversation.

Besides using pauses to emphasize important words in formal speech, native speakers of English usually pause after phrase or clause boundaries, or, in other words, after a "thought group"—words that logically "go together," such as noun phrases, prepositional phrases, or complete, short sentences (Chafe 1987; Pawley and Snyder 1983). Speakers generally do not pause and "break up" the flow of their speech before the end of a phrase or clause. But even native speakers do not always pause in the "right" places—sometimes they hesitate because they do not know what to say next, because they have made a mistake or want to correct or repair something they said, or because they are searching for a particular word.

Step 1: Predict This exercise asks learners to predict where pauses and word stresses will occur in native speaker speech. Thus, they will need a transcript of a tape of native (or expert) speaker speech. Ideally, it would be helpful to have two transcripts for the whole class to use: one of formal speech, such as a television or radio news broadcast or a formal lecture; and one of informal, conversational speech. If possible, the instructor can provide the class with these transcripts, or learners may have transcripts from the activities in chapter 3.

To gather these data "from scratch," instructors can tape-record a native speaker in informal and formal settings and then prepare the two transcripts for the whole group to use. For this prediction activity, it is not important to transcribe every filler ("uh," "um"), backchannel ("yeah," "right"), or partial word (e.g., if the speaker starts a word then stops and rephrases), but it is important to make sure that each transcript includes all the full words that the speaker uses.

A transcript is distributed to the class. Before listening to the tape, students mark the transcript with underlines (_____) under the words that they expect to have strong stress, double or dark underlines (_____) under the information focus (the word that has the greatest stress in the sentence), and slashes (/) between words where they expect that there will be a pause. They check their predictions with a partner, then listen to the tape and see how accurate their predictions were. (There may be some differences of opinion, even after listening to the tape. If there is access to technological support, such as the Visipitch or the CSL/Computerized Speech Lab, which visually charts stress and pauses between words, this can be helpful.)

Based on their results, students answer the following questions.

1. What kinds of words are stressed? What makes certain words more important than other words in the sentence? Give two or three examples from your transcript, explaining why stress was used in each case.
2. When do pauses occur? Are there other reasons for using pauses besides emphasizing important words? Give examples from your transcript.

Step 2: Plan For this activity, data consist of any audiotape or videotape of each learner speaking, accompanied by a transcript (preferably done by the learner and checked by the instructor). A sample of extended speech is most appropriate, as opposed to a brief comment or two made by the learner. Thus, the learner-prepared data from Additional Activity 9A, a complete narrative, or Activity 11, an informative talk, would be good candidates for this activity. If learners are not going to be doing these activities, see the suggestions for transcribing speech in chapter 2 (under "Working with Spoken Language Data") and the suggestions for choosing story topics in Activity 9, Step 2—a method for eliciting a sample of extended talk.

Step 3: Collect data Learners transcribe one or two minutes of their own speech. As with the native speaker data used in Step 1, it is not important to transcribe every filler, backchannel, or partial word, but it is important to make sure that all full words are transcribed, so that others who examine the transcript can easily read through it and make sense of it.

Step 4: Analyze Learners trade transcripts with a partner so that they are not working with their own spoken data. This is appropriate since they will be analyzing the transcript and then comparing their predictions to what actually happened. Learners are given the following instructions (modeled after Wennerstrom 1991), preferably to do as homework:

First, predict which words are likely to be stressed (underline these in pencil), which words are likely to be strongly stressed (underline these in dark pencil or twice), and where pauses are likely to occur (mark these with a slash in pencil). Then listen to the tape and mark the actual stressed words and pauses in ink.

Learners then discuss their findings with the speakers whose data they analyzed. In pairs or groups, learners complete the following chart for each speaker, giving two or three examples for each category.

Data Collection Sheet for Activity 15
Analysis of Successes/Problems

Word Stress

(Write out the whole sentence. In some cases it might also be helpful to write out a sentence or two before and a sentence or two after, if the context gives you clues about why certain words are important.)

Strengths	Weaknesses
(important words that were stressed)	(important words that were not stressed)

Pauses

(Write out the whole clause, sentence, or group of sentences.)

| Strengths | Weaknesses |
| (pauses used appropriately) | (problematic pauses) |

After learners have worked in small groups to analyze errors, the large group/whole class re-forms to discuss their findings—the successes and "typical" errors they noticed in their data. In Step 1, for example, learners may have noticed that words in a sentence are stressed when they contain main ideas or new information or when they stand in comparison or contrast to each other. Step 1 also provided the opportunity to observe that nonnative and native speakers often pause for reasons other than emphasis.

Step 5: Generate With this activity, the fact that each learner provides data for the analysis (Step 4) has already ensured that they generate language themselves. But this activity can be particularly valuable if it is repeated at some later point, especially if learners are given opportunities to practice what they have learned. (See the Learner/Teacher Feedback section for citations of textbooks that address this purpose.)

Learners can audiotape their own speech in any of the formats suggested in Step 2 or in any context where they are required to speak for an extended period of time (i.e., more than a comment or two). Informal contexts, such as an oral dialogue journal or pair conversations, might produce slightly different results than more formal or academic settings. If learners are interested in examining their speech as it is produced in different registers, they can tape-record speech in an informal setting if their data in Step 3 were produced in a formal setting, or they can tape-record speech in a formal setting if their data in Step 3 were produced in an informal setting. It is possible, however, that the differences will be slight, unless their planning time and/or use of notes was notably different in the more formal setting.

Step 6: Review Since one objective of this activity is for learners to become conscious of the ways in which they can work on improving their speech, it is important that learners analyze their own data at some point, looking specifically for the kinds of problems pointed out in the analysis in Step 4. Another method of analysis is to employ an observer in a small group of three or four students who provides feedback to speakers on the particular structure or feature they want to work on (see Additional Activity 3A).

Learner/Teacher Feedback: The opportunity for learners to examine how native or expert speakers use pauses and word stress is often enlightening to learners, since they find that although native speakers tend to pause after a "thought group," it is also natural for them to pause when searching for a word, especially in unplanned speech, or when moving to a new topic. In this activity, learners may discover that opinions about what sounds "smooth" may differ, which is interesting in itself, since it reinforces the notion that listeners are active participants, with different impressions of speakers' skill or "fluency."

In addition, students are often encouraged by this activity since they may discover that monitoring their own speech for stress and pauses is a relatively "accessible" activity that comes much more easily than an awareness of grammar and pronunciation problems. Thus, follow-up work is likely to be fruitful in emphasizing learners' natural strengths and in improving their self-confidence. There are several excellent textbooks that work on stress, parsing, rhythm, and intonation: see Morley 1996 for suggestions; also see Hagen 1988; Hagen and Grogan 1991; Wennerstrom 1991; Celce-Murcia, Brinton, and Goodwin 1996.

Activity 16

Reductions and Contractions   Spoken Language, Informal Settings

Macro level   Micro level

Objective: This activity focuses on the reductions that occur in normal spoken English. Learners are directed to observe reductions in native speaker speech and then to practice producing them in their own speech.

Background: Learners in a foreign language setting who have had little experience listening to native speaker speech are often baffled when they hear authentic English spoken in informal contexts, since spoken English bears little resemblance to written English. In North American English, unstressed syllables are reduced, contractions are almost always used except in the most formal contexts, and sounds and even whole words are often dropped (this is called *ellipsis*).

Teachers of ESOL believe that it is important to explicitly teach these features characteristic of rapid, informal spoken English to learners who will need to listen to and speak to native speakers of English (Morley 1996; Celce-Murcia, Brinton, and Goodwin 1996). It is also believed that sustained systematic practice that both exposes learners to the features of "fast" native speaker speech and also provides them with practice in producing these features themselves in context can be effective. Thus, this activity can serve as an introduction to one of the broadest phenomena of natural, everyday English: reduced speech. As with most of the micro features associated with accuracy, further practice and concentrated work are recommended, and for the features targeted in this activity, some excellent textbooks accompanied by tapes are available (e.g., Celce-Murcia, Brinton, and Goodwin 1996; Hagen and Grogan 1991; Hagen 1988).

Step 1: Predict This exercise asks learners to predict where reductions and ellipses will occur in native speaker speech. As in Activity 15, it is possible to use a transcript of native speaker speech that learners first read through, marking syllables or words that they predict will be reduced or dropped. Another way to complete this step is to have learners select a short section of a written text, predict which syllables or words will be reduced or dropped, and then have a native speaker read the passage in fast, relaxed English. However, if a more controlled approach is desired, this step might be better done as an elicitation activity that targets four general areas: reduced syllables, dropped syllables, contractions, and dropped words.

Reduced syllables. Most function words (prepositions, conjunctions, articles) and unstressed syllables often have vowels that are reduced to an "uh" sound, which is represented in dictionaries and pronunciation textbooks by the symbol /ə/ (called a *schwa*). For example, in the following sentence, the vowels with ə over them are pronounced with the schwa sound.

/ə/   /ə/   /ə/   /ə/?   /ə/
I believe that most Americans think that their families are important.

Constructions that are commonly reduced in spoken English are "going to," which sounds like "gonna" when it is reduced; "want to," which sounds like "wanna" when it is reduced; and "have to," which sounds like "hafta" when it is reduced. Sometimes such reductions occur in fiction writing, if the author wants characters' speech to appear "natural."

To familiarize themselves with reductions, learners predict which vowels in the following sentences (or sentences they make up) will have the schwa sound, and write /ə/ over them. Learners also predict if there are likely to be other common reductions. Then learners ask a native (or expert) speaker to read the sentences in fast, natural English, to see if their predictions are accurate. Learners can tape-record the native speakers as they read, then listen to the tape with a partner to check their predictions.

1. I have about three more chapters to read before I'm finished.
2. Then I'm going to make some tea and relax.

3. I'll probably go to bed at about eleven.
4. That's a lot earlier than when I usually go to bed.
5. But I've had a long day and I have to do a lot of work tomorrow, so I want to get a lot of sleep tonight.

Dropped syllables. In some words, unstressed syllables in the middle of words are dropped completely in some dialects of fast, spoken American English. (This is called *ellipsis.*) For example, many native speakers pronounce the words below by dropping the syllables replaced by '.

      fam'ly
As your family grows up, you'll be glad that you spent the money on a

      cam'ra   diff'rence   prob'ly
good camera. It will make a difference, since you'll probably be inspired to take a lot more photos of your children.

To familiarize themselves with dropped syllables, learners predict which syllables in the following sentences (or sentences they make up) will be dropped, and they rewrite the word with ' replacing the dropped syllable. They then ask a native (or expert) speaker to read the sentences in fast, natural English, to see if their predictions are accurate. They can tape-record the native speakers as they read, then listen to the tape with a partner to check their predictions.

6. The vegetables that my husband used to grow were delicious.
7. He was an organic farmer, and his memories of his farming days are mostly pleasant.
8. He loved farmers' markets, but he was uncomfortable with the business end of things.
9. It made a big difference when I helped him with his bookkeeping.
10. I didn't find that kind of work very interesting, but I also have fond memories of the markets.

(Note: Students may find that they have different results, depending on the native speaker who reads the sentences. Some speakers do not drop syllables, and some that might in a more natural spoken context [i.e., when they are talking with each other] may be more careful to pronounce each syllable when they are asked to read. More natural results are one advantage of using a tape of native speakers talking in a conversation or in another informal situation rather than eliciting spoken language from a written prompt. The disadvantage in doing this is that there is less control over what is said, and although there are sure to be some reductions and dropped words or syllables, there might not be examples of the four major "areas" introduced in this activity.)

Contractions. In informal spoken North American English, it is common for most auxiliary verb + *not* combinations (should not, cannot, will not, do/did not) to be contracted (shouldn't, can't, won't, don't/didn't). Other common contractions occur with *will* (I'll, she'll) and forms of the verb *to be* (I'm, they're) and with *what* and *have/has* (What've you decided? = What have you decided?; What's she done now? = What has she done now?) and *that* and *would/had* (That'd be nice = That would be nice; That'd already been done = That had already been done).

To familiarize themselves with contractions, learners predict where native speakers would use contractions in the following sentences (or sentences they make up), then ask a native (or expert) speaker to read these sentences in fast, natural English (telling them to use contractions if they normally would), to see if their predictions are accurate. Learners tape-record the speakers as they read, then listen to the tape with a partner to check their predictions.

11. What have I been doing for the last year?
12. That is a good question.
13. Well, I have been working a lot, and actually I should not let myself get so stressed out about work.
14. If I had had more time, and if I did not have so many bills to pay, and if I were not such a workaholic, I would have gone traveling.
15. My partner is the kind of person who will actually go traveling rather than just talk about it like I do.

(Note: Again, remember that some speakers will insist on reading every word, rather than reading as if they were really talking, so learners' findings may differ.)

Dropped words. Sometimes in informal spoken English, the first word or words in short questions are dropped. Short questions or requests sometimes drop the words *Do you, Did you, Would you,* and *Have you* when followed by a form of the verb *to get.* Instead of speaking the full form of the question, they start instead with the main verb.

To familiarize themselves with dropped words, learners predict the words that native speakers would drop in the following short questions (or questions they make up), then ask a native (or expert) speaker how they would shorten the questions in informal speech and to read the questions in their fast, shortened forms. Learners tape-record the speakers as they read, then listen to the tape with a partner to check their predictions.

16. Do you mind if I smoke?
17. Oh, have you got a problem with my smoking?
18. Do you remember when my dad asked you about smoking?
19. Would you mind telling me what you said to him?
20. Hey, are you mad at me? Why didn't you answer my questions?

Step 2: Plan For this activity, learners first examine authentic native speaker speech for reductions and contractions; then produce speech, working from a script; then analyze their own speech produced in a spontaneous, informal context. Thus, the first step is to tape-record informal native speaker speech, since the phenomena occur here rather than in more formal, planned speech.

Learners can use native or expert speaker speech from any of the previous activities in which they collected data in informal contexts; many of the activities in chapter 3 required this kind of data collection. Or they can tape-record "fresh" data: live conversations are appropriate, as are television or radio programs in which the context is informal (e.g., television sitcoms or casual interviews, rather than more formal interviews or news broadcasts).

Step 3: Collect data Learners tape-record at least five minutes of native or expert speakers engaged in informal talk. This can be done in groups or by individuals, preferably as homework.

Step 4: Analyze data Learners listen carefully to their tapes, writing down all examples of reductions and contractions along with their full "translations"—the full words that would have been used if they had not been reduced or contracted. These can be organized under the four categories presented in Step 1, as in the following chart.

The instructor can determine how extensively this task should be done. In five minutes of talk, there could be numerous examples of different kinds of reductions and ellipses. Looking for reduced vowels alone can be exhaustive, since it is obligatory for many unstressed vowels to be reduced to /ə/. Thus, it is suggested that the teacher limit the number of examples in the first category (reduced syllables) to twenty. It is also advantageous to fix the total number of examples in the next three categories: there are likely to be many contractions but not necessarily many dropped syllables or words. Thus, depending on the quality of the data and the dialect of the speaker, a total of twenty for the following three categories together is not too overwhelming a number and amounts to thirty minutes of work or less for intermediate learners.

Data Collection Sheet for Activity 16
Reductions and Contractions

Reduced and Dropped Syllables

(Write out the full sentence. Write the reductions above the words; indicate with /ə/ when appropriate. Indicate dropped syllables with ' above.)

1.

2.

3.

etc.

Contractions and Dropped Words

(Write out the sentence as spoken. Write out full, uncontracted words below the contraction. Write out "missing"/dropped words below.)

1.

2.

3.

etc.

After completing their lists, learners can discuss their findings in a group discussion, noting similarities and proposing general rules about reductions and contractions, and comparing these hypotheses to the introductions to the four categories presented in Step 1.

Step 5: Generate Learners now read the sentences they transcribed in Step 4 that contain reductions and contractions, imitating the native speaker produced data. They can tape-record their readings and compare them with the native speaker readings, or they can work with a partner to critique their readings. A supervised language lab is an appropriate setting for this task, since an instructor or supervisor could provide feedback to the learner.

Learners then work together in partners or groups creating dialogues that draw from the examples they found in their data. The goal of this step is for students to create short, meaningful role plays that can be performed in front of others and evaluated in terms of the reductions and contractions students used. These dialogues can resemble the data they gathered in terms of content, or they can diverge from the content. The important thing is that learners gain practice in using reductions and contractions that naturally occur in "real" discourse.

Since one objective of this activity is for learners to become conscious of the ways in which they themselves do or do not incorporate native-like reductions and contractions into their own speech, it is important that learners analyze their own data at some point. Thus, the next step is for learners to speak spontaneously, without a script, yet maintaining consciousness about the use of reductions and contractions. The data prepared in Additional Activity 9A, which elicits a complete narrative from the learner, would be a good candidate for this activity, as would a conversation or discussion in which all participants contributed more than brief comments.

Step 6: Review This self-directed analysis examines where each learner used or did not use contractions and reductions. Thus, detailed transcriptions, done by the students, are helpful. First, students transcribe their own speech as spoken, trying to replicate it in terms of authenticity (e.g., if "going to" is pronounced in its reduced "gonna" form, it should be written that way).

After transcribing a minute or two of speech, learners work alone or with a partner to review their use of contractions and reductions. Each time a word or syllable was used or reduced appropriately, the student marks it with a check (✔); if a contraction or reduction could have been used but was not, the student circles that word or words, writing the reduction or contraction out above it on the transcript.

Learner/Teacher Feedback: Learners often express appreciation at getting the "facts" about fast English, especially if they have previously had little exposure to authentic, informal speech or have had little practice with authentic listening materials. Some confess that their first face-to-face interactions left them baffled about whether they were even speaking English, but when they discover that most, if not all, language learners encounter similar problems when they first encounter real native speakers of the target language, there is some comfort.

However, learners are often initially discouraged about their own capabilities to produce speech that sounds "native-like" in terms of reductions. Learners appreciate the fact that native speakers do not always use reductions and contractions and the fact that in more formal situations, full forms are more likely to be used. Another way to prevent learners from being discouraged about their own abilities to "speak like native speakers" is to break down the types of reductions into more manageable components (the four categories presented in Step 1) and to encourage further, more systematic work. There are excellent ESOL textbooks that expose learners to different features of "fast English" and provide them with practice on a more step-by-step basis. (See Background for citations of such textbooks; further recommendations are provided in the Suggested Readings and References section at the end of this chapter.)

Finally, some instructors find that when learners analyze native speaker speech for reductions, this can be a can-of-worms type of activity. So many reductions are not covered in this introductory activity: such features as the flap /ɾ/, linked words (Activity 17), other common reductions not treated here (*of* = *v*), and so on may all be the source of some consternation. However, as with the many other discourse analysis activities presented throughout this book, these observations can also be exciting to students, since, after all, they are the ones who are noticing the phenomena and grappling with them to make sense of them. They, not the teacher or another expert, are the language researchers who define the research problem and settle on the challenges they choose to continue with.

Activity 17

Linking   Spoken Language

Macro level   Micro level

Objective: This activity is intended to help heighten learners' awareness about how words are linked together in English and to help learners use linking more consciously and effectively in their own speech.

Background: Often learners who have not been exposed to naturally paced "fast" English are baffled when they first hear native speakers' speech. One of the features characteristic of rapid, informal spoken English that teachers believe should be explicitly "taught" is the phenomenon of linking. This can be introduced to learners by presenting the two most common kinds of linking: (1) when a word starts with a vowel, it is connected, or linked, to the previous word if that word ends with a consonant (e.g., "She's unhappy" sounds like "She-zunhappy"); (2) when the end of a word has the same sound as the starting sound in the next word, the two words are connected, or linked (e.g., "She felt terrible" sounds like "She felt-errible" since the end of *felt* and the start of *terrible* share the same one sound, *t*).

Step 1: Predict This task asks learners to predict where linking will occur in native speaker speech. Thus, they need a transcript of a tape recording of native (or expert) speaker speech. As with Activity 15, ideally the whole class can work together with one transcript so that this introduction to linking can be efficiently presented. In this case, it would be helpful if the instructor provided members of the class with the transcript, or learners may want to loan a transcript for this purpose to the instructor.

However, class members may want to do this step of the analysis individually or in small groups, and there is no reason why this should not happen. If learners need to gather data for this assignment "from scratch," a native speaker or expert speaker can be tape-recorded in either informal or formal settings, since linking occurs in both. For this prediction task, it is not important to transcribe every filler ("uh," "um"), backchannel ("yeah," "right"), or partial word (e.g., if the speaker starts a word then stops and rephrases), but it is important to make sure that all the full words that the speaker uses have been transcribed.

Learners choose a transcript of at least thirty seconds to one minute of tape, which is an adequate amount of time for different occasions of linking to occur. Before listening to the tape, learners join together the words that they expect to be linked with a ⌢ symbol on the transcript. For example, "She gave up her seat" would be marked "She gave⌢up her seat," since you might expect that a word starting with a vowel would be linked to the consonant preceding it.

Learners check their predictions with a partner. Then they listen to the tape and see how accurate their predictions were. There may be some differences of opinion, even after listening to the tape. For example, some words may sound connected to one person and not to another. (Access to a technological aid, such as the CSL/Computerized Speech Lab, a machine that visually charts linking and other phenomena, is helpful.)

Based on their results, learners answer the following questions.

1. Are all consonants in every word pronounced?
2. What kinds of words are linked? (Think in terms of whether they start and end with vowels or consonants.)
3. To illustrate your answer in the preceding question, give two or three examples of linking from your transcript.

Step 2: Plan For this activity, data consist of an audiotape or videotape of each learner speaking, accompanied by a transcript (preferably done by the learner and checked by the instructor). A sample of extended speech (thirty seconds to one minute of speech, rather than only a brief comment or two made by the learner) is probably adequate.

Step 3: Collect data Learners tape-record themselves speaking for an extended turn of thirty seconds to one minute, then transcribe this. As with the native speaker data used in Step 1, it is not important to transcribe every filler, backchannel, or partial word, but it is important to transcribe all full words, so that those reading the transcript can easily understand it.

Step 4: Analyze Learners trade transcripts with a partner so that they are not working with their own spoken data. This is appropriate for this step since they will be comparing predictions about how words are linked with what the speaker actually did. Learners first predict which words are likely to be linked, indicating this by connecting the words together with ⌢ in pencil. Then they listen to the tape and mark the actual linked words in ink.

Learners then discuss their findings with the speakers whose data they analyzed. In pairs or groups, learners complete the following chart for each speaker, giving two or three examples for each category.

Data Collection Sheet for Activity 17
Analysis of Successes/Problems

Linking

(Write out the whole sentence.)

| Strengths | Weaknesses |
| (words that were linked appropriately) | (words that should have been linked) |

After learners have worked in small groups to analyze linking, the large group/whole class can re-form to discuss their findings—the successes and typical "errors" they noticed in their data. Some learners may have no problems with linking and may find that linking seems to come naturally to them; others may notice that there speech seems "choppy" and broken up by a lack of appropriate linking.

Step 5: Generate With this activity, the fact that each learner provides data for the analysis (Step 4) has already ensured that they generate language themselves. But for those learners who noticed problems in the way they linked words, this activity can be particularly valuable if it is repeated. Thus, learners should audiotape and analyze a "fresh" sample of their own speech.

Another direction that this activity can take is further work on listening comprehension. Students who do not find linking in their own speech a challenge may consider it more valuable to do more transcription of "fast" native speaker speech. They can listen to audiotapes and compare their transcriptions, a useful endeavor for noticing how, in normal fast-paced native speaker speech, words are chained together into one long string.

Step 6: Review Like the other pronunciation activities in this section, one objective of this activity is for learners to become conscious of the ways in which they can work on improving their speech. For learners who need to work on linking, therefore, it is important that they examine their own data and notice improvements that they have made.

For learners who chose to do further work in listening, this is the time to again pool data for the purpose of discussing general rules of linking. It is also an appropriate time to talk about features that initially confused them when they listened to native speakers: dropping the initial *h* from a word and linking that word is likely to be one of those phenomena (What did he do? = What didee do?; I'd like to see her = I'd like to see-er).

Learner/Teacher Feedback: This activity is extremely useful for students who encounter problems with understanding fast English, since linking is one of the central features of natural, everyday English. In addition, learners usually discover that monitoring their own speech for linking is a relatively accessible activity compared to looking for grammatical "errors" and certain pronunciation problems. Learners also find that linking can greatly build smoothness, or fluency, in their speech, and some are encouraged to find that they already tend to naturally link words.

Activity 18
Problematic Vowels and Consonants   Spoken Language

Macro level   Micro level

Objective: This activity is designed to help learners become aware of the sounds in English that they need to work on. It also is intended to introduce them to self-monitoring and to designing follow-up pronunciation practice programs that can help them target the vowels and consonants they find difficult or troublesome.

Background: Learners are sometimes hyperaware of the sounds in English that are hard to pronounce and that are likely to sound less than native-like when they make them. However, some students of English are not particularly conscious of their pronunciation problems, especially if they tend to be the type of learner who is more intent on communicating and interacting than on monitoring for accuracy. It is perfectly appropriate that learners do focus on communication, especially if they are living or working in an English-speaking country and are generally effective communicators whose listeners usually do not experience comprehension problems.

However, many learners are motivated to work on improving their pronunciation. Depending on native language, difficult consonants for many nonnative speakers include the /th/ sound (as in **th**in and **th**is); /r/ and /l/; /f/, /v/, and /w/; and the /kw/ sound (as in **qu**ick). Some of the vowel contrasts that are especially difficult (for low-intermediate nonnative speakers and others) are /i/ and /I/ (as in s**i**t versus s**ea**t) and /ey/ (as in d**ay**), /ɛ/ (as in n**e**xt), and /æ/ (as in c**a**t).

Hagen and Grogan 1991 is an especially useful text for working on particular sounds in context. But because of the difficulty of improving pronunciation, Wennerstrom's (1991) suggestion is useful: she suggests that learners consider a four-level approach to pronunciation practice. Learners practice a particular sound first at (1) the word level and next at (2) the text level—reading aloud a written text. The next level is (3) the outline level, where students make a written outline to use as notes, continuing to concentrate on one particular sound. The final level is (4) the free speech level—spontaneous talk on any topic.

Step 1: Predict Learners focus on one or two consonants or vowels (or minimal pairs) that they feel they need to work on. They may be able to identify, without any prompting, which one or two sounds they could use help on. If not, the preceding suggestions about typically difficult vowels or consonants (see Background) may be helpful. In addition, many pronunciation books have a diagnostic section that can aid learners and instructors in identifying troublesome or difficult vowels and consonants.

Another way for learners to "diagnose" their own areas of pronunciation difficulty is for them to tape-record a short segment of their speech in which they talk for at least thirty seconds to one minute. This could be a segment in which they read aloud a short written passage (a paragraph or two). Alternatively, it could be an excerpt of talk—either a conversation in which the learner's turn is more than a brief comment or two, or a segment from a monologue (a story or informative talk, such as those produced in Activities 9 and 11). At this point in the activity, it is not necessary for learners to diagnose all their pronunciation problems; they just need to identify one or two sounds that they experience difficulty with.

Since it is sometimes hard for learners initially to "hear" their own pronunciation errors, it may be helpful for learners to trade their audiotapes (of them speaking for thirty seconds to one minute) with each other or to hand in these tapes to their teacher. The listener selects one or two sounds that either cause difficulty in comprehension or sound clearly "accented." The instructor may want to confirm that these sounds are in fact sounds that the learner can use some help with, since in a foreign language setting, it is sometimes hard for nonnative speakers with a common L1 to notice or "hear" each other's accents.

In fact, in some areas of the world where English is spoken as an "alternative first language" along with the native tongue (e.g., Malaysia, India, Zimbabwe, Nigeria), speakers of a common dialect will share the same phonetic characteristics. Thus, an "accent" is only foreign when encountered by speakers of a dialect that is different and/or is considered standard. Note also the differences in pronunciation by speakers of British English, Australian English, and North American English. All these areas, where English is the first or only language spoken, can be broken down even further, and speakers characterize speakers of dialects outside of their own as "accented" (e.g., people from the southeast region of the United States have a "southern accent").

The difficult vowels and consonants presented earlier (see Background) are often considered problematic for all learners who share a first language other than English. For low-level learners especially, these may be the sounds to target. In this case, this diagnostic step can be bypassed.

Step 2: Plan Once learners (or the instructor) have determined which one or two sounds they would like to concentrate on initially, they design a short program that will allow them practice in those sounds. Following Wennerstrom's (1991) suggestion, learners target this sound at four levels. First, they practice the sound or sounds at the word level; they write out a list of ten to twenty words that contain the sound or sounds and underline each occurrence. (Targeting more than two sounds makes it difficult to maintain consciousness about accuracy; thus it is recommended that only one or two sounds [or minimal pairs] be targeted.) In the next step of this activity, learners will read aloud these words, focusing on accuracy of the one or two sounds they are targeting.

Learners find a short written text and again underline each occurrence of the sound(s) they are targeting. They can write their own texts if this is preferable, especially if the sound occurs fairly rarely: /z/ and /j/ are examples of such sounds. It is helpful if texts are "authentic" in the sense that they are not unrelated sentences, since it is helpful for learners to gain some practice in monitoring for accuracy with a specific focus yet also producing meaningful text in the sense that there is some coherence.

The third level of pronunciation practice does not rely so heavily on written texts, and the fourth level does not at all. For practice of level 3, students make a written outline to use as notes, continuing to concentrate on one or two particular sounds. Finally, for practice of level 4, they talk spontaneously on any topic. When planning for these latter two practice exercises, learners should take some care that the sounds they are targeting will be generated. With many phonemes, this will happen naturally, but with sounds that are not frequently occurring, the words from the list produced in the first level may be useful in planning.

Step 3: Collect data This step involves tape-recording the four levels of practice that learners planned for in Step 2. First, they record themselves reading their lists of words; next, they record themselves reading their text. It helps to have an audience for the last two steps since it is sometimes hard for people to speak spontaneously without having someone who is really listening and responding. Thus it is recommended that learners work in pairs or groups while they give both the talks that they have prepared outlines for (level 3) and the spontaneous talks on topics of their choice (level 4).

Step 4: Analyze It is recommended that learners first work together to analyze each other's data, since it may be initially difficult for learners to be objective about accuracy in their own speech. Although there are exceptions, learners working for the first time with self-produced data tend to be overly critical about their pronunciation and may not notice their own successes, whereas it is likely that, when listening to another student's talk, a listener can be positive yet at the same time constructive, especially if the listener has collaborated with the speaker on previous discourse analysis activities.

Learners should be sure to tell their listeners what specific sound or sounds they are working on, since at this stage it is probably not helpful to move into a more general critique of pronunciation problems, and since learners themselves have already determined what they want to focus on. Because they are focusing on discrete sounds, listeners/evaluators will need to listen to each section of the tape of their classmate two or more times.

In the first three practice sections (the reading aloud of words and of texts and the speaking from an outline), it is helpful if the listener/evaluator has the speaker's written texts and notes to refer to. The evaluators listen, following along with the text, and circle any words that were hard to understand. They should then check to see if the word was hard to understand because of the sound that is targeted or because of another problematic sound, and if the latter is the case, they should let it pass for now. It is also important that they point out cases where the sound was clear and "native-like."

For the task at the free speech level (level 4—spontaneous talk), it can be extremely helpful to the listener/evaluator if the speaker has prepared a transcript or notes after giving and tape-recording the talk. This can help the listener/evaluator focus on the particular sound the learner is targeting, especially if the words that contain those targeted sounds are underlined. Transcript preparation is also helpful for learners, since they must monitor carefully what they said and how they said it. As with the other three practice tasks, the listener/evaluator circles words that were hard to understand (because of problems with the targeted sounds) and gives feedback on the cases where the targeted sound was not problematic.

If a transcript or notes are not available (i.e., if the learner chooses not to provide such), the listener/evaluator instead writes down words that were hard to understand, stopping the tape and relistening whenever necessary. After listening to this section, the listener/evaluator can work alone or with the speaker to decide if the comprehension problem is because of the targeted sound. If not, at this point it might be best ignored.

Step 5: Generate Since one objective of this activity is for learners to become conscious of their pronunciation development, it is important that learners analyze their own data at some point. Thus, either they can replicate the method for producing and collecting data suggested in Step 2, or they can take a less structured approach to producing spoken data. They can tape-record themselves engaged in any spontaneous or planned talk. (If it is heavily planned, with all words containing the targeted sound written out, for example, learners may also want to produce data in a more spontaneous framework.)

Learners may want to focus on the same one or two sounds they worked on earlier, or they may choose to target another problematic vowel or consonant. Alternatively, they may decide to use spoken data that are unmonitored—that is, in which learners had not focused on maintaining consciousness about the accurate pronunciation of certain sounds. Thus, there are many options for generating data in this step.

Step 6: Review Learners can approach this analysis in the same way they did in Step 4, only this time they listen to their own spoken language data. Again, it is recommended that learners transcribe a segment of their tapes because of the insight this can provide and the accuracy that is necessitated. If learners were concentrating on monitoring a particular sound (or sounds) when they taped themselves talking, they can simply jot down the words that contained these targeted sounds. However, noting the phrase that contains the word/sound may actually be more helpful, since how words are linked may have an effect on the pronunciation of individual sounds.

If learners were not focusing on particular words when taping but wanted to get a more general sense of what seemed to cause them difficulty, a complete transcript is helpful. Following along with the transcript, learners listen to themselves in talk and circle words that sound "heavily accented," seem hard to comprehend, or are the source of repair. A research notebook is an appropriate tool for keeping track of this analysis. In it, learners list sounds that they need or want to work on, design tasks that provide practice with this sound at the four levels described earlier (see Background), log the time that they spend concentrating on pronunciation work, and keep track of progress, noting successes and changes that they perceive.

If this is the first time learners have "self-diagnosed," or analyzed their own self-produced data, it is helpful to have an instructor or another class-mate respond to the learners' own analyses and focus on the strengths and successes. This can serve as a validity check, verifying learners' own analyses. It can also help to encourage those learners whose first attempts at self-analyses were overly critical.

Learner/Teacher Feedback: Working on problems with pronunciation may at first seem overwhelming to the novice learner and teacher. Thus, a structured approach such as Wennerstrom's (1991) is appealing, since focusing on a sound at the word level is easier than trying to monitor for a particular sound at the free speech level.

Developing accuracy in pronunciation is an ongoing process, in part because it is difficult to maintain consciousness about micro features when effective communication, rather than accuracy, is the goal. Thus, it is advisable to do self-monitoring analyses often. If learners have identified what specific phonemes they need or want to work on, there are excellent textbooks and tapes on the market that are appropriate for individual work, in and out of the language laboratory. (Hagan and Grogan 1991 and Wennerstrom 1991 are examples of such textbooks; further recommendations are provided in the Suggested Readings and References section at the end of this chapter.)

With commitment, progress can be notable, as learners will see if they extend their evaluation of samples of their speech over a span of time. For this reason, learners often find that a research notebook benefits them, since they can keep in it a record of their development over time. For this reason, too, it is more fruitful if instructors can keep the emphasis on learners' successes in pronunciation, rather than on their problems. They are more likely to find that there are successes if students have decided what sounds specifically they want to work on and how, in a structured way, they can practice these sounds.

Sample Activities 19–22: Grammar

Activity 19

Present Perfect versus Simple Past   Spoken Language

Macro level   Micro level

Objective: This activity is the first of two designed to introduce learners to research in the usage of a particular grammatical structure—in this case, the contrast between use of the present perfect and the simple past. A second objective of this activity is to introduce learners to designing practice activities that incorporate the chosen structure into learners' own speech so that accuracy is enhanced.

Background: The intent of this background section is to provide a brief introduction to present perfect versus simple past usage. For teachers and learners who need more than just this "refresher," most grammar books that target the low-intermediate level or higher will be useful in providing more detail. (Also see suggestions at the end of this chapter in the Suggested Readings and References section.)

In brief, the present perfect is used to connect the past and the present: the present perfect tells us about something that began in the past and continues to the present. (Example: I've lived here a long time. Implication: I'm still living here now.) In contrast, the simple past is used to talk about something that happened at a specific time in the past. (Example: I lived here in 1990. Implication: I don't live here anymore.) The simple past shows when something happened; the present perfect is used when the experience or the length of time is more important than when it happened.

The present perfect is used to frame or introduce a general idea, whereas the simple past follows up on this general "framing" to give specific details. (Example: I've lived here a long time. I first moved here in the 1970s. That's when I went to college at Western Washington University in Bellingham.)

Step 1: Predict Learners consider whether present perfect usage is ever guaranteed and whether it is ever required. Learners can work with other students to think of situations where the present perfect is likely to be used. In considering what questions would elicit the present perfect, students should think of contexts that focus on duration or on the experience rather than on a specific time. Questions beginning "Have you ever . . . ?" or "How long have you . . . ?" are likely to do this. (Students might look in grammar textbooks for other ideas.)

When students have found a topic that they think will elicit present perfect usage, they can work with a partner or group to develop a set of interview questions that talk about when things happened and for how long. With each question, they should guess whether the answer will require present perfect usage or not.

Step 2: Plan This stage is the time to plan on who students will interview—a native or expert speaker, if possible, or more than one, if that is appropriate. Learners will also need to decide how structured they want the interview to be. For example, does each group want to have one person ask a set of questions, one after the other, or do they want to leave room for questions that might naturally arise? Do they want the interviewee to feel free to elaborate? Is it acceptable for all members of the research group to ask questions, and if so, do they want to take turns or have room for more spontaneity?

This is also the stage for refining the interview questions. Students can do this by piloting, or "trying out" questions on each other. Is there a way that a question can be changed so that it is more likely to require an answer that uses the present perfect? (A change that makes the question sound too artificial should not be made.) Also, the set of questions can be checked for coherence in terms of topic: Does one question naturally follow up after the previous question and lead to the next? Where might the speaker be expected to elaborate?

Step 3: Collect data Learners conduct and audiotape or videotape their interview(s). If they had intended to interview just one person but find that the interview is shorter than expected, it may be appropriate to extend the interview to others. The goal is to collect natural-sounding samples of a native or expert speaker talking.

Step 4: Analyze Learners listen to their recorded interview(s), focusing on verb tense usage. Was the present perfect ever used? If not, were there cases where it could have been used? Was the simple past used correctly?

As a whole class, learners discuss their findings, being sure to address questions that emerged in the predicting and planning stages. For example: Was the present perfect used at the times they predicted it would be? Is it possible to make any general statements about the use of the present perfect?

Step 5: Generate Part of the objective for this chapter's activities is for learners to generate language using the structures targeted. For this activity, a natural way to do this is for learners to elaborate on the topics chosen by the different research groups and to tape-record this talk, with each person talking for at least one minute. This step could be done formally and thoroughly, imitating the interviewing formats chosen by the research groups in steps 2 and 3.

Alternatively, this step could be conducted less formally, as a discussion. Suppose the topic chosen was people's hobbies or activities. One person might initiate the discussion with a question: "Have you ever collected anything? Stamps, coins, or . . ." Another person can respond to the question. There is no need for people to talk only about themselves; it is interesting and appropriate to talk about other people's collections as well.

For the purposes of this activity, it is important that learners generate language on topics that could (but may not) involve present perfect usage. Because of the earlier stages of this activity, it is possible that learners will be more conscious about their verb tense usage—more specifically, about when to use the present perfect and when to use the simple past. Or they may find that they do not monitor (or think about) how they talk about a particular topic at all, because they are more intent on what they are talking about. The next step is an opportunity for learners to check this and, in the process, to gain some awareness about their use of or avoidance of the present perfect.

Step 6: Review Learners analyze the tape-recorded data they produced in Step 5, addressing the following questions: Was the present perfect ever used? If not, were there cases where it could have been or should have been used? Was the simple past used correctly?

It is appropriate for learners to first analyze their own data and then have their analyses checked by a classmate and/or an instructor. The check can confirm validity and can also reinforce learners' self-analyses.

Learner/Teacher Feedback: There might initially be some resistance to this kind of activity, especially if learners are used to having grammar exercises provided for them. It is my experience that this resistance can be easily overcome if learners are motivated to improve their English and participate in structuring their learning; it is helpful if the instructor is enthusiastic about a discourse analytic approach to understanding, using, and analyzing language.

Even learners new to these kinds of activities generally find that an activity structured in this way is useful. First, they discover that they need to have some understanding of the structure under investigation in order to think of questions that might elicit the structure. Thus, the predicting and planning stages of this research project can be helpful as a grammar refresher.

Second, the results of their analyses, both of native/expert data and their own data, help learners build confidence in their own investigatory skills. It is enlightening for nonnative speakers to learn that native speakers do not necessarily "follow the rules" of formal prescriptive grammar: such grammatical structures as the present perfect may turn out to be used infrequently, even at points where present perfect usage would be appropriate.

Third, learners who consider themselves good at learning grammar are sometimes excited about participating in research that examines "real," as opposed to textbook, grammar. One student who did this activity asked me why grammar textbooks do not have "activities like this." (This was before the 1993 publication of the series of *Grammar Dimensions* textbooks edited by Larsen-Freeman; otherwise I would have answered, "They do.")

Activity 20

Conditionals   Spoken Language

Macro level   Micro level

Objective: This activity is the second of two designed to introduce learners to research in the usage of a particular grammatical structure—in this case, conditionals. As with Activity 19, a second objective of this activity is to introduce learners to designing practice activities that incorporate the chosen structure into learners' own speech.

Background: The intent of this background section is to provide a brief general introduction to conditionals. For more specific information, teachers and learners can consult any grammar book that targets the low-intermediate level or higher; see the suggestions for further readings in the Suggested Readings and References section at the end of this chapter.

Conditionals, also called if-then statements, are usually perceived as being of two main types. *Real conditionals* talk about situations that are likely to happen. (Example: If it's cloudy, I'll bring my umbrella.) *Unreal,* or *hypothetical, conditionals* talk about situations that are unlikely to happen (Example: If I had the money, I'd buy a boat. Implication: I probably won't be able to buy a boat, since I probably won't ever have the money) or about situations that are impossible (Example: If Elvis were alive today, he'd be a loser. Implication: This is impossible, since he's not alive).

Step 1: Predict Learners can work with other students to think of situations where both kinds of conditionals are likely to be used. As students consider what questions would elicit conditionals, instructors might hint that questions with *if* in them are likely to do so and that the topic of superstitions is a way of eliciting a complete conditional—both a conditional clause and a main clause. (Students might look in grammar textbooks for other ideas.)

When students have ideas for eliciting conditional usage, they can work with a partner or group to develop a set of interview questions. For each question, they should predict the form of the answer: Is a conditional required? Is it likely that the respondent will use a complete conditional (conditional clause and main clause) or just a main clause?

Step 2: Plan This stage is the time to plan on who students will interview—native or expert speakers, if possible, and more than one if the questions require only short answers. Learners will also need to decide how structured they want the interview to be. The interview questions will help to determine what is appropriate.

This is also the stage for refining the interview questions. Students can do this by piloting, or "trying out" questions on each other. Is there a way that a question can be changed so that it is more likely to require an answer that uses the conditional? (A change that makes the question sound too artificial should not be made.)

Step 3: Collect data Learners conduct and audiotape or videotape their interview(s).

Step 4: Analyze Learners listen to their recorded interview(s) and write down all examples of conditionals just as they were said. As a whole class, learners discuss their findings, being sure to address questions that emerged in the predicting and planning stages. For example: Were conditionals used at the times learners predicted they would be? Were complete conditionals used at the times learners predicted they would be? Is it possible to make any general statements about conditional usage?

Step 5: Generate Part of the objective for this chapter's activities is for learners to generate language using the structures targeted. For this activity, a natural way to do this is for learners to hold a tape-recorded discussion in which they elaborate on the topics chosen by the different research groups. This step could replicate the question-and-answer format chosen by the research groups in steps 2 and 3, or new topics and questions might emerge.

For the purposes of this activity, it is important that learners generate language on topics that could (but may not) involve conditionals. It is possible that learners will be more conscious about their conditional usage, or they may find that they are not conscious of this because they are more intent on what they are talking about. The next step is an opportunity for learners to check this and, in the process, to gain some awareness about their use of or avoidance of conditional usage.

Step 6: Review Learners analyze the tape-recorded data they produced in Step 5, addressing the following questions: Was the conditional used appropriately? Were there cases where it could have been or should have been used?

It is appropriate for learners to first analyze their own data and then have their analyses checked by a classmate and/or an instructor. The check can confirm validity and can also reinforce learners' self-analyses.

Learner/Teacher Feedback: This activity is a good one for learners of various levels. It is my opinion that grammar books sometimes present conditionals in an overly complicated manner. Research into conditionals in authentic spoken language discourse often turns up some surprises, namely, that (1) the conditional clause is often omitted if it is understood as part of the context (for example, when questions are asked with *if* in them, the conditional clause is usually not repeated in the answer) and (2) there are many more options besides *will* and *would* for the verb in the main clause (Branch 1995). This information can be exciting for learners to discover, since it is not always presented in textbooks. In addition, it is always interesting for nonnative speakers to learn that native speakers do not necessarily "follow the rules" of formal prescriptive grammar.

Activity 21

Child Language Acquisition — Spoken Language

Macro level — Micro level

Objective: The goal of this activity is to heighten learners' awareness about the grammatical structures that are difficult for children learning English as their native language, as evident in their "errors." In addition, learners reflect on how their own speech fares in terms of their findings: have they "mastered" the structures that are difficult for children, or are these structures problematic for them, too?

Background: "Mistakes" are considered a natural part of the learning process for children learning their own native language. Most of their errors are grammatical, although children also have a notably different pronunciation and a simpler vocabulary than adults. Most laypeople—in this case, people who do not study language—are aware of some of their own children's errors, especially those they consider "cute." Moskowitz (1985), a child language acquisition researcher, suggests that this perception comes from the fact that the errors children make are transparent and systematic: it is easy for adult native speakers to understand why certain mistakes in syntax are made. For example, children overgeneralize the past tense *-ed* endings for all past tense verbs, even irregular verbs ("go" becomes "goed" instead of "went"; "break" becomes "breaked" instead of "broke").

Step 1: Predict Learners note how much coverage is given to different structures in a grammar book that they are familiar with. Then learners discuss the structures that cause the most difficulty for them. Is their difficulty consistent with the amount of coverage in the grammar book they are examining? In other words, does an appropriate proportion of the book focus on the problematic grammatical structure?

Learners then discuss their textbook examination findings in terms of what structures they predict will prove hard for children to learn. What mistakes do young children make? What mistakes do their parents or caregivers notice?

Step 2: Plan There are several possibilities for ways of conducting research on this topic if this activity is done in an English-speaking country. Ideally, researchers personally observe and interact with young children. If they are parents or know young children, interacting with the children they know is the best way to go, since children are likely to talk to someone with whom they have an established relationship. Day cares, preschools, or elementary schools often allow short-term observers, especially if the observers offer some help (e.g., with an activity). Most universities and colleges have information on children's schools and day cares for their employees. Or a staff or faculty member who has young children might be able to provide information on possible observation sites.

In EFL settings, students might interview parents of young native English-speaking children about "typical" (or "cute") mistakes their children make. Even if the children are no longer young and no longer making errors, sometimes parents can remember mistakes with language that their children have made. But students should be prepared to sort through parents' stories about their children that may or may not be related to the topic of language!

Finally, other possible sources of information are journals or books on language acquisition (these tend to provide much more detail than a learner may want, depending on the source) and television shows or movies that have young children as characters (ages two to four usually are the times when children are in the thick of the rule-formation process).

Step 3: Collect data Individuals or research teams of two or three students (more than that might be intimidating to a child) collect data in their chosen research sites. If tape-recording is feasible, it is advantageous, since tapes can be reviewed at leisure later. In situations where it is possible to talk with a child, it might be helpful to be prepared to ask some simple questions about the child's recent past (e.g., what the child did earlier in the day), the child's present (e.g., what the child is doing now), other people that the child knows and interacts with, and so on. The researcher should feel free to ask the child to repeat what she or he said if it is not clear, especially if there is lots of time and an already established relationship.

If tape-recording the child's speech is not possible, a research team of two is probably a good idea, since one person can do the talking while the other person takes notes in her or his research notebook. These notes will probably have to be brief and may consist only of occasional utterances that the child makes. (If the child is doing a lot of talking, it will be impossible to write down everything that is said.) If it is clear that what the child is saying is incorrect in terms of standard adult grammar, then the learner/researcher can jot down the errors that the child makes. The researcher should also make notes about the context of the talk—the general topic and the time frame (e.g., Is the child talking about last month? last year?). This is likely to be important, since context determines in part which structures should be used.

Step 4: Analyze Learners pool their data, making a list of the kinds of errors they (or the parents of the children) have noticed. They then conduct a group discussion on their findings, especially considering the ways that these findings relate to their predictions (in Step 1) about errors they would expect children to make. In addition, they should discuss how their discoveries of "typical" language errors by children correspond to their evaluations (also in Step 1) of the coverage assigned to difficult structures in grammar books.

Step 5: Generate This stage is reserved for a comparison between the observed language errors of children and the learners' own speech. Do children and adult learners tend to make similar errors? There are several ways of approaching this step, depending on the age of the children who were the source of the "errors," the awareness learners have of their own grammatical difficulties, and the contexts in which the adult speech under consideration is produced (some errors, for example, are not likely to occur in adult learners' speech if they are too topic specific).

One objective of this activity is for learners to become conscious of the ways in which they themselves make or do not make errors like those that they noticed in children's speech. To maintain a focus, it is best to work on one or two types of grammatical error, rather than the whole range of errors that they might have uncovered in their data on children's speech.

If learners determine that the errors they noticed in children's speech are likely to occur frequently in a wide variety of contexts and with a number of topics (e.g., verb tense usage), a short sample (one minute) of learners' own speech in spontaneous talk would be appropriate. If there is not an existing speech sample (a tape and an accompanying learner-made transcript), learners can generate data by speaking spontaneously, without a script, while attempting to maintain consciousness about the error or errors they are focusing on. The data produced in Additional Activity 9A, which elicits a complete narrative from the learner, would be a good candidate for this activity, as would conversations or discussions in which all participants contributed more than brief comments.

If the error that learners choose to focus on occurs relatively infrequently, research teams may want to design interview questions that are likely to elicit the structure (see Activities 19 and 20 for discussion on designing such questions). In this case, students can take turns interviewing each other and audiotaping these interviews, the goal being to use the targeted structure in spontaneous, unplanned speech.

Step 6: Review It is good practice for students to first analyze their own data and then have a classmate and/or instructor check this analysis. Learners analyze their own self-produced data to see how their use of the targeted structure compares to their findings on children's language. Was the structure problematic for the adult learners/researchers, too? Or does a particular structure seem to have been mastered, since it appears to cause no problem in the learners' speech?

It is useful here to pool findings and, in a group discussion, to hypothesize whether or not certain errors are generally hard for most or all adult learners at a particular level. Did other classmates have similar results? Another possibility is that errors are individually determined, that is, that there does not seem to be a pattern across all learners/researchers participating in this project. And finally, learners will want to discuss whether particular grammatical structures tend to cause problems for native speakers of a particular language.

A research notebook is an appropriate tool for keeping track of this analysis. In it, learners list the structure(s) that they need or want to work on or that they feel they have "mastered" and no longer need to work on; design tasks that provide practice with this grammatical structure; log the time that they spend concentrating on grammar; and keep track of progress, noting successes and changes that they perceive.

Learner/Teacher Feedback: It would be difficult to do this activity without a pool of child native speakers of English. In Zimbabwe, where English is widely spoken and is the medium of instruction in schools, students used as data sources both Zimbabwean children and my young U.S.-born children. (I also found some excellent child-care providers out of the deal!)

This project is not limited to "academic" language students. For example, it has been undertaken by beginning-level recently arrived U.S. immigrants—mothers whose young children are in day cares or preschools with children who are native speakers of English. This activity has proven to be appealing for almost all participants who have done it, in part, I suppose, because language learning can be freshly perceived as universal—something that everyone goes through. To see that native-speaking children who are actively learning a language also actively make errors can be a thrilling discovery. Learners get the sense that they are not alone in their language-learning voyage.

Activity 22

Problematic Structures   Spoken Language

Macro level   Micro level

Objective: This activity is designed to help learners become aware of the grammatical structures in English that they need to work on. It also is intended to introduce them to self-monitoring and to designing follow-up practice programs that can help them target the grammatical structures they find difficult or troublesome.

Background: At the low-intermediate level, a number of grammatical structures may be problematic for learners. Some typical errors are using the wrong verb tense (e.g., using the simple present instead of the present perfect), making mistakes in number (subject-verb disagreement; making noncount nouns plural—e.g., "informations"), incorrect formation or avoidance of the passive (at points where it is appropriate), and wrong choice of prepositions.

Like pronunciation, grammar is best approached in steps. It is helpful for learners to first be aware of the types of errors they are likely to make and the ones that are more serious in terms of interfering with listeners' comprehension. Peer evaluation of speech may be especially useful in determining this.

Teachers of grammar have long noted that learners benefit by concentrating on one structure at a time. Acknowledging that there are different types of learners is important, too: some learners benefit from explicit attention to the rules that govern a structure; others may learn more efficiently by using the structure in context. A recent series of textbooks that incorporates what we know about the learning of grammar is the four-volume *Grammar Dimensions* edited by Larsen-Freeman (1993; 2d ed., 1997). This series would be appropriate for individualized follow-up work at all levels, since its range is from beginner level (volume 1) to advanced (volume 4), and since each unit concentrates on one particular structure.

As with pronunciation, learners are sometimes aware of the structures in English that are likely to be the source of grammatical errors (e.g., many Japanese students shudder at the English article system). Other students, however, are not particularly conscious of their grammar problems, especially if they tend to be the type of learner who is more intent on communicating and interacting than on monitoring for accuracy. Again, in many situations, it may be perfectly appropriate that learners focus on communication, especially if they are living or working in an English-speaking country and if they are generally effective communicators whose listeners usually do not experience comprehension problems. But many learners are motivated to work on improving their grammar, especially if they are engaged in the process.

Step 1: Predict Learners will focus on one grammatical structure that they feel they need to work on. They may be able to identify, without any prompting, what they need to work on to improve grammatical accuracy. If not, the preceding suggestions about typically difficult structures (see Background) may be helpful. In addition, most grammar books are designed to target difficult structures for learners at various levels and thus could also serve as a basis for self-diagnosis.

Another way for learners to diagnose their own areas of difficulty is for them to tape-record a short segment (thirty seconds to one minute) of their speech. Formal settings, such as rehearsed speeches, are likely to produce different structures than informal conversations. For example, relative clauses and lengthy subordinate clauses are used less in informal than in formal contexts (Tomlin 1994; Gass 1984), and it is typical for native speakers in informal conversation to use short independent clauses and fragments rather than complete, well-formed, complex sentences. In other words, the grammar of spoken language may appear, on close examination, quite different than that of written language. Thus, different problem areas are likely to be noticed in speech samples elicited in different contexts. At this point in the activity, it is not necessary for learners to diagnose all their problems with grammar; they need only identify one structure that causes errors.

Since it is sometimes difficult for learners initially to "hear" their own grammatical errors, it may be helpful for learners to trade their audiotapes (of them speaking for thirty seconds to one minute) with each other or to hand in these tapes to their teacher. The listener selects one structure where an "error" is made more than once (in terms of standard prescriptive English). The instructor may want to confirm that this structure is in fact worthy of further work (e.g., for beginning learners, it would be inappropriate to work on distinctions between indefinite, definite, and zero articles; using *a* versus *an,* though, may warrant attention at this level).

Step 2: Plan Once learners (or the instructor) have determined which structure they would like to concentrate on initially, they design a short program that will allow them practice with that structure on three levels, starting with a highly controlled activity in sentence construction. First, they write out a short passage that contains several occurrences of the structure they want to practice. They can read these passages aloud to each other, with each learner first alerting his or her listener about the structure the learner wants to focus on, so that the listener pays special attention to it. Learners who are working on the same structure can be paired up; this provides practice in listening for the structure.

In the next part of this step, learners make a written outline to use as notes at the next practice level, in a discussion in Step 3, continuing to concentrate on one structure. In Step 3, they will also practice at a third level, talking spontaneously on any topic. When planning for these latter two practice exercises, learners should take some care that the structures they are targeting will be generated. With many structures (e.g., verb tense), this will happen naturally, but with structures that are not frequently occurring, the passage generated in the first level of this step may be useful in planning.

Step 3: Collect data This step involves tape-recording the learners' two talks: the one in which learners use a prepared outline and the one where they talk spontaneously on any topic. Since it is difficult for most people to talk naturally without a responsive audience, it is recommended that learners work in pairs or groups while they give both the talks that they have prepared outlines for and the spontaneous talks on topics of their choice.

Step 4: Analyze Learners listen to the tapes of themselves speaking, paying special attention to the structure they were concentrating on, and making an analysis like that begun in the following chart.

Data Collection Sheet for Activity 22
Analysis of Successes/Problems

Grammar

(Write out the sentence or phrase containing the error. If context is important for determining accuracy, add a sentence or two that was said before/after the sentence or phrase.)

What was said:

What should have been said:

Learners can shift their focus if another structure has turned out to be problematic.

It is recommended that learners first work together to analyze each other's data, since it is likely that at least some students will be focusing on the same structure. In addition, learners working for the first time with self-produced data tend to be overly critical about their grammatical accuracy and thus to have difficulty noticing their own successes, whereas it is likely that when listening to another student's talk, they can be positive yet at the same time constructive, especially if the students have collaborated on previous discourse analysis activities.

Learners should be sure to tell their listeners what structures they are working on, since at this stage it is probably not helpful to move into a more general critique of grammatical problems, and since learners themselves have already determined what they want to focus on. For the task at the free speech level introduced in Activity 18 (level 4—spontaneous talk), it can be extremely helpful to the listeners/evaluators if the speakers have prepared a transcript or notes after they have given and tape-recorded their talks. This can help the listeners/evaluators focus on the particular structures the learners are targeting. Transcript preparation is also helpful for the learners, since they must monitor carefully what they said and how they said it. The listener/evaluator reviews the speaker's analysis, adding to it if there are other examples of errors with the structure focused on. The listener/evaluator also gives feedback on the cases where the targeted structures were not problematic. If a transcript or notes are not available (i.e., if the learner chooses not to provide such), the listener/evaluator instead writes down examples of problems with the structure, stopping the tape and relistening whenever necessary.

Step 5: Generate Since one objective of this activity is for learners to become conscious of their development in grammatical accuracy, it is important that learners analyze their own data at some point. There are many options for generating data in this step. Learners can replicate the method for producing and collecting data suggested in Step 2, or they can take a less structured approach to producing spoken data and tape-record themselves engaged in any spontaneous or planned talk. (If the chosen talk is heavily planned, with all examples of the structure written out, for example, learners may also want to produce data in a more spontaneous framework.)

Learners may want to focus on the same structure they worked on earlier, or they may choose to target another problematic structure. Alternatively, they may decide to use spoken data that is unmonitored—that is, in which learners did not focus on maintaining consciousness about the accuracy of a particular structure.

Step 6: Review Learners can here approach their analysis in the same way they did in Step 4, only this time they listen to their own spoken language data. Again, it is recommended that learners transcribe a segment of their tapes, because of the insight this can provide and the accuracy that is necessitated. If learners were concentrating on monitoring for a particular structure when they taped themselves talking, they can simply jot down the phrases and sentences that contained this targeted structure. However, a more thorough transcription may actually be more helpful, since the context of the utterance is likely to determine what structure should be used.

If learners were not focusing on a particular structure but wanted to get a more general sense of what seemed to cause them difficulty, a complete transcript is helpful. Following along with the transcript, learners listen to themselves in talk and circle grammatical errors. A research notebook is an appropriate tool for recording this analysis. In it, learners list structures that they need or want to work on, design tasks that provide practice with this structure at the three levels described in Step 2, log the time that they spend concentrating on work in grammatical accuracy, and keep track of progress, noting successes and changes that they perceive.

If this is the first time learners have "self-diagnosed," or analyzed their own self-produced data, it is helpful to have an instructor or another classmate respond to the learners' own analyses and focus on the strengths and successes. This can serve as a validity check, verifying learners' own analyses. It can also help to encourage those learners whose first attempts at self-analyses were overly critical.

Learner/Teacher Feedback: Working on accuracy may at first seem overwhelming to the novice learner and teacher. Thus, a structured approach, such as the one described here (based on Wennerstrom 1991), is appealing to both learners and instructors. Developing accuracy is an ongoing process, in part because it is difficult to maintain consciousness about micro features when effective communication, rather than accuracy, is the goal. Thus, it is advisable to do self-monitoring analyses often if it is important for learners to improve their grammatical accuracy. (Sometimes this is not important.) And if learners have identified what specific structures they need or want to work on, there are excellent textbooks and tapes that are appropriate for individual work, in and out of the language laboratory. (See recommendations in the Suggested Readings and References section at the end of this unit.)

With commitment, progress can be notable, as learners will see if they extend their evaluation of samples of their speech over a span of time. For this reason, learners often find that a research notebook benefits them, since they can keep in it a record of their development over time. For this reason, too, it is more fruitful if instructors emphasize learners' successes in grammar rather than their problems.

Sample Activities 23–26: Vocabulary

Activity 23

New Words — Spoken Language

Macro level — Micro level

Objective: This activity is designed to help learners focus on words that they do not recognize in the course of talk and develop strategies for guessing their meaning. Ultimately this activity will help learners analyze and associate new words in meaningful ways and thus build their vocabulary.

Background: Nation (1990) points out that understanding vocabulary in spoken language is a different task than understanding while reading, in part because of the pace and informality of spoken language. Audiotaping talk provides the opportunity for learners to attend more closely to words that they do not know or recognize. In the course of talk and under the demands of real time, talk continues. Thus, it is possible to "gloss over" unknown words in a continued stream of talk; in other words, listeners may hear words but not comprehend them (and not realize that they do not comprehend them). In the interest of attending to the current talk, these unknown words are not usually objects of attention unless they are recognized as the source of confusion and misunderstanding. In that case, the conversation can break down because of them, and they can become the conscious source of repair (Segalowitz 1993).

Once words are recognized as new or unknown, context clues can be helpful in guessing the meanings of these words. In spoken language, the talk that precedes the new word and the shared knowledge between speaker and listener provide this context. However, most language teachers (e.g., see Sokmen 1992) now agree that noticing new words and guessing their meaning does not guarantee that these words will be "learned" and retained. Instead, new words need to be associated in meaningful ways.

Step 1: Predict Where do learners hear new words? What real-time spoken language situations cause difficulty in listening comprehension? In this step, learners identify one or two settings where they have experienced difficulty understanding the speech of native speakers of the target language.

Once a learner has identified a setting, he or she should think about whether this setting is challenging for all listeners learning the language or causes listening comprehension problems for this learner only. In other words, is the difficulty idiosyncratic, and if so, why? Or is this setting (with native speakers of other languages) likely to cause difficulty for people learning any language?

Step 2: Plan Learners team up to form research teams with others who have identified the same setting as a challenging one in terms of their listening comprehension skills. These research teams then decide how and where to collect a data sample of talk that occurs in this setting. For example, if news broadcasts are the setting identified, does the research team want to audiotape a radio news program, videotape a national television news program, or both? If the fast speech of television sitcoms is challenging for the research team, what television show would they like to audiotape or videotape? If academic lectures are the identified setting, can members of that research team agree on one speaker or field of study as the data source, or might data collection best be done individually?

Step 3: Collect data This step involves simply taping the speech in the setting agreed on in Step 2. In research teams or individually, learners review their tapes and identify either (a) short segments (one minute or less) that are particularly hard to understand or (b) five to ten occasions where a particular word or phrase is "new" or hard to understand.

Step 4: Analyze This step is best done in research teams for the purposes of collaborative listening and problem solving. First, members of a research team listen to each other's difficult segments that were selected as part of the data collection process. It is most effective to transcribe these difficult excerpts, since this may reveal that certain of the listening difficulties were not because of new or unknown words but were due to characteristics of "fast speech": the linking of words, reductions and ellipses, and so on. (Also see Activities 16 and 17.) Learners eliminate the possibility that the manner of articulation caused the problem in listening comprehension. (Did the speaker speak very quickly? Was there competing noise that made it hard to hear?)

If the problem in understanding was due to a particular word that is new or unknown, then learners can propose meanings for these words. In other words, they guess the meaning from context. So that everyone has a chance to guess, it is helpful for learners to write down their guesses individually and then discuss them as a group. If no one knows for certain the meaning of the word, they can work together to decide which guess is the best.

At this point it is appropriate to look up the word in a dictionary to check the accuracy of the guesses. It is possible that slang expressions or phrasal verbs will not be found in some dictionaries; thus, it is helpful if there is access to a good but relatively accessible dictionary, such as the *Longman Handy Learner's Dictionary of American English* (Steadman 1992).

The next stage in the analysis is to determine what clues helped learners to guess the meaning of the unknown word or phrase. For example, did the speaker give examples or describe experiences that helped to explain the meaning of the word? Were learners able to figure out the meaning because they knew what kind of word it was (noun, verb, adjective, adverb)? Learners try to trace the logic that originally helped them to guess the meaning of the word. Sometimes this may be difficult, since this thought process may not have been conscious. However, if learners can bring to consciousness their strategies for guessing from context, this may help them in future encounters with new words and phrases.

Step 5: Generate In this step, learners think of ways to associate the new words they learned in Step 4 with words they already know. It is appropriate to use a research notebook for this step.

Sokmen (1992) suggests that learners develop "word maps" and conduct "word association surveys" as ways of remembering new words. To develop word maps, learners brainstorm to think of all the words that come to mind when they hear the word or phrase from Step 4 that they are focusing on. One person in a group can be assigned to be the recorder to write down all the group members' words. Or this step can be done individually, with each person being sure to write down all the words she or he can think of, without censoring anything. Then learners review their word lists and circle the words and phrases that go together.

Finally, learners reorganize their lists into word maps, which show more explicitly why the circled "clusters" of words go together. In other words, each circle of related words and phrases is analyzed: Why do the words and phrases go together? What do they have in common? For example, are the circled words related to each other because they are synonyms or antonyms? Do the circled words describe some similar thing (e.g., a situation or condition)? Once this unifying "reason" is identified, it is written down and serves as a label, with the related words/phrases written under it. (See Sokmen 1992, 12, for an excellent example of this word-mapping process.)

To conduct the "word association surveys" that Sokmen also recommends, learners in research groups interview native or expert speakers about what words "go with" a particular new word or phrase (those defined in Step 4). For example, learners ask, "What word do you think of when you hear the word . . . ?" (giving the word under consideration). Results are pooled and examined for common associations that the interviewees had. Learners can write down these common word associations in their research notebooks.

Step 6: Review This step provides the opportunity for learners to review the new words they have learned. This can be done informally, with learners "trading" their entries in their research notebooks—the new words along with the word maps and/or the common word associations. If desired, they can copy down the words and phrases they think will be useful to them, along with the definitions.

Or learners may find it more helpful to work further with the word lists they themselves have created. It can be a challenge to think of a context that can incorporate some of these new words in a coherent way. If this is possible, learners can write passages that use some of these new words, or they can prepare and deliver short talks (with notes) in which they use some of their new words. It is recommended that a time and page limit be set; one minute or one page is usually adequate. This activity can be done as a game, with each person giving the short talk or presenting the written passage for others to read. Members of the class can vote on who created the most sensible, coherent passage and used the most new words.

Learner/Teacher Feedback: It is my experience that learners are unfailingly eager to work on developing their vocabulary in this way—by listening closely to a segment of speech that "rushed by" during their first listen, due to real-time processing. One of the problems with this activity, though, is that learners are sometimes hesitant to give up the leisure that listening to audio-taping can afford. In other words, it is hard to go back to listening in real time once one has had the luxury of audiotaped material, which can be reviewed again and again, in great detail.

Learners also remark that it is hard to learn and remember new words that are spoken in the course of talk and even to recognize that there is a new word or phrase. But a majority of learners who have done this activity come to realize that their first listen (in real time) did not seem problematic because there were enough contextual clues to "carry" the meaning and that their deeper analysis of new words expanded on their initial processing of the words. In other words, this activity can be confidence building in the sense that learners realize that they already possess some real-time processing skills.

Finally, although I have never followed up this analysis of new words with the word map activity that Sokmen (1992) recommends, teachers who have done so report that the activity is both easily learned and fun for students.

Activity 24

Specialized Words   Spoken Language

Macro level   Micro level

Objective: This activity encourages learners' understanding of the fact that specialized "areas" or topics within a field may use field-specific vocabulary that is not widely known outside that field. This activity is also intended to build skills in vocabulary research and to teach new words.

Background: Some learners have the notion that adult native speakers of a language know most of the words there are to know, and it can be surprising to them to discover that learners who work in specialized fields or know about specialized topics may know words unknown to native speakers.

Step 1: Predict Learners choose a topic or field that is interesting to them and that is likely to use some specialized vocabulary. For example, students in a degree program at a college or university may want to pursue research in a topic in their field of study. Others may want to learn about a hobby, sport, or leisure activity. One of the objectives of this activity is for learners to give a short talk that introduces their topics to other members of the class and uses specialized vocabulary pertaining to that topic (Brenner 1994). Thus, an ideal topic is neither too broad nor too narrow. Too broad of a topic may call for general vocabulary only; too narrow of a topic may require too much explanation about technicalities. Some topics chosen previously by students are baseball, jazz, gardening, fighting forest fires, MTV (music television), wines, language acquisition, and genetic engineering.

Step 2: Plan Once learners have settled on a specialized topic or field, they can join up with others interested in the same topic to form research teams. It is possible, though, that learners may not share an interest in the topics others choose, and if this is the case, individuals can pursue topics independently.

The long-term objective of this activity is for learners to deliver short talks (three to five minutes in length) on their chosen topics, using new words that they have researched. These talks can be descriptive overviews that introduce the topic: the student-chosen topics of genetic engineering and language acquisition were talks of this type. Or they can give a general orientation to some aspect of the topic: for example, students interested in gardening talked about weed control and the basics of garden design; a baseball talk described the basic rules and scoring methods of the game for an audience unfamiliar with the game except in a general way.

During the course of this research, learners will find out about ten new specialized words pertaining to their topic; they will define these words and practice using them aloud. At the planning stage of this activity, however, the goal is for learners to further define their topic and to think about sources of information on their topics. It is appropriate that learners initially use written sources to get ideas about their topic, to narrow them further, and to think about who might know more on the subjects and who might be accessible interviewees. For academic subjects, lectures or college courses (especially introductory survey courses) might be appropriate starting places. For other topics and areas, places (and possible interviewees) to consider are music or sports events, meetings or conferences, and local radio talk shows.

Once a topic has been further defined, learners may want to think about what information they are interested in hearing more about and what kinds of questions they might ask of someone knowledgeable about the topic. As with any interview, it is important to think about what strategies might best elicit information on the chosen topic. For example, would structuring the questions beforehand be helpful, or would it be best to "see where the conversation goes"? It is also important to think about which people are likely to be able to serve as sources of information; they need not be "experts" but should be knowledgeable about and interested in the topic.

It is likely that ten (or more) new words will emerge in the course of getting information about the topic. In other words, it may not be necessary to ask an interviewee directly about specialized vocabulary words ("Can you tell me a specialized word related to this topic?"). However, in informal situations it is perfectly appropriate for a learner hearing a new word in the course of the talk to ask, "What does that word mean?"

Step 3: Collect data Learners conduct research on their topics, with these two objectives in mind: (1) a list of ten new field- or topic-specific words and their definitions; (2) notes, an outline, or an informal "sketch"/idea for a short talk that describes the topic to other members of the class or provides a brief orientation to the learner (see the description of the different types of talks in Step 2). Learners will use the new words in the context of their talks, but it is not necessary to force the use of all ten words.

Step 4: Analyze Learners examine their list of ten words and answer the following questions.

1. How did you come up with each word and its definition? Was it "found" in a written or spoken context? Did you guess the word from context, and if so, how, or what was the logic? (See Activity 23 for more information on this.) Or was the word directly defined, in speaking or writing? If it was directly defined, describe this a bit more; for example, did the written or spoken source give examples, say what the word is "like," explain or illustrate the word with visual "help" (a drawing, an object, gestures or facial expressions)?
2. Are these all field-specific words in that they are used only to talk about this particular topic? Or can they be used in other contexts?

3. Are the new words related to each other? For example, are some of the words general and others specific? Are any of the words synonyms or antonyms of each other?
4. What kinds of words are they: nouns, verbs, adjectives, or adverbs? Can you think of other words with similar forms (e.g., other nouns ending in *-tion;* other adjectives ending in *-ed* or *-ing;* etc.)?

Learners practice saying the words aloud, first as individual words and then in context (in a sentence or as part of a short description or definition), preferably with someone listening. On words that learners are unsure of, they can check with others who are able to judge whether the pronunciation is accurate or can be improved. Learners determine whether the word's pronunciation seems unusual or seems to obey the rules that they are aware of.

Step 5: Generate Learners give their talks to other members of the class, in small groups if that is preferred. Audience members should write down any new words they hear, but after a talk is finished, they should concentrate on the content of the talk and ask any questions that come to mind.

After this, audience members compare their lists of words with the speaker's, and if there are people interested in learning the field-specific words, the speaker/researcher can orally help these people assign meaning to the words on their lists. Or the speaker/researcher may want to distribute a copy of the written word list and the definitions (some students like to do this before they give their talks).

Step 6: Review Learners should be sure that their research notebooks are up to date. In it should be, at the minimum, their own lists of words from Step 3, any interesting notes on the analysis of these words (the findings of Step 4), and any trouble they might have had in defining or explaining these words to others when they gave their talks. The research notebook is also the place to list the words and definitions of interest from other students' research.

Learner/Teacher Feedback: This activity is almost always fun for students to do and entertaining for the class as a whole, since class members comprise the audience for each student's talk. The only problem I and other instructors have encountered with this activity is that some learners choose topics that are either too specialized or unappealing or uninteresting to other members of the class. To address this problem, one instructor made the topics "public" at an early stage and had class members take a (written) vote in order to eliminate unpopular topics.

However, even highly specialized topics can be interesting to others if presented in a way that identifies how the issues or features described are of current relevance. For example, this activity has been used in an ESP (English as a Specific Purpose) setting in China, where students, mostly scientists, gave short poster presentations that incorporated new field-specific vocabulary and that provided a brief orientation to their fields of study, pointing out what issues were considered currently most important and worthy of research to others in that specific field.

Activity 25

Objective: This activity is designed to help learners focus on transition words and phrases in a formal talk or academic lecture, in order to understand the structure of the talk and the relationships between different sections of the talk. Ultimately the goal of this activity is to enable learners to use transitions appropriately in their own formal talks.

Background: Research in listening comprehension suggests that learners who can understand the organization of a formal talk or lecture are better able to "fill in" meaning when there are individual words that they do not know (Flowerdew 1994). In other words, tuning into the cues that are marked by transition markers is a skill that can enhance overall listening comprehension abilities. It has been suggested that a reason for this is that an understanding of how a talk is structured can activate schema and thus stimulate predictive skills, an important element of listening.

For example, in introductions to talks or lectures, structural clues can be traced to specific words and phrases. Speakers often start out with statements that indicate what their goal is or what the audience will be able to do after hearing their speech ("After hearing my lecture, you will be able to list the three main causes of . . ."; "Today I am going to describe the situation surrounding . . ."). Transition words and phrases within the body of the talk can reinforce or move away from this structure, indicating, for example, when points are related to each other in terms of a list or a chronology ("First," "Following this," "Finally"), when ideas are causally related ("Because," "Consequently," "Therefore"), and also when points compare or contrast with each other ("In contrast," "Similarly").

Step 1: Predict In this activity, students will listen to a talk or lecture that is of interest to them. Thus, they will need to decide what kind of informative talk best suits their purposes. On a North American college campus, there are likely to be plenty of opportunities for students to attend live talks on a variety of topics. In other North American settings and in non-English-speaking countries, learners may need to rely on radio or television news programs.

The following questions can encourage learners to think about the transition markers likely to be used in the data they will collect. (It is helpful if learners have some general information on the topic and purpose of the talk or lecture they will observe.)

1. Knowing what you know about the topic and purpose of the talk you will audiotape, what key verbs might be used in the introduction? Some possibilities might be *analyze, compare, list, explain,* or *describe.* In other words, what do you predict that the speaker will do in the talk or lecture? What do you guess the objective is?
2. Given your predictions about the objective of the talk, what are some of the ways that important points might be emphasized? List several transition words and phrases that the speaker might be likely to use.

Step 2: Plan For this project, students will observe/listen to a formal talk or lecture and later analyze in more detail the vocabulary used to mark transitions. As usual, it is preferable to audiotape or videotape talks, so that learners can be specific in their analyses. Working in teams is encouraged, especially if learners share interest in the same topic and/or field of study.

Step 3: Collect data In teams or individually, learners observe and listen to a talk. Audiotaping is, of course, an acceptable data collection method, but videotaping is ideal, since the entire event, including the accompanying non-verbal information, is then available for viewing. Both audio and video recordings allow closer examination of the more micro-level transition markers.

If neither audiotaping nor videotaping is possible, the activity is still useful, especially with the collaboration of students who work in research teams. Members of a research team take notes on the words and phrases that they felt marked transitions; then, as a means of triangulation, they compare these notes with other team members as part of their analysis.

Step 4: Analyze Data can be analyzed in small groups, individually, or, if a tape of a lecture is especially interesting and clear, as a whole group. Learners review their taped lectures, listening closely for all transitions. Were there words and phrases that gave important clues into the structure of the talk? Were there words and phrases that showed the relationships between parts of the talk? These should be written down, along with the sentence or two that preceded and followed these transitions and structural clues. Detailed transcriptions are not necessary (and not possible if the talk was not audio-taped), but there should be enough information for student researchers to recall how the transitions that they heard fit into the talk in terms of the surrounding context. Learners should also consider whether there were other features that marked the transitions. (For example, sometimes speakers pause in order to emphasize words or phrases; see Activity 15 for other suggestions.)

After noting all the words, phrases, and other features that marked transitions or that gave important clues about the structure of the talk, learners will evaluate these in terms of their purpose and meaning. For example: What words and phrases show that a new idea is being introduced? How is cause or effect talked about? What words or phrases in the introduction described the objectives of the talk? This part of the analysis can be done as a group, with learners compiling their results in a chart like the following.

Sample Student Analysis for Activity 25
Transition Words and Phrases

New Idea	Cause or Effect	Comparison/Contrast	etc.
First of all	Because	Similarly	
Now I'm going to . . .	Consequently	A parallel feature . . .	

It is possible that learners may have listened to a lecture or talk in which the speaker did not structure the talk or use transitions. In this case, learners should discuss what the speaker could have done that would have made the talk clearer. Were there points where transition markers should have been used? In other words, what words or phrases might have made the structure of the talk clearer to the audience?

Step 5: Generate All learners who want to should have the opportunity to develop and deliver a short formal talk or lecture that incorporates the transition markers and structural clues appropriate to the subject. However, it is important to consider time constraints and course objectives when determining the length of the talks. Topic selection should also be discussed so that the student-chosen topics are not too narrow or specialized or too general and unfocused. Talks should be taped if possible.

If learners want to practice speaking spontaneously, it may be appropriate for them to prepare an outline from which they will speak and then to rehearse (but not memorize) their talk beforehand. If learners are inclined to read aloud texts that they have written out word for word, it may be helpful for them to first hear examples of formal, read talks that illustrate the variety of reading "styles." Learners will then hear for themselves that good speakers do not sound like they are reading and that speakers who rely heavily on their text often come across as boring and mechanical sounding.

To address their reading style in their own talks, learners may want to develop a scale with which audience members evaluate the naturalness of their speech (e.g., a five-point scale on which 1 = sounds very natural/spontaneous and 5 = sounds read/mechanical). This evaluation could be done anonymously, if preferred.

Step 6: Review The first step in the analysis of student-delivered talks can involve note taking by the class members who serve as the audience. This can help to demonstrate to the speaker whether or not the organization of the talk was clear to listeners. Then, since it may be difficult for learners themselves to objectively evaluate how they incorporated transition markers and provided information about the structure of their talk, peer evaluation is recommended. Learners can work together with the tapes of their talks, finding examples of the words, phrases, and other features that marked transitions or that gave important clues about the structure of their talks. Peer evaluators can also discuss how each talk could have been strengthened and the structure made more clear to the audience (i.e., what transition markers or structural clues could have been used but were not).

A tape of the talk can supply the peer evaluator with additional information, and it can be especially useful data for self-analysis. Each learner should transcribe at least a portion of their talk, to verify their peer evaluator's observations and to closely monitor their own use of transition markers and structural clues.

Learner/Teacher Feedback: Some students find this kind of activity exciting. Before doing this activity, many students believe that their listening comprehension ability is entirely reliant on knowing every word that is said; thus, it can be enlightening for them to realize that tuning into specific types of words is a relatively easy way to understand more.

This kind of activity is not new for teachers of listening comprehension, but it is new for many instructors to have their students conduct the research themselves, collecting data from lectures and talks that they are interested in. Instructors who were first-timers at using this approach reported success with this particular activity. Since students determine what data to use, they are engaged with the material. At the same time, instructors find that looking for structural cues in formal talks is a relatively straightforward task for their students and boosts their confidence in their listening comprehension abilities. One word of warning: some talks are done very casually (haphazardly?), and in these cases, the use of *formal* transition markers are limited. Thus, it may be helpful for students to choose material from lectures that are done more formally.

Activity 26

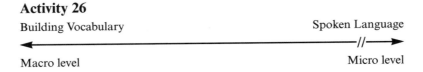

Building Vocabulary   Spoken Language

Macro level   Micro level

Objective: This activity is designed to help learners build their vocabulary by examining their own audiotaped speech and rephrasing words and phrases that did not "work."

Background: Language students at all levels feel the need for vocabulary improvement. Low-level learners are especially conscious of points in the course of talk where the "right word" is not accessible; even adult native speakers of a language sometimes experience this problem. To compensate, speakers develop strategies: they use words from their native language in place of the unknown word (this is called language switch); they "foreignize" words by applying morphological and phonological rules from one language to a base word from the other language; they approximate by using related words; they use circumlocution to describe something without attempting to use the unknown word; and they coin new words (Yule and Tarone 1990; Faerch and Kasper 1983). Some learners may not be conscious of these strategies, especially if they are engaged in communicating, but many learners are motivated to work on improving their vocabulary and are interested, retrospectively, in what they did during the course of talk.

Step 1: Predict Learners first predict communicative situations in which they are likely to have difficulty saying what they want or what they intend. They can discuss with each other possible sources of this difficulty: Is it because they are not sure about the appropriate way to say something in particular situations? Or are there hesitations because of problems with grammar? Not knowing the right word(s) usually has some role in communication problems. Learners discuss whether or not they believe this is the case for them.

Vocabulary used in informal settings is likely to differ from that used in formal settings, such as rehearsed speeches. Specialized topics are also likely to use words that might sound unusual in an informal conversation (see Activity 24). Native speakers typically use vocabulary that is quite "common" (i.e., low-level) in conversation; slang and idioms are high-frequency items in this context as compared to their usage in formal contexts (Nation

1990, chapter 2). Thus, different problem areas are likely to be predicted for different contexts.

Step 2: Plan Once learners have determined what contexts are likely to be troublesome for them in terms of vocabulary, they plan their data collection procedures. If informal conversation with native- or expert-speaking peers is typically difficult for the learners, then audiotaping a conversation would be appropriate. If fluency (i.e., lack of automaticity or "smoothness") is generally a problem, as it is for many low-level learners, then perhaps a small group discussion with other members of the class would be an appropriate data collection site.

Step 3: Collect data Learners tape-record a short segment (one to three minutes) of their speech in the contexts they have chosen, in spontaneous or planned talk. (If they choose a heavily planned talk that approximates reading aloud, then they should also produce data in a more spontaneous framework.) Native or expert speakers need not be involved as speakers, since learners will be focusing on their own speech. However, it is important that learners be engaged in real communication in order to get some perspective on their own vocabulary usage during authentic interactions. Thus, speech samples of the learner engaged in talk, like those in Activity 1 (conversation) and Activity 9 (storytelling), would be appropriate, as would a discussion based on a controversial topic (see Rooks 1996 for up-to-date discussion topics and ideas).

Step 4: Analyze Learners listen to their tapes and write down examples of places where they feel, in retrospect, that they had difficulty expressing themselves. Sometimes these places are easy to locate because the learner notices his or her hesitations or the use of strategies with which the learner tries to "get the point across" to the other speaker without using the unknown or unavailable word. At other times, vocabulary difficulties can be recognized because of the repair initiations from the other speakers (e.g., "What? I don't understand").

If some learners are not able to locate any problems with vocabulary, it may be helpful for them to trade their audiotapes (of them speaking for one to three minutes) with other learners or to hand in these tapes to their teacher. The listener of a tape selects points where it would have been possible for the learner to say something differently—and more "effectively," according to the listener.

In the case of hypercritical learners, the instructor may want to confirm cases where a word or phrase could in fact have been said "better" and note cases in which what was said was perfectly understandable and appropriate, at least in the mind of the instructor. However, learners themselves are best able to determine when they did not express themselves to their satisfaction.

Learners examine their talk for five to ten examples of places where they had wanted to use a certain word that was not available or known to them or where they feel they could have improved their communication by saying something differently. Then they focus on the examples that are definitely vocabulary related rather than grammar related, since vocabulary is the focus of this activity. They write these examples down in a list like that outlined in the following chart, and in cases where it is possible to narrow the problem to one particular word, they circle that word.

Data Collection Sheet 1 for Activity 26
Vocabulary Self-Analysis

What I said that could have been said better/differently:

(Write out the complete sentence and a sentence or two before and after. If the problem was due to one word, circle it.)

1.

2.

3.

etc.

Step 5: Generate Once learners have determined which excerpts they would like to concentrate on, they rephrase what they said (in retrospect, of course) in writing. To do this, they can use any sources that are helpful: they can brainstorm with each other to elicit words, they can refer to a thesaurus or dictionary, or they can ask native or expert speakers how they might phrase something (e.g., they might say, "I was trying to describe such and such. How might you describe this?").

When they have found the "right" word or rephrased the problematic wording so that it is satisfactory to them, they rewrite what they said in a list like that outlined in the following chart.

Data Collection Sheet 2 for Activity 26
Vocabulary Self-Analysis

What I said that could have been said better/differently:

1.

2.

etc.

What I could have said instead:

1.

2.

etc.

Then learners share their findings with each other, speaking from notes or, if it is preferred, reading their "new" versions aloud. If this is the first time learners have "self-diagnosed," or analyzed their own self-produced data, it is helpful to have an instructor or another classmate respond to the learners' own analyses and focus on the strengths and successes. This can serve as a validity check, verifying learners' own analyses. It can also help to encourage those learners whose first attempts at self-analysis are overly critical. It is helpful, for example, for learners to hear comments about cases where the targeted vocabulary does not seem problematic or in need of "better" expression.

Step 6: Review Since one objective of this activity is for learners to become conscious of their development in vocabulary, it is important that learners record their findings in a research notebook. Along with a list of new words or phrases that they discovered in the course of this analysis, learners also can design tasks that provide practice with these new vocabulary items. For example, they can prepare short talks, in which the use of these new words or phrases is contextually appropriate. In addition, in their research notebooks learners can log the time that they spend concentrating on work in vocabulary and can keep track of progress, noting any successes and changes that they perceive.

Learner/Teacher Feedback: Learners generally like this activity. Most speakers of a language not "native" to them feel frustrated at some point by their lack of fluency (or automaticity/smoothness) but are able to do little about this problem in the course of communicating. Other learners are sometimes pleasantly surprised when they listen to their tapes and find few problems in the way that they communicated. But even these learners claim they benefit from this activity, since there is always room for improvement and always a curiosity about "better" ways to say things. In addition, if one of the learners' goals is a more ready access to slang, idioms, and other "native-like" ways to say things, this activity can be fun and entertaining and can evolve into a "refresher" of current popular usage.

For Teachers: Discussion Questions

1. Think of approaches to teaching vocabulary, grammar, and pronunciation that you have used or have been exposed to, as an instructor or as a student. Could any of these be considered discourse analysis activities?

2. The activities in this chapter all target micro-level features. Can it be argued that any of the targeted structures or features in this chapter's activities are actually a bit farther away from the micro-oriented end of the scale of language features and more toward the macro-oriented end of the scale?

3. As with the collection of sample activities in chapter 3, it is claimed that the structures and features targeted in the set of activities in this chapter are best focused on in a greater discourse context. Are there any reasons for working on these structures in "isolation"—at the word or sentence level?

4. All of the activities in this chapter allow learners the opportunity to produce data samples that they then review and analyze; usually they generate data in Step 4 and review and analyze their self-produced data in Step 5. Besides the techniques mentioned here, can you suggest other ways that learners could incorporate self-monitoring of their own learner-generated speech samples?

5. If you are an oral skills instructor, consider what you are expected to teach in your language class. Could any of the structures and features that you concentrate on be supplemented with discourse analysis activities? Design a short discourse analysis activity that targets the needs of your students.

Suggested Readings and References

Celce-Murcia, M., D. Brinton, and J. Goodwin. 1996. *Teaching pronunciation: A reference for teachers of English to speakers of other languages.* New York: Cambridge University Press.

This is an excellent textbook for training instructors of ESOL to teach pronunciation. It provides an overview of the English sound system and presents techniques for diagnosis of problems, teaching, and correction. These techniques range from highly structured exercises to holistic, discourse-based communicative activities, in which students function as researchers, collecting self-produced data and monitoring their own speech. Thus, this book is an in-depth yet accessible resource book and teaching guide.

Hagen, S., and P. Grogan. 1991. *Sound advantage: A pronunciation book.* New York: Prentice Hall.

Accompanied by audiocassettes, this book focuses on the elements considered essential for successful pronunciation. Not only are the difficult vowels and consonants covered, but also treated are features not always covered in traditional pronunciation textbooks: stress, intonation, linking, reductions, ellipses, and so on. Observations about native speaker speech are integrated into the explanations, thus motivating learners to take an interest in natural discourse.

Larsen-Freeman, D., ed. 1993. *Grammar dimensions: Form, meaning, and use.* 4 vols. Boston, MA: Heinle and Heinle. 2d ed., 1997.
Volume 1: Badalamenti, V., and C. Stanchina
Volume 2: Riggenbach, H., and V. Samuda
Volume 3: Thewlis, S.
Volume 4: Frodesen, J., and J. Eyring

This four-volume series is designed to help English language learners use grammar accurately, meaningfully, and appropriately. Thus it integrates the study of form (syntax), meaning (semantics), and use (pragmatics) in order to focus on each dimension of grammar where it poses the biggest challenge for students, at different levels of their acquisition process. Exercises provide the opportunity for learners to engage in communication that is meaningful, while certain activities put learners in the role of discourse analysts who examine structures as they appear in natural language, both written and spoken.

Nation, I. S. P. 1990. *Teaching and learning vocabulary.* New York: Newbury House.

> Based on the premise that a systematic approach to vocabulary development is advisable, this book is a good and thorough resource on teaching and learning vocabulary. It summarizes much of the pre-1990s literature on vocabulary acquisition and offers many ideas for designing and implementing vocabulary lessons. It also provides discussion of the many aspects of vocabulary acquisition.

Sokmen, A. J. 1992. *Common threads: An interactive vocabulary builder.* Englewood Cliffs, NJ: Prentice Hall.

> This vocabulary book is unique in its open-endedness: it is a generative workbook that relies on students to structure their own vocabulary studies and to work on the words they find most useful. In this sense it is also interactive, since, as stated in its introduction, students work with each other to engage in the process of "making sense out of the lexicon" (ix). The fifty vocabulary activities presented in the book, most of them discourse-based, are rich, varied, and theoretically sound, offering students explicit ways to expand, organize, store, and retrieve vocabulary. Thus, this book is an excellent textbook for students as well as a useful resource book for teachers of vocabulary.

Wennerstrom, A. 1991. *Techniques for teachers: A guide for nonnative speakers of English.* Ann Arbor: University of Michigan Press.

> This book, described in the Suggested Readings and References section of chapter 3, is also relevant follow-up reading for people who want more information about aspects of pronunciation, specifically prosodic features of speech. In this book, designed for international teaching assistants (ITAs), learners analyze micro-level features such as word stress, contrastive stress, and pauses, first in the speech of native speakers who demonstrate on an accompanying video these speech patterns and teaching techniques, then in their own speech. Learners are encouraged to audiotape or videotape all short activities, with opportunities for structured follow-up evaluation. Thus, this book can serve as a source of discourse analysis activities that target micro-level features of pronunciation.

Badalamenti, V., and C. Stanchina. 1997. *Grammar dimensions: Form, meaning, and use.* Vol. 1. 2d ed. Boston, MA: Heinle and Heinle.

Branch, B. 1995. Course project for English 575: Pedagogical Grammar. University of Washington M.A.TESOL Program, Seattle.

Brenner, P. 1994. Course materials, English Vocabulary and Idioms course. University of Washington ESL Center, Seattle.

Carter, R., and M. McCarthy, eds. 1988. *Vocabulary and language teaching.* Applied Linguistics and Language Study Series. New York: Longman.

Celce-Murcia, M., ed. 1991. *Teaching English as a second or foreign language.* Boston, MA: Heinle and Heinle.

Celce-Murcia, M., D. Brinton, and J. Goodwin. 1996. *Teaching pronunciation: A reference for teachers of English to speakers of other languages.* New York: Cambridge University Press.

Chafe, W. 1987. Cognitive constraints on information flow. In R. Tomlin, ed. *Coherence and grounding in discourse.* Amsterdam/Philadelphia: John Benjamins.

Connor, U. 1996. *Contrastive rhetoric: Cross-cultural aspects of second-language writing.* New York: Cambridge University Press.

Connor, U. 1991. Discourse analysis and writing/reading instruction. *Annual Review of Applied Linguistics* 11:164–80.

Ellis, R. 1995. Interpretation tasks for grammar teaching. *TESOL Quarterly* 29 (1): 87–105.

Faerch, C., and G. Kasper. 1983. On identifying communication strategies in interlanguage production. In C. Faerch and G. Kasper, eds., *Strategies in interlanguage communication,* 210–38. New York: Longman.

Flowerdew, J., ed. 1994. *Academic listening: Research perspectives.* New York: Cambridge University Press.

Ford, C. 1993. *Grammar in interaction.* New York: Cambridge University Press.

Fox, L. 1987. On acquiring an adequate second language vocabulary. In M. H. Long and J. C. Richards, eds., *Methodology in TESOL: A book of readings,* 307–11. New York: Newbury House.

Frodesen, J., and J. Eyring. 1997. *Grammar dimensions: Form, meaning and use.* Vol. 4. 2d ed. Boston, MA: Heinle and Heinle.

Gardner, R., and W. Lambert. 1972. *Attitudes and motivation in second language learning.* Rowley, MA: Newbury House.

Gass, S. 1984. A review of interlanguage syntax: Language transfer and language universals. *Language Learning* 34:115–32.

Goffman, E. 1981. *Forms of talk.* Philadelphia: University of Pennsylvania Press.

Hagen S. 1988. *Sound advice: A basis for listening.* New York: Prentice Hall.

Hagen, S., and P. Grogan. 1991. *Sound advantage: A pronunciation book.* New York: Prentice Hall.

Horowitz, R., and S. J. Samuels. 1987. *Comprehending oral and written language.* New York: Academic Press.

Krashen, S. D., and T. D. Terrell. 1983. *The natural approach.* Hayward, CA: Alemany Press.

Kroll, B., and R. Vann. 1981. *Exploring speaking-writing relationships: Connections and contrasts.* Urbana, IL: National Council of Teachers of English.

Larsen-Freeman, D., ed. 1993. *Grammar dimensions: Form, meaning, and use.* 4 vols. Boston, MA: Heinle and Heinle. 2d ed., 1997.

Larsen-Freeman, D. 1991. Teaching grammar. In M. Celce-Murcia, ed., *Teaching English as a second or foreign language,* 2d ed., 279–95. Boston, MA: Newbury House.

Larsen-Freeman, D., and M. Long. 1990. *An introduction to second language acquisition research.* New York: Longman.

McCarthy, M. 1990. *Vocabulary.* Language Teaching Series. New York: Oxford University Press.

Morley, J. 1996. Second language speech/pronunciation: Acquisition, instruction, standards, variation, and accent. In J. E. Alatis, C. A. Straehle, M. Ronkin, and B. Gallenberger, eds., *Georgetown University Round Table on Languages and Linguistics 1996: Current trends and future prospects,* 140–60. Washington, DC: Georgetown University Press.

Moskowitz, B. A. 1985. The acquisition of language. In V. P. Clark, P. A. Eschholz, and A. R. Rosa, eds., *Language: Introductory readings,* 45–73. New York: St. Martin's Press.

Nation, I. S. P. 1990. *Teaching and learning vocabulary.* New York: Newbury House.

Ochs, E. 1979. Planned and unplanned discourse. In T. Givon, ed., *Discourse and syntax,* Syntax and Semantics Series, vol. 12, 51–80. New York: Academic Press.

Pawley, A., and F. H. Snyder. 1983. Two puzzles for linguistic theory: Native-like selection and nativelike fluency. In J. C. Richards and R. W. Schmidt, eds., *Language and communication.* New York: Longman.

Pienemann, M. 1984. Psychological constraints on the teachability of language. *Studies in Second Language Acquisition* 6 (2): 186–214.

Riggenbach, H., and V. Samuda. 1997. *Grammar dimensions: Form, meaning, and use.* Vol. 2. 2d ed. Boston, MA: Heinle and Heinle.

Rooks, G. M. 1996. *Non-stop discussion workbook: Problems for intermediate to advanced students of English.* 2d. ed. Boston, MA: Heinle and Heinle.

Rutherford, W. E. 1987. *Second language grammar: Learning and teaching.* New York: Longman.

Seal, B. D. 1991. Vocabulary learning and teaching. In M. Celce-Murcia, ed., *Teaching English as a second or foreign language,* 2d ed., 296–312. Boston, MA: Heinle and Heinle.

Segalowitz, N. 1993. Skilled performance, practice, and the differentiation of speed-up from automatization effects: Evidence from second language word recognition. *Applied Psycholinguistics* 14:369–85.

Steadman, A., ed. 1992. *The Longman Handy Learner's Dictionary of American English.* New York: Longman.

Sokmen, A. J. 1992. *Common threads: An interactive vocabulary builder.* Englewood Cliffs, NJ: Prentice Hall.

Thewlis, S. 1997. *Grammar dimensions: Form, meaning, and use.* Vol. 3. 2d ed. Boston, MA: Heinle and Heinle.

Tomlin, R. 1994. Functional grammars, pedagogical grammars, and communicative language teaching. In T. Odlin, ed., *Perspectives on pedagogical grammars,* 140–78. New York: Cambridge University Press.

Yule, G., and E. Tarone. 1990. Eliciting the performance of strategic competence. In R. Scarcella, E. Andersen, and S. Krashen, eds., *Developing communicative competence in a second language,* 179–94. New York: Newbury House.

Wennerstrom, A. 1994. Intonational meaning in English discourse: A study of nonnative speakers. *Applied Linguistics* 15 (4): 399–420.

Wennerstrom, A. 1991. *Techniques for teachers: A guide for nonnative speakers of English.* Ann Arbor: University of Michigan Press.

Appendixes

Appendix 1
Sample Handout for Students—Activity 1. Turn Taking

(Also see page 69, Step 2: Plan in Activity 1, for an explanation of these samples.)

Conversation Turn-Taking Activity

The Purpose of This Activity

This activity will help you become more aware of how people converse in (North American) English. You will see some of the ways that speakers take turns in conversation, and you will learn strategies for conversation turn taking, so that you can feel more comfortable participating in conversations.

What You Need to Do

1. Find a conversation partner

You will need to find someone to talk with, and you will tape-record your conversation. If you cannot find or do not know any native speakers of English, find someone who you consider an "expert" speaker of English—someone who has lived in an English-speaking country for many years or someone whose English is very good. It is best if you can find someone who you already know and are comfortable with—a friend or a roommate, for example. If you are doing this activity in your English class, your teacher can also make suggestions about where to find a conversation partner. For example, is there a conversation exchange program in your English language center? Do you live near native speakers of English? Is there a tutoring center that you visit regularly? All of these places might be suitable for finding a conversation partner.

2. Tape-record a conversation

a. After you have found someone to talk with, be sure they understand that you need to tape-record part of your conversation for your English class. Your teacher and classmates do not need to know your conversation partners' names. And if there is any part of your conversation that you or your conversation partner feels is too personal, do not use it—erase this part of the tape, or record another conversation.

b. Test your tape recorder! It is very frustrating to think that you are tape-recording an interesting conversation, only to find that your tape recorder has not been working.

c. You can talk about anything. Do not plan on what you are going to say. If you know each other, you will have plenty to talk about—people that you know in common, things you have recently done or seen, activities that you know about or want to learn about, and so on. If you are meeting for the first time, you might want to talk about where you both come from, what you are studying or where you are working, family members, things you like or dislike, customs that are different from each other or the same, and so on. It is OK to have some ideas about topics of conversation, but do not write down any questions. The more natural the conversation is, the better.

Appendix 2
Student Data Samples—
Activity 1. Turn Taking

(Also see pages 72–73, in the Learner/Teacher Feedback section of Activity 1, for an explanation of these samples.)

Transcription conventions:

[[	overlap—the point where one speaker started speaking while the other continued to speak
=	"latch"—one speaker's turn immediately follows a previous speaker's turn; turn's are "latched" together
(hh hh)	laughter "particles"—syllables of laughter
-	immediately following word as in "They have- they"; the word (*have*) is abruptly ended
(.8)	number in parentheses = length of gap/silence in seconds, in this case .8 seconds/eight-tenths of a second
(.)	"micro pause"—a very short hesitation in the speaker's speech
:	vowel extension—vowel is lengthened/drawn out (also called "sound stretch")
(( ))	commentary about how something is said—transcriber's perception
xxx	incomprehensible

Transcript 1

The native speaker (NS) is a roommate/friend of the language learner. The language learner (LL) is a Japanese student in a high-intermediate English conversation class. She collected these data for her assignment on turn taking, Activity 1 in this book.

1 NS: Well what do you think about um mothers who um have their baby
2   [and they
3 LL: [Uh-huh
4 NS: leave them in garbage cans.
5   (1.5)
6 LL: Huh? What do you (s[
7 NS: [They have- they have their baby?
8 LL: My mom?
9 NS: No no (hh) Not your (hh hh) m- Mothers.
10 LL: Uh-huh. (mothers) Uh-huh.
11 NS: They have their baby?
12 LL: Uh-huh.
13 NS: And then- they leave it in garbage cans.
14   (.8)
15 LL: Garbage?
16 NS: Garbage cans. Like big garbage c(hh)ans. Outside of businesses.
17 LL: Uh-h[uh
18 NS: [and apartments
19 LL: Ahh . . . [. . .
20 NS: [You know what I mean?
21 LL: No I don't know. I d- I understand Garbage.
22 NS: Ye[ah. You know dumpsters? where- You know our garbage.
23 LL: [Garbage.
24 LL: Garbage?
25 NS: Uh-huh
26 LL: Ah yeah
27 NS: Yeah. And they'll have a baby and they'll leave it in there
28   (2.0)
29 LL: Uhyu:h? ((tone displays shock))
30 NS: Yeah. For someone to- to take it or for it to die.
31 LL: Die? Ahh . . . Like a (xxxx[x((incomprehensible)) xxx
32 NS: [Mm-hm
33 LL: I know. ((clears throat)) What do yo[u
34 NS: [It's mean.
35 LL: What's mean?
36 NS: No- It's mean. It's mean.
37 LL: Mean.
38 NS: Yeah (hh hh) It's bad.
39 LL: It's bad. Uh- I know ((xx mumbles xx x[x xx))
40 NS: [Mm-hm
41 LL: Because baby is not thing is y'[know

42 NS: [Baby's what?
43 LL: Not Thing. Baby is a animal- (hh) I (hh) don't know. Humor
44 NS: Human ye[ah
45 LL: [So I can't do that. I can't do that. I can't sell, I
46   can't- I can't (throw) garbage[
47 NS: [Throw it awa[y.
48 LL: [Throw away.
49 NS: Yeah.
50 LL: But- I can't kill because it's human.

Transcript 2

The native speaker (NS) is an elderly woman, who is the language
learner's landlord—she rents her guest house to the language learner.
The language learner (LL) is a native speaker of Chinese. She collected
these data for her assignment on turn taking, Activity 1 in this book.

1 NS: That means you should have lots m[ore birthdays.
2 LL: [Oh I see. I see. I see. In our
3   country we: (.8) is a (.4) people (.8) uh: (.6) when they: (.3) have a
4   birthday (.3) we just family cel- celebration. Not like
5   Amer[ica.
6 NS: [No friends?
7   (.7)
8 LL: Yea:h. No. They just-uh neat- eat-uh noodle. Means the:: (.) they
9   live the long long time. Like the noodles. Very [long. Not like here.
10 NS: [Uh:
11 LL: Here is uh they=
12 NS: =Well she had- a lot of her family were here. Her daughter
13   [(.3) who lives in
14 LL: [Mm-hm
15 NS: Washington (.) [I dunno if you remember seeing her. Very pretty
16 LL: [Oh: I see.
17 NS: young woman.=
18 LL: =Uh-h[uh.
19 NS: [She flew in specially.
20 LL: Oh I see.
21 NS: From Washington D.C. (.) to be with her mother on her special day.
22 LL: Oh I see.=
23 NS: =And her grandson was here.
24 LL: Uh huh.

25   (1.0)
26 LL: Oh, grandson?
27 NS: Right.
28 LL: Yesterday?
29 NS: Yeah.
30 LL: Did I meet?
31   (.5)
32 NS: Uh:m (.) he was a young man. You probably met him.
33 LL: Mm-[hm
34 NS: [Maybe you don't remember.

Appendix 3
Sample Student-Generated Chapter
(excerpts)—Activity 7. Speech Events

(Also see page 99, Step 6: Review in Activity 7, for an explanation of these excerpts.) The following examples were drawn from a chapter on complaints, one of several student-made chapters (four to eight pages each) on different speech events. Although lightly edited for the purposes of easier reading, all examples and comments are students'.

Complaints

Phrases for introducing the complaint

Excuse me, Sir/Madam/Dr./Mr./Ms. . . . May I take   Formal
   a moment of your time? I have a problem that I'd
   like you to hear about.
Excuse me. May I take a moment of your time? There's a
   problem I need to talk with you about.
Excuse me. There's a problem that you should hear about.
   (Directly describe problem, no mention of
   who caused problem.)
I'm afraid you/your company/(name of business) made a mistake/
   (describe the action/source of problem).
You/your company/(name of business) . . .
   (. . . directly describe problem/assign blame).
(Shout your complaint directly.)   Informal

Pointers

1. In informal situations, you do not need a long introduction to the complaint. A brief one is OK, or you can directly start with the complaint.
2. If you directly complain without a polite introduction, this can sound rude.
3. Be careful! It is not always easy to judge the situation. If you do not know what to expect (if they listen to your complaint or not), it is probably best to start out with a polite introduction. If no success, more direct is OK.
4. Getting angry and shouting usually is not successful. But if you have a temper and if they don't honor your complaint, then why not? Depends on person and situation.

Dialogues

Situation 1. You get your test back from your teacher. It says F (45 points). But you add up your points and the grade should be C (65 points). What should you do and say?

1. Formal situation—if the teacher is high rank/professor, if their style is formal, if the class is a large class.

   Student: Excuse me, (teacher's title/name). May I take a moment of your time?
   Professor: Certainly.
   Student: I'm afraid there's a problem.
   Professor: Yes? What is it?
   Student: I added up the points on this test, and I think my grade was not added correctly. (Show professor the test)
   Professor: (looks at test, adds up marks) I see. Yes, you're right. I'll change your grade immediately.
   Student: Thank you very much for your time.
   Professor: You're welcome.

2. Less formal situation—if the person's style is informal, if the class is a small class, you know each other well and you are relaxed together.

   Student: I think there's a problem here.
   Teacher: Oh really?
   Student: Yeah, I counted up my points and I should get C not F.
   Teacher: OK, let's check. (looks at test) Yes, you're right. I'm sorry! I'll change it right away in my records.
   Student: Thanks.
   Teacher: No problem! I thought you shouldn't do so bad to get an F!

Situation 2. You bought an expensive jacket (pullover with zipper) at a big department store, but when you take the jacket home, you notice the zipper is broken.

Can be formal or informal situation. Some big department stores in the United States have a special person to discuss problems. Go to the place called "Returns" or "Exchanges."

Store employee:	May I help you?
Customer:	Yes, thank you. I'm afraid there's a problem with this jacket. I just bought it yesterday. When I took it home to try it on, the zipper was broken.
Store employee:	Do you have the receipt?
Customer:	Yes, it's right here. (show receipt)
Store employee:	Super. You can go and find another jacket and then come right back here.
Customer:	Thank you very much.

Pointers

Always keep your receipt when you buy anything in the United States!

If you wait too long to go back to the store (one week or more), you will have problems. So, double-check your purchases.

Situation 3. You have been sitting in a restaurant for fifteen minutes and the waiter still has not come to your table. You notice that the people who sat down less than five minutes ago have already been waited on. What do you do and say?

Situation 4. You bought a bus ticket at the bus station, but when you get on the bus, the bus driver collects the ticket, looks at it, and gives it back to you. He tells you that your ticket is not for the place you are going to—the place the bus is going to—but for another place. You realize that the ticket seller sold you a ticket to the wrong place. What do you do and say?

Appendix 4
Sample Student-Written
Character Portrayal—Activity 10. Style

(Also see page 117, in the Learner/Teacher Feedback section of Activity 10, for an explanation of these writings.) This sample was submitted by a native speaker of Shona, one of the indigenous languages of Zimbabwe. The spoken version is the interviewer's translation into English from Shona, the language used for the original interview.

I = Interviewer (the student who contributed this sample)
T = Tsitsi (not her real name)

Spoken Version

I: Eh . . . how did you come to . . . eh . . . you know what I mean . . . to be involved in this thing considering that, you know, that society does not approve?

T: You know . . . some of these things happen just like that. I never intended to become a commercial sex worker in my life and nobody, I mean no young girl would say that she wants to be one when she grows up. No. Circumstances force you to. You see? The next thing you are deep into it and you lose yourself in it if you follow what I am digging.

I: Um-hmm . . . but what would you really attribute as the particular forces, I mean what are the circumstances you alluded to which made you what you are today? Like there must be something, you know? That made you start on this thing.

T: Oh . . . that one. I get it. It stands like this. My parents are poor and I am the only girl among six boys and all the boys are sent to school and I do not because I am a girl and a girl just wait to be married so why waste money on someone who will be looking after someone else's family so it's better to educate boys. So they say. So that's how things stand. And

· 220 ·

nowadays no man is willing to marry or pay *lobola* [bride-price] for a girl who did not go to school and is staying in the rural areas no matter how beautiful and upright you are. So with no money to buy myself an undergarment or such things, I was left with no other choice but to do as other girls in the nearby township do. I just started to hang around at the township and I was so marketable on the first days and I could say it was really paying. That's how I got started on this thing. It's not like I want to be called names behind my back but there is nothing else for me on this earth. I have to survive my own way. Only that only.

I: I see. That's very interesting, but before I go further on that I have one more question.

T: Mm-hm?

I: How are you managing now in this business given that it's now flooded and there is also the scare of AIDS to your prospective customers?

T: I manage so and so, like one day you get something to feed and cover yourself and other days you get nothing. And about the AIDS scare . . . eh . . . it's no surprise and I am not even worried about it. Like I don't care if I have it myself because I resigned myself to death long back when I started this. Now I only wait for the day. I can not go back to society again. Never. I am a taboo. An outcast. I will die here and I don't care all the same.

Written Version

I did not want to be a prostitute in my life but economic hardships forced me to engage in this practice. My parents are poor and the fact that I am a girl worsened things because a girl is sidelined when it comes to education and other priorities. I am a victim of the gender issue and the only way I can survive is to be a prostitute, simply because I can not wait to be married knowing that no one will ever marry me. I got into this business and now I can not get out at all because I have to face the spiteful society and I can not stand that. I will die a prostitute. I don't even care how dangerous the business is as in the light of health hazards like AIDS. I will be grateful to know I have got the disease because it will claim my soul soon. I don't care if I die at all. I chose this and I will die of it.

Challenges Faced in Doing This Activity

I encountered a number of problems in translating from our native language, Shona, into English. The girl, being uneducated, used a mixture of Shona and broken English, which I suppose must have been gotten from the jargon of the trade which is usually appealing to prospective customers, who are English speaking. The girls would be trying to portray that they are educated and English is regarded as an important language, despite that it was heavily abused in the interview with broken grammar. I corrected this in the Written Version but not in the Spoken Version.

Another thing is that I had to repeat a question in different ways so that Tsitsi could actually get the meaning. This resulted in a lot of repairs which lengthened the whole interview. The interjection of "You know what I mean" is testimony to the efforts made to ensure the conversation flowed. The phrase has some slangish intonations which are associated with those who think that they know English language better. In actual fact, Tsitsi used this phrase in its English form and she used it quite often. I felt that I should leave some of these repairs and hesitations in the Spoken Version for it to sound more lifelike.

The other problem is that the answers from Tsitsi were stretchy, long, and difficult for me to translate, also because of grammatical faults. This is testimonied by the excessive use of the conjuction "and." An excessive use of phrases, produced one after the other, which is common in spoken instances, was rampant and somehow made the translation into English difficult, especially given the fact that the tape recorder was not functioning well. Repetition of statements and words with similar meanings was also a problem, as it often caused loss of direction of the conversation. A lot of wording would be employed, yet the matter would be small. Especially in the Written Version, I tried to avoid some of this repetition, but I wanted to keep a sense of Tsitsi's mood and style of speaking.

Some of the words used in Shona do not allow for direct translation, as the meaning is sometimes distorted and it becomes difficult to really straighten things out. Phrases such as "only that only" when delivered in Shona have meaning but are relatively meaningless in English. In the Spoken Version I left some of these in anyway, but I reduced the Written Version to what I considered essential for both the story and for Tsitsi's character.